New Paradigms
for Bible Study

New Paradigms for Bible Study
The Bible in the Third Millennium

Edited by

*Robert M. Fowler,
Edith Blumhofer, and Fernando F. Segovia*

T & T CLARK INTERNATIONAL
A Continuum imprint
NEW YORK • LONDON

T & T Clark International, Madison Square Park, 15 East 26th Street, New York,
NY 10010

T & T Clark International, The Tower Building, 11 York Road, London SE1 7NX

T & T Clark International is a Continuum imprint.

Cover design: Laurie Klein Westhafer

Library of Congress Cataloging-in-Publication Data

New paradigms for Bible study : the Bible in the third millennium / edited by
Robert M. Fowler, Edith Blumhofer, and Fernando F. Segovia.
    p. cm.
Includes bibliographical references and index.
  ISBN 0-567-02660-4 (pbk.)
  1. Bible—Study and teaching. I. Fowler, Robert M. II. Blumhofer, Edith Waldvogel.
III. Segovia, Fernando F.
  BS600.3.N48 2004
  220'.071—dc22

                          2004006912

Printed in the United States of America

04 05 06 07 08 09   10 9 8 7 6 5 4 3 2 1

Table of Contents

Foreword

The Challenge of New Paradigms for Bible Study

Robert M. Fowler

The inspiration for this book was a symposium entitled "Futuring the Scriptures: The Bible for Tomorrow's Publics," held at Bible House, the headquarters of the American Bible Society, in New York City, on February 6, 1999. The symposium was co-sponsored by ABS's Research Center for Scripture and Media (Robert Hodgson, Jr., Director, assisted by Robert M. Fowler) and the Public Religion Project of the University of Chicago Divinity School (Martin E. Marty, Director; Edith Blumhofer, Associate Director). Representing such diverse areas of expertise as biblical studies, history, theology, graphic arts, communications, journalism, and business, a panel of sixteen individuals spent an entire Saturday engaged in a lively discussion of the future of the Bible among its various audiences as we move into Third Millennium of Christian history. A large audience was present at Bible House for the symposium, both to listen to the panelists' conversation and to offer their own comments and questions at opportune moments during the day. In an ABS report on the symposium, the following issues were identified as the main threads of the conversation:
- Open Canon versus Closed Canon
- Cultural Diversity and Religious Pluralism versus the Uniqueness of the Christian Message, the Bible, and Revelation
- Continuity versus Discontinuity in the Biblical Message
- The Medium versus the Message
- Traditional Approaches versus new Approaches to the Bible's Authority
- The Bible of the 21st Century: Issues of Racism, Sexism, and Anti-Semitism

The symposium was so stimulating that many of us who had planned, participated, or attended began to discuss how we might harness the energy that had been unleashed on that day. In the months afterward, Bob Hodgson and I realized that an attractive way to fulfill some of the promise of the symposium would be to publish a collection of essays inspired by the topics that had emerged from it. Fortuitously, the American Bible Society had just begun its "New Paradigms for Bible Study Project." Created to seek new directions for ABS to pursue in the coming millennium, this project had three major areas of concern:

- the "pluralistic and postmodern ideologies" of our increasingly global and multicultural age
- the tremendous impact of new electronic media
- the need to develop new resources for Bible study within these emerging new paradigms

Happily, the topics of discussion that had arisen in the "Futuring the Scriptures" symposium were exactly the kind of issues that the "New Paradigms" project was intended to explore. Accordingly, we began to brainstorm what a book inspired by the symposium and guided by the vision of the New Paradigms Project might look like. First, the editorial team of Robert Fowler, Edith Blumhofer, and Fernando Segovia was formed. All of us had participated in the original symposium, either as a planner (Blumhofer), a participant (Segovia), or both (Fowler). The three editors then recruited several others who had either helped to plan the symposium (Martin Marty), had been panelists (Lamin Sanneh and Richard Thieme), or had been present in the audience (Mary Hess and Randy Litchfield). Finally, casting our net as widely as possible, we recruited the remaining contributors (A. K. M. Adam, Mark Fackler, Robert Fortner, Kwok Pui-lan, Abraham Smith, John Stackhouse, and R. S. Sugirtharajah). The volume that has resulted is a remarkable collection of essays that richly fulfills the spirit of that original symposium and succeeds in dreaming some of the dreams of the future that the ABS New Paradigms Project was intended to elicit.

The essays in this book can be organized under two broad themes. The first theme is the implications of communication media generally, and the emerging electronic media in particular, for readers of the Bible. The second is how pluralism, multiculturalism, and globalism will affect those who will use the Bible in the Third Millennium.

Under the theme of communication media and the Bible, we have chosen to begin the book with a topic that received much attention in the original symposium and was one of the three pivotal concerns of the ABS New Paradigms Project: the Bible and electronic media. A. K. M. Adam opens the book by arguing that in an era of increasingly diverse electronic multimedia, our old fixation on the primacy of the printed word must be resisted, in order to exploit the full potential of the new media. Robert S. Fortner outlines the history of communication, especially regarding the

Bible, and discusses how digital electronic media are beginning to provide new metaphors for life in postmodern culture. In what is surely the most 'futuristic' piece among our essays, Richard Thieme describes the sociological and psychological transformations that we are all living through at this historical moment of media transformation. He asks what it might mean to enter sacred space in an era where we seem to be living more and more of our everyday lives in cyberspace.

Two more essays follow that also deal with the Bible and communication media, but these are concerned with the publication of more traditional printed Bibles. (Along with Jay David Bolter, one may observe that the dawning of the Digital Age is simultaneously the "Late Age of Print" [2].) These two essays deal with innovative and opportunistic Bible publication efforts, one of them in the United States and the other in the United Kingdom. Mark Fackler discusses the publication of "niche Bibles," produced and marketed mostly in the U.S., for narrowly defined Christian audiences. Fackler raises thoughtful questions about the paradox of the popularity of such Bibles, replete with carefully tailored 'helps' and personally toned commentary, among Christians for whom the words of the Bible alone are supposed to matter above all other words. By contrast, R. S. Sugirtharajah discusses the publication in the United Kingdom of the Canongate Pocket Bible: individual books of the Bible, employing the King James Version, with each volume introduced by a novelist, pop musician, literary critic, scientist, or some other cultural luminary. This Bible publication effort aims, therefore, not at churchgoers, but primarily at a secularized British audience. Sugirtharajah raises intriguing questions about the implicit moralizing and, indeed, re-colonizing gestures implicit in such a clever marketing scheme, aimed at a "post-Christian," postmodern, secular culture.

Turning to the second broad theme of the book—pluralism, multiculturalism, and globalism—we have four essays devoted to "context-based and ideologically-committed readings" of the Bible (see below, p. 105). Abraham Smith examines "hidden texts" within African-American culture, instances drawn from African-American literature, music, or art that powerfully engage the Bible. In particular, Smith explores several cultural expressions arising out of the Harlem Renaissance that echo biblical themes. Kwok Pui-lan conducts a provocative analysis of the biblical book of Ruth, from an Asian, feminist, post-colonial perspective. Lamin Sanneh discusses the practice of vernacular language Bible translation by European missionaries, which had the unforeseen and unintended result of empowering indigenous, colonized peoples. John G. Stackhouse, Jr., offers a primer on the basics of evangelical Christianity, with particular focus on that tradition's high regard for the Bible. He reviews challenges that are emerging to the evangelical pledge always to use the Bible, "yesterday, today, and tomorrow."

Also under the rubric of pluralism, multiculturalism, and globalism, our last two essays are by specialists in religious education. These are probably the most down-to-earth essays in the collection, discussing in eminently practical ways how Bible study might be conducted in local communities of faith in the Third Millennium. Mary Hess invites us into the dialogue between the Bible and pop culture, providing a wonderful discussion of how people in faith communities might engage "the Other" in contemporary life. Randy G. Litchfield helps us to imagine what Bible study might look like in the local community of faith of the future. Litchfield takes seriously the characteristics of the postmodern era in which we live, and he offers helpful recommendations for organizations such as the American Bible Society, who hope to produce Bible study materials for local congregations—a fitting conclusion to a set of essays aspiring to dream dreams and see visions of "New Paradigms for Bible Study."

As to who should have the very last word in the volume, who better than Martin Marty? Marty was one of the organizers of the original symposium at Bible House; he moderated the discussion that day; after dinner that evening, he reviewed, summarized, and wrapped up the day. We editors could not imagine anyone better suited to wrap up a book arising out of the symposium, so we were delighted when Marty agreed to perform such a parallel service for this collection of essays. In his Afterword, Marty adroitly reviews all the essays in the volume, focusing on the energizing tension between "the past and what has nearly arrived" that runs throughout the collection.

Finally, some words of thanks are in order. I could not have edited this book alone: Edith Blumhofer and Fernando Segovia were valued and trusted collaborators, from beginning to end. Special thanks goes to Robert Hodgson, now a senior staff member at ABS, with whom I worked closely to plan the original symposium, and who engaged me to take on this project. This book is yet another noteworthy product of ABS's late and lamented Research Center for Scripture and Media, so ably direct by Bob during its all-too-brief lifespan. At T & T Clark, thanks goes to Henry Carrigan and Amy Wagner, who worked with us so capably to get this book into print. A huge debt of gratitude is owed to Paul Soukup, S.J., who skillfully produced camera-ready pages for the book, and to Anteres Anderson, who edited the index. Both are at Santa Clara University.

Works Consulted

American Bible Society
    N.D. *Futuring the Scriptures: The Bible for Tomorrow's Publics*. New York: American Bible Society. [Report on symposium of the same title on February 6, 1999, at Bible House, New York City]
Bolter, Jay David.
    1991 *Writing Space: The Computer, Hypertext, and the History of Writing*. Hillsdale, NJ: Erlbaum, 1991.

1

This Is Not a Bible

Dispelling the Mystique of Words
for the Future of Biblical Interpretation

A. K. M. Adam

At this point, projections based on the present are worse than useless. And that, of course, is exactly how matters stand at the turn of the millennium when it comes to technology. We've never experienced a period of such rapid change—especially when it comes to the web. Making predictions in this kind of environment isn't just foolhardy; it can be a kind of denial. "Tomorrow will be much like today"— yeah, you *wish*!

—David Weinberger

He spent some time with the holoscope, studying Elias's most precious possession: the Bible expressed as layers at different depths within the hologram, each layer according to age. The total structure of Scripture formed, then, a three-dimensional cosmos that could be viewed from any angle and its contents read. According to the tilt of the axis of observation, differing messages could be extracted. Thus Scripture yielded up an infinitude of knowledge that ceaselessly changed. It became a wondrous work of art, beautiful to the eye, and incredible in its pulsations of color.

—Philip K. Dick (65-66)

What is "the present" for biblical scholarship? The present typically involves attaining fluency (or, more realistically, reading competence) in a variety of languages; inculturation in the somewhat parochial world of academic biblical studies; and immersion in the vast secondary literature that the biblical-criticism industry continually generates. The present focuses acute attention on *words*, the words that comprise our Bibles and the words with which we represent those (biblical) words.

What does the future—especially the future of cybermedia—hold for academic biblical scholarship? I am less foolhardy than the many prognosticators who can assert with confidence the ramifications of the World Wide Web, hypertext, digital video, streamed audio and video, and digital publishing (to name but a few media convulsions that bear on the future of biblical scholarship). After all, who would have understood the ramifications of Europe's discovery of movable type when the first Bibles were printed on Gutenberg's press? Whatever specific changes develop over the years to come, the advent of electronic media will catalyze a complex of circumstances that biblical scholars in the age of printing have successfully avoided so far, even in the face of film and video media, and the dimensions of these new domains of biblical interpretation can not be estimated on the basis of the way things are right now.

Those who espouse detailed predictions of the discipline's future remind me of a scene from my elementary-school education. A number of my childhood's classrooms featured tall rolling gantries that held television sets, televisions that were ostensibly available to usher me into the brave new world of broadcast education. As I recall, we occasionally watched a weekly science program, and once a year may have seen a televised version of a great book or play, but almost as often the sets were used to watch the Pittsburgh Pirates' baseball games. The cost of those large-screen sets per instructional hour of use must have been enormous, and the cost per *effective* hour of use was vastly greater. Someone had imagined that the future of pedagogy lay in class-period-length instructional programming on "educational" broadcast channels, and the Board of Education had invested in that vision of the future only to encounter the reality that there were few instructional programs to watch, the programs available did not necessarily match the instructional schedule of every elementary school in the city, and many of the programs simply showed in two-dimensional black-and-white pixels what our science teacher could have shown us in three-dimensional, colorful flesh.

Unduly specific predictions about the future of biblical studies in an intellectual economy shaped by cybermedia risk the dusty fate of my elementary-school television sets. As David Weinberger points out, when conditions are changing rapidly, predictions are a risky business. Especially when the *rate* of change is exceptionally rapid, when the very categories of change are themselves changing, we are wiser to wait and see what happens than to invest our resources in one particular version of what will surely come tomorrow—no matter how firmly that anticipated future is asserted, no matter how roundly it is endorsed. Our waiting need not be idle, however; patience affords us the opportunity to prepare for the changes that will be borne upon us by weaning ourselves from some of the constants that define the status quo. Recognizing some elements of the present as transitory effects of a changing disciplinary field, we can equip ourselves to pursue biblical studies *differently* as the field modulates around us.

With a view to the relation of biblical interpretation to cybermedia, then, I propose two propaedeutic recuperations: first, a demystification of *words* as means of communication, and, second, a relaxation of what has been the constitutive hostility of modern academic biblical studies to *allegory*. At the heart of both these proposals lies a sensitivity to the explosive breadth of means for communicating information in cyberspace. Academic biblical scholars need to awaken to a range of communicative practices that extends far beyond the print media in which we typically subsist; one might well ask, "If a picture is worth a thousand words, why can't we have more illustrations and fewer multivolume sets in our commentaries?" Once we admit a richer span of communicative options, however, we will need an articulate mode of criticizing these representations, and it is for this purpose that learning some lessons from allegorical interpretation may better equip us for future interpretive ventures.

Demystifying the Word(s)

The circumstances most liable to change in our future resist precise articulation, in part because they are effects of the *structure* of biblical scholarship as academic institutions have defined it. The discipline of biblical studies has grown up at the intersection of divergent, often conflicting, forces driven by theological interests, secular academic interests, and the broad cultural currents of nineteenth- and twentieth-century European and American modernity. The confluence and divergence of these formative influences has produced an academic field whose central practices and guiding metaphors derive from a particular model of *translation*. The academic biblical scholar's job of work allows and requires him or her telling an audience what the Bible means, how the texts written in ancient Hebrew and Aramaic and in Hellenistic Greek should be expressed in contemporary European and American vernaculars. Unfortunately, practitioners of academic biblical scholarship do not usually appreciate the wisdom of scholars in the field of translation (whose practical emphasis itself sometimes occludes *other* interpretive problems—problems of theoretical hermeneutics that biblical scholars have been dealing with, or hiding from, for centuries). Instead of benefiting from the work of theoreticians and practitioners of translation, academic biblical scholarship shows a persistent inclination toward a fantasy of a perfect one-to-one equivalence.

Even the goal of "fidelity" to the biblical text, the hallmark of the American Bible Society's ceaseless efforts to bring the Bible to all audiences, can sometimes be haunted by the perfect-translation fantasy. A rich notion of "fidelity" embraces far more than grammar and lexicography, but when a particular paraphrase or a new-media representation of a biblical passage dissatisfies its critical readers, they are apt to attribute their frustration to the "freeness" of the paraphrase or the remoteness of the video production from the biblical text. We should, however, distinguish the matter of "free paraphrase" or of the metaphorical distance between two media from the matter of "fidelity": as translators have long known, one may sometimes attain the greatest fidelity to a biblical expression only by a very free paraphrase, and one might argue that passages from Ezekiel or Revelation are more effectively communicated with images than with words.

One powerful constituent in the problem of biblical studies' past and future lies in the persistent mystification of verbal communication, which practitioners of biblical studies often reduce to communication in print, as though there were no noteworthy distinction between oral words, hand-written words, and printed words. Scholars collaborate in perpetuating a myth that (printed) words are a unique, semi-divine product with unearthly qualities. Because (printed) words do such an admirable job of facilitating communication, scholars have often jumped to the conclusion that words must possess special properties that constitute them as a uniquely appropriate medium for expression, imbued with "meaning" in something of the way that scientists once believed that combustible materials were imbued with a fiery essence or that soporifics contained a dormitive property. If words work, these scholars reason, they must work on the basis of intrinsic meanings.

The mystique of words derives further currency from theological reasoning. The first verse of John's Gospel, the opening verses of Genesis, the genre of prophetic oracles, and the principal modes of Jesus' teaching (particularly his teaching in parables) seem to mark verbal communication as God's communicative medium of choice. The proposition that God's choice to make known the record of divine truth in verbal form—as writing, *Scripture*, ἡ βίβλος—then seems to warrant our regarding words as miniature vessels of potential revelation, whereas inductions from non-verbal visual phenomena, from sublime sound or heady scent, can be dismissed as forms of "natural theology."

To the contrary, however, words—spoken or written or printed—are not the unique vessels of meaning that our interpretive practices often imply them to be, even when we do not adhere to that premise self-consciously or explicitly. Not only words, but also physical gestures, non-verbal sounds, images, even smells, convey meaning in ways different from, but associated with, linguistic expression. Our hermeneutics, preoccupied with the fantasy of the perfect translation, concentrate almost to the point of exclusivity upon words. We concentrate not simply on words but devote most of our attention to *printed* words.

Be it conceded right away that language has proven an inestimably versatile and effective means of communication. When my children have fallen asleep, I can often manage to make my ideas evident to my wife in gesticulation and grimace, without spoken words, but I do not propose that words are a bad idea and should be abandoned, or that they are so radically ambiguous as to be indistinguishable from cubist paintings or thrash rock'n'roll. Words have made possible tremendous, powerful, convincing, highly-effective acts of communication. Indeed, we who are profoundly (decisively?) shaped by the effects of language can hardly imagine the scope and force of words' influence on every aspect of human life. Neither I nor anyone I know wishes to undervalue linguistic communication.

At the same time, I do not wish to *over*value language, ascribing to it mystical properties that go beyond the social conventions that give it currency. Communication does not depend on spoken or written language ("written" in the sense of spelled-out words). One can effect understanding on the basis of gestures, pictures, or inarticulate sounds. If one allows a background dependence on language—as language itself generally depends on some sensuous acquaintance with the phenomenal world—then communication can get on quite well without explicit recourse to verbal language, as speakers of sign language can testify. Drivers cannot usually speak directly to one another, but they find ways of communicating with car horns, gestures, and noteworthy automotive maneuvers, and internationally-recognized symbols guide drivers' navigation in areas where they do not understand the local language. Words form an extraordinarily strong, labile, productive medium for the social interactions that sustain meaningful connections among (other) words, images, sounds, experiences—but we need not posit the *necessity* of verbal language for such social connections. Some social conventions can sustain some associations of meaning and experience even in the absence of verbal language.

That is to say, the success with which humans often use words to communicate does not imply that words constitute the quintessence of communication. Words prove especially useful for communicating particular kinds of information under particular circumstances, but their outstanding usefulness does not make an argument for their *necessity*.

Neither ought we to conclude that words provide a paradigmatic mode of communication, so that our theories of interpretation need only account for words in order to claim completeness. Once we entertain seriously the possibility that legitimate interpretation may involve more than providing word-for-word alternatives, the power and the prominence of non-verbal communication oblige us to offer theories of interpretation that do not treat non-verbal communication as an incomplete, insufficient, primitive, non-scholarly offshoot of the (verbal) *real thing*. A hermeneutic that works only for *words* is itself incomplete and insufficient.

Nor does the theological argument for treating words as the paradigmatic instance of communication carry decisive weight. Though the Word became flesh and dwelt among us, the Word was not manifest as a part of speech or a siglum; the Word effected communion with humanity by *becoming human*, not by becoming an inscription. The Bible foregrounds instances of verbal communication from God but reports a variety of other means by which God makes the divine will known. God communicates not exclusively through (evidently) verbal communication but also through visions and through physical demonstrations, and one would be foolhardy who determined that God might not communicate in yet other ways. The prophets received visions as well as verbal bulletins, and God commanded that they pass along their divine messages by enacted communication. Paul insists that the created order itself communicates something of God's identity in Romans 1. Indeed, even those who construe the word *logos* in John's Prologue flatly as "word" oversimplify the semantic breadth of the term in Greek (as its common Hebrew partner, *dabar*, likewise covers much more semantic terrain than just "word"). This caveat applies all the more since John deploys the term in a setting that lacks the contextual markers that might tend sharply to limit plausible construals of that noun. The doctrine of the incarnation itself should serve as a warning that exclusively verbal revelation was not sufficient in itself; God chose *body English*, as it were, as the medium for the fullness of communication. Where Protestant theologies—which in some instances show a marked aversion to physical or sensuous dimensions of human life, preferring abstractions, thoughts, and words to images, matter, and action—prospered with the advent of printed communication and widespread literacy, other traditions have maintained the theological importance of communication in visual arts, in physical movement, in sound and smell and taste. While arguments for emphasizing verbal communication identify a legitimate strand of biblical and theological reflection, words should not be permitted to eclipse iconic, active, aural, olfactory, gustatory, and tactile aspects of theological discourse.

If we dispense with the mystical-vessel model of verbal meaning, we are not bereft of resources for explaining the relative stability of literary understanding nor the effectiveness of verbal communication. Proponents of "meaning" often construct the hermeneutical alternatives only as: either "words *have meanings*" or "any word can mean any thing." This illegitimately excludes a pivotal range of middle terms that provide quite adequate accounts of communication. The social conventions that undergird communication are strong, deep, and quite elastic (though not infinitely so). In most regards words are indeed more stable and effective a means of communication than other media. Other means of communication, however, have benefits of their own, as traffic signs, musical compositions, and fine cooking—or, to remain in the sphere of theological practice, church architecture, hymnody, incense, the elements of communion, and even pot-luck suppers—all demonstrate.

Scholars have become accustomed to fixating so unwaveringly on words that they will espouse theories whose shakiness could readily be brought to light by framing them graphically. To choose a simple, common example, New Testament scholars frequently draw exegetical conclusions about the relative dates of documents or sayings by assaying the Christologies that the texts reflect or the degree to which the texts show concern about the delay of the parousia. Such reasoning might be represented graphically by the charts in the figure on the next page. In each case, as a document's Christology moves toward a more exalted understanding of Christ or as it shows a greater degree of anxiety over the return of the Lord, that document may be presumed to date from a later period. Of course, scholars feel free to fudge their relation to these (presupposed) charts. If a document that scholars feel strongly to date from the late first century shows robust confidence that the Lord will come soon, said scholars can point out that the apparent confidence is intended to allay the fears of the community to which the text is addressed. If a late document includes a passage that evinces a low Christology, the passage in question may be an older tradition that the editors included intact; conversely, if an early text shows signs of a high Christology, we may conclude that a later editor has emended the document.

Few scholars would uphold so bald a presentation of their reasoning. The heuristic value of Christology or *Parusieverzögerung* for dating New Testament texts presumably complements other, more rigorous criteria. Yet anyone who looks at the graphs that accompany this page and thinks hard about the geographical, theological, and cultural diversity that characterize the earliest years of the Christian movement must recognize how tenuous such criteria must be: *any* assumptions about a predictable

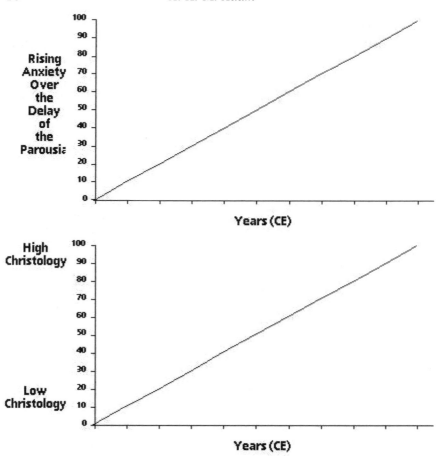

correlation between chronology and either Christology or eschatology stand to falsify or mislead historical reason at least as much as they stand to aid it. A Galilean from whom Jesus of Nazareth exorcised a persistent demonic presence would probably hold to a higher Christology than a casual bystander who overheard snippets of a parabolic discourse, though both lived and reported their impressions of Jesus at the same time. A wandering Christian prophet might proclaim the nearness of the Day of the Lord just across town from a corner where a sage Christian teacher offered aphoristic counsel on how to live wisely and long.

The charts in this illustration are, of course, oversimplifications of more complex hypotheses. If one wanted to represent these hypotheses more fairly, one might, for instance, allow that anxiety over the delayed parousia was not a linear but a parabolic function. Or one might plot Christology against years in a scatter-chart, allowing for greater variability in the distribution of data. Then, however, one would run into the difficulty that scholars assign dates to the documents in question largely on the basis of the hypotheses that we are illustrating. The data points do not scatter much, because they have to a great extent been located with reference to the assumed validity of the hypothesis. While we can observe patterns of transition from one sort of outlook to another, the variety of particular circumstances and of human responses to those circumstances preclude our vesting the patterns we observe with the regularity that could undergird deductions about when or where or why. Sometimes visual representation of a hypothesis helps clarify just what the hypothesis entails and how much credit that hypothesis deserves.

The question of visual representation, however, reaches beyond the value of interpreting historical-critical data and hypotheses with graphs or charts. Words are themselves sensuous phenomena, whether aural or visual. A word written is not simply the same as a word printed. A word printed in Century Schoolbook type is not simply the same as a word printed in **Cooper Black** or Comic Sans. Will the *Journal of Biblical Literature* ever adopt a hard-to-read, grungy typeface as its standard? The way one presents a verbal message casts the message in a particular light. Those who have read applications for college admission or a job opening will have to acknowledge that not all words are presented equally—a point that fueled the transition from typewriting to computer word processing, from impact printers to laser and inkjet printers.

Words signify, in other *words*, not only by the letters that constitute the word or by the meaning that we conventionally associate with the word, but also by the appearance of the word—and the visual context within which that word appears. René Magritte, the master-teacher of the paradoxes of interpretation, wrought a career of painted and printed essays on just this aspect of the relation of words to images. He is best known for such works as "L'usage de la parole I" ("The Use of Words I"), a painting that combines the large painted image of a pipe with the written legend, "Ceci n'est pas un pipe" ("This is not a pipe"). The painting reminds viewers that the painting is not a pipe; it is a two-dimensional *representation*, significantly enlarged, of a three-dimensional implement. Further, the painting may prompt viewers to recognize that the words "*un pipe*" (and the demonstrative "*Ceci*") are not a pipe, either. Verbal language and graphic illustrations offer two means for representing objects, concepts, and relations, but these media do not escape their status as representations.

In a less well-known article for *La révolution surréaliste* in 1929—at about the same time he was painting "L'usage de la parole I"—Magritte sketched an eighteen-part essay on the relation of words and images. The essay comprises small line drawings, each with a caption

positing a theoretical-interpretive point. The first, for example, shows the shape of a small leaf with the label, "le canon"; of this, Magritte observes, "An object does not belong to its name to such an extent that one couldn't find it another that suits it better" (60; all translations from this article are my own). Another drawing shows a human profile between the letters "a, b," and "n, o," which in their turn are followed by the perspective drawing of a rectangular solid: "In a painting, the words are of the same substance as the images." In yet another, Magritte reminds his reader that "An object never serves the same purpose as its name or its image." The essay challenges a reader's propensity to think of words as ontologically distinct from images, as possessing intrinsic properties associating themselves with their referents or rendering them particularly efficacious for interpretation. Had Magritte been particularly interested in biblical interpretation, he might seventy years ago have begun reminding his readers of the long-standing tradition of interpretation in statuary, in stained glass, in woodcuts, in icons; our sense of the breadth of biblical interpretation might already have extended to cope not only with Milton, Mozart, Doré, and Eschenbach, but also to Dali, DeMille, and Lloyd Webber (and in a more modest way, theologian/cartoonist Fred Sanders).

Observers sometimes suggest that our disciplinary constrictions arise from biblical scholars' "linear thinking," from our being "too linear." If by "linear" one means "logical" or "analytic," the accusation probably does not hold water. If, on the other hand, the accusation means "captive to one-dimensional approaches to multidimensional problems," then the accusation is demonstrably false. At least thirty or forty years ago, biblical scholars attained two-dimensionality by recognizing the legitimacy of such approaches as literary, sociological, political, and certain postmodern criticisms. The residual problem lies in the extent to which our two-dimensionality underachieves in a world of polydimensional communication; in that sense, we are not too *linear* but too *planar*. Biblical scholars have been able to finesse this limitation by emphasizing verbal communication in our main areas of productivity (our orientation toward verbal communication, in articles, books, the oral presentation of papers, and so on) and in our industrial by-products (biblical theology and preaching, each imagined as a subordinate discipline to the regnant critical methodocracy). Like inhabitants of Edwin Abbott's *Flatland*, we construe the limitations of our imagination and experience as limitations of what can be imagined. Our evasive maneuvers, however, will not keep cybermedia at bay much longer, and our planar interpretive consciousness will be flung—prepared or unprepared—into a polydimensional interpretive cosmos.

When we contemplate the kinds of differences that the future of electronic media will bear upon us, we can see all the more clearly the importance of learning how to relativize the importance of words in our disciplinary practice. It takes no Nostradamus to notice that the means of producing digital video and animations have come more readily and more inexpensively into the hands of non-professionals and that the tools available to professionals have become vastly more powerful. As the vacation slide show moved over to make room for videotape presentations when the price of videotape cameras diminished to fit the budget of bourgeois Europeans and Americans, so the diminishing cost and complication of digital video production will in all likelihood increase the amount of information we encounter in that medium. By the same token, the most sophisticated examples of digital-media video and animation will become inestimably more complex and convincing. As anyone can testify who compares the elementary-school reports their computer-literate children compose with the reports from their own childhood, visual information has become increasingly *available* as a tool for communication, and every sign points toward that trend continuing and accelerating. Pictures, animations, and video will not supplant words, but they will become ever more prominent as supplement, as context. The interpretation of words alone will not suffice to account for this additional contextual matter. And interpretations *in* words alone will likewise seem increasingly paltry, when with so little extra effort one can illustrate one's remarks with three-dimensional virtual models of the synagogues of second-century Palestine, or dynamic diagrams of Solomon's social network, or animations of the dragon and the beast from Revelation—or something more like the holoscopic, pulsating colors of the Bible that Philip Dick describes.

Relaxing Hostility to Allegory

As academic biblical interpretation moves more rapidly and comprehensively into domains other than the printed word, practitioners will need to learn how to *evaluate* interpretations on unfamiliar terms. Under present circumstances, the dominant critical question posed to (verbal) interpretations consists principally in whether they appropriately honor the historical context of the text's origin; such questions well suit a discourse of interpretation that trades in propositions as its currency. When interpretations involve not only verbal truth-claims about interpretive propositions, but also shapes, colors, soundtracks, and motion, the matter of historical verisimilitude recedes among a host of other questions. The questions that most obviously fit cybermedia interpretations are more familiar from the worlds of film criticism, art criticism, and literary criticism (though this latter appears in this context in a mode less concerned with authorial intent and "original audiences" than with contemporary assessments of literary effect). These criteria feel awkward and subjective at present, but the effect of imprecision derives from the interpreters more than from the interpretive approaches. Scholars unfamiliar with construing biblical texts on any basis other than that of historical accuracy fumble and grope as they reach beyond the boundaries of their familiar practices. When academicians eventually become habituated to thinking aesthetically or ethically or politically about their interpretations, these modes of interpretation will seem no more subjective than interpretations based on varying assessments of historical probability.

One need not read tea leaves to suggest such a prospect. Brilliant scholars from eras past have deployed non-historical criteria freely in evaluating texts and interpretations. Critics who found a passage's apparent literal meaning offensive applied ethical criteria to ground their conviction that the text must then mean something different from the literal sense. Medieval interpreters who saw edifying instruction in a biblical story made free to depict that scenario graphically without the constraints of historically-appropriate costume or topography. Handel's *Messiah* confidently presses the case for a Christological reading of Old Testament passages that bear no obvious messianic overtones when read in their historical social context. In such examples biblically-erudite interpreters generate profound interpretations of texts without recourse to historical reasoning.

Interpreters from other cultural moments devised sound readings of biblical texts inasmuch as their social contexts provided cues that clarified the sorts of interpretation that might be encouraged and the sorts of interpretation that should be stopped. Handel would have had no basis for making sense of claims that his *Messiah* illegitimately misconstrued the *historical* import of the Old Testament passages he cited. Philo sensitively recognized that his readers might be affronted by Lot's drunken liaisons with his daughters, so he couched his exposition of the passage in terms of the relations of various intellectual faculties to one another. And at a moment when the cultural world of biblical interpretation trembled and warped under the stress of impending technological revolution, anonymous scholars composed the woodblock compositions that became known as the *Pauper's Bible,* a mixture of graphic and verbal interpretations of the gospel, combining images drawn from the Old Testament and the Gospels, from pious legend and deuterocanonical narrative, to summarize a vast intertextual account of salvation history in forty woodcuts.

The woodcuts themselves represent what Edward Tufte calls a "confection," a compilation of various sorts of images and information in a communicative ensemble whose whole vastly exceeds the sum of its parts. Several editions of the *Pauper's Bible* divide the printed (or hand-drawn) page into as many as eighteen small frames, each contributing a short text, the depiction of a character, or a scene from a biblical narrative (the number of frames in a given edition of the *Biblia Pauperum* may vary; one at hand shows twenty frames, another twelve). The eighteen frames do not simply stack up figures and texts in a jumble; instead, the illustrations and quotations constitute an interpretive context for the gospel passage that the central panel depicts. The illustrations in one frame echo visual motifs from the others, calling attention to connections between the illustrated passages that are absent from the literal sense of the quoted passages. They show the biblical figures in clothing and situations proper to the fifteenth-century milieu of the woodcuts' composition, quietly making contemporary sense of the ancient writings. The careful arrangement of text and illustration—shaped by years of interpretive tradition and reproduction—encode and encourage a harmonized interpretation of the Bible's message.

The *Pauper's Bible* intimates one direction of post-print-media confections of biblical interpretation. Whereas modern biblical interpretation depends almost exclusively on the verbal media of print and its interpretive practices are haunted by the fantasy of a perfect translation, the *Pauper's Bible*s mingle form and color with text (handwritten text, in some versions; woodcut text, in others). When we compare this premodern multimedia interpretive exercise to its modern successor, we are likely to recognize that the *Pauper's Bible* lies closer to the frames, images, and text of a web page than to the lengthy expositions of contemporary academic scholarship. Add a few QuickTime animations, a streamed-audio background, and hyperlinks to other pages, and the fifteenth-century *Pauper's Bible* already fits the present-day media world more comfortably than does the twentieth-century *Journal of Biblical Literature*.

The anonymous evangelical confections of the *Pauper's Bible* bring us round, at last, to the second point I would press regarding the future of biblical interpretation as we modulate from a typographic interpretive culture to a cybermedia interpretive culture. The *Pauper's Bible* testifies to the pivotal role that a disciplined imagination plays in biblical interpretation. For the past two centuries, interpreters' imaginations have been policed by criteria native to the discipline of historical analysis; other approaches have been permitted to extend the range of biblical interpretation, to add a second interpretive dimension, only so long as they orient themselves toward the pole-star of historical soundness. Thus, literary criticism of the Bible frequently highlights the supposed editorial seams that enable historical interpreters to isolate distinct strands of a tradition; similarly, social-scientific interpreters foreground the social conventions of the Ancient Near Eastern and Hellenistic cultures from which the

Testaments emerged. Historical reason determines the modern limits of legitimate interpretation.

Imaginations informed by cybermedia will not sit still for the ponderous police of historical authentication. New media will oblige interpreters to extend the range of their interpretive and critical faculties—and the further our endeavors extend from the exclusively verbal interpretive practice of contemporary biblical scholarship, the less pertinent the fantasy of perfect translation and the *imprimatur* of historical verification will seem. New media will teach us new criteria. But as the *Pauper's Bible* reminds us that the work of biblical interpretation has in past times communicated well in images, so the allegorical imagination that funded the *Pauper's Bible* can provide clues for the directions that critical interpretation may take in new media.

The contributors to ancient and medieval theology found in allegorical interpretation a device for expounding the Bible in the light of what they understood to be its plain sense, its more refined theological sense, its moral import, and its adumbration of things to come. Contrary to glib denunciations of this interpretive mode, their practice of the *quadriga* did not permit them to make Scripture say whatever they wanted, but brought to their consciousness the pertinent constraints on the range of permissible meanings. (The Reformation *topos* that allegorical interpretation makes a wax nose of Scripture, that can be twisted and reshaped in any way one likes, overlooks several salient characteristics of wax noses. Most important of these is that one cannot simply wrench a wax nose into twists and corners, flat stretches and pits, and still claim that it is a "wax nose"—any more than a potter can claim that her fresh-from-the-kiln ceramic vessel is a lump of clay. There are limits beyond which one cannot deform a wax nose without forsaking any claim to rhinosity—but, within those limits, one may alter the shape of the wax nose as need dictates. That is the *point* of a wax nose.) The *quadriga* teaches four sets of criteria with which to evaluate representations of biblical texts; the fourfold approach to allegorical interpretation was not a license to permit imaginations to run wild but a set of channels to guide interpretive imaginations. Those channels rely for their cogency not on intrinsic properties of words but on an aptitude for drawing correlations, *confections*, that satisfy the imaginations of their readers. The allegorical criteria operate apart from the assumption that some property intrinsic to words provides the sole legitimating standard for critical interpretation, and they honor the inevitability that interpretations will go divergent directions without necessarily diverging from legitimacy.

Concluding Comments

The *quadriga* will not return in its premodern contours (though we could do worse). It may, however, stimulate thoughtful interpreters to authenticate their own electronic-media representations less compulsively on historical analysis or on their approximations of a phantasmic perfect translation. These alternative criteria need not exclude the authority of historical studies: where interpreters want to make historical claims, they will always have to back those claims up with historical warrants. But as our capacity to imagine and interpret the Bible expands in ways that only a foolish forecaster would venture to specify, we stand only to benefit from observing the ways that our forebears dealt with assessing non-historical and non-verbal representations of the Bible. Some scholars will insist that the conventions of the nineteenth and twentieth centuries have established unsurpassable canons of hermeneutical validity, such that all representations from this day forward must pass the tests of historical and philological precision. If they are right, then all we need do to prepare ourselves for the oncoming wave of new media is to study ever harder the repertoire of historiographic and grammatical insights that they

have handed down to us. They wisely commend to us the treasury that those insights offer. When change sweeps around and past us, however, we prepare best for an unforeseeable future by looking beyond the words with which our teachers enriched and bounded our understanding. We need to look beyond one or two dimensions of meaning and expression, to acquaint ourselves with as full a range of interpretive possibilities as we can, and to seek a critical engagement with that range of representations that honors the richness of our interpretive imagination to which we are heirs, of which we are stewards on behalf of our neighbors and our successors.

Works Consulted

Abbott, Edwin A.
    1884   *Flatland: A Romance of Many Dimensions.* New York: Dover Press, 1992.

Biblia Pauperum
    1859   Introduction and bibliography by J. Ph. Berjeau. London: John Russell Smith.
    1867   Edited and introduced by Pfarrer Laib and Franz Joseph Schwarz. Zurich: Verlag von Leo Wörl.
    1967   Introduction, notes, and subtitles by Elizabeth Soltész. Budapest: Corvina Press.
    1969   Introduced, transcribed, and translated by Karl Forstner. Munich: Verlag Anton Pustet.

Dick, Philip K.
    1981   *The Divine Invasion.* New York: Pocket Books.

Eichenberg, Fritz
    1992   *Works of Mercy.* Edited by Robert Ellsberg. Introduction by James Forest. Maryknoll: Orbis Books.

Labriola, Albert C., and John W. Smeltz
    1990   *The Bible of the Poor* [Biblia Pauperum]. Pittsburgh: Duquesne University Press.

Magritte, René
    1929   "Les mots et les images." *La révolution surréaliste*, 12 (December 15): 32-33. Reprinted: Pp. 60-61 in *Écrits complets*. Ed. André Blavier. Paris: Flammarion, 1979.

McCloud, Scott
    1994   *Understanding Comics: The Invisible Art.* New York: Harper Perennial. [Originally published in 1953 by Kitchen Sink Press.]
    2000   *Reinventing Comics: How Imagination and Technology Are Revolutionizing an Art Form.* New York: Perennial.

Sanders, Fred
  1999a *On Biblical Images: Dr. Doctrine's Christian Comix, Vol. 1.*
          Downers Grove, IL: InterVarsity Press.
  1999b *On the Word of God: Dr. Doctrine's Christian Comix, Vol. 2.*
          Downers Grove, IL: InterVarsity Press.
  1999c *On the Trinity: Dr. Doctrine's Christian Comix, Vol. 2.* Downers
          Grove, IL: InterVarsity Press.
  1999d *On the Christian Life: Dr. Doctrine's Christian Comix, Vol. 2.*
          Downers Grove, IL: InterVarsity Press.
Tufte, Edward R.
  1997   *Visual Explanations: Images and Quantities, Evidence and
          Narrative.* Cheshire, CT: Graphics Press.
  1990   *Envisioning Information.* Cheshire, CT: Graphics Press.
  1983   *The Visual Display of Quantitative Information.* Cheshire, Conn.
          Graphics Press.
Weinberger, David
  2000   "Predictions." *All Things Considered* (August 22).
          <http://www.npr.org/ramfiles/atc/20000822.atc.08.ram>.

2

Digital Media as Cultural Metaphor

Robert S. Fortner

Perhaps the main difficulty we have in discussing new paradigms is the necessity of jettisoning the old ones. There are two main reasons for this. First, in order to recognize when a paradigm shift occurs, we can only look for it using old lenses, because that is all we have until a new pair arrives. But as anyone who has had to go through several different and progressively more corrective lenses can tell you, the problem is to be able to know when you are ready for the new pair. As your eyesight worsens, you lose track of what clear vision truly is and simply do not recognize the necessity or the advantages of changing lenses. Second, all of us live within what Baudrillard called "hyper-reality," a reality of multiple layers of interpretation, each dependent on those before it and each separating us just a little bit further from the actual events being interpreted.

There are three aspects of this hyper-reality that affect the Christian response to Scripture. First, we often assume that our own interpretation of Scripture is identical to the historical interpretation of the church, or, if we realize that ours is different, we may assume that it is the result of superior insight or the development of understanding from which our forebears could not benefit. We have what Herbert Butterfield (1965) called a "whiggish" view of our own history. The most obvious form of this is dispensational theology. In other words, we do not recognize the hyper-reality for what it is. It is masked by our own assumptions.

Second, we desire—somewhat paradoxically—to see Scripture as it was seen originally. As John McManners put it, we want to understand it as a "religion of the word—the 'Word made Flesh', the word preached, the word written to record the story of God's intervention in history" (11). In other words, we have an intense desire to imagine that the "word made flesh"—or at least our understanding of that concept—is the same as it has always been. We reify the language applied to God, Christ, and Spirit and fail to see the layers of interpretation that have resulted in our current understanding.

Third, we insist on the continuing work of the Holy Spirit today. This insistence—and I do not mean to imply by this term that I doubt this

21

continuing work—leads us to a sense that our experience of faith is not separated from that of the Israelites of 2000 years ago, but continues to be a first-hand witnessing of God's redemptive work in history. Somehow our own personal experience is thought (at least subconsciously) to cut through the hyper-reality that would otherwise compromise historic Christianity.

This is not the place, and neither am I the historian, to establish the true "reality" of the "word made flesh" in the first century. I will leave the description of those historic events to others. But I would begin with the comment of Henry Chadwick, who writes that "before the time of Irenaeus [c. 180], the sacred books of the Christians were in the main the Hebrew Bible, 'law, prophets, and writings' or 'Old Testament.' The tradition of the words of the Lord were largely oral, and even after the canonical gospels were freely circulating, second-century citations of Jesus' teaching often suggest oral rather than written transmission" (30-31). Chadwick's comment suggests the existence of hyper-reality, in that even those closest to Christ's ministry, life, miracles, and teachings, understood him and his work through an oral tradition for some time after his death. Only later did the written Scripture that we take for granted as the definitive, canonical record of the Word achieve the widespread acceptance that we have assumed.

While this is perhaps common knowledge—so common that we fail to recognize its significance—it also suggests the largely hidden contribution of communications technology in constructing the hyper-reality of faith. In other words, the means of communication has had significant but unacknowledged impact on the way human beings think about their world, relationships, history, and faith.

Communications historians have typically divided history into three broad eras: oral culture, writing and print culture, and electronic culture. These are not perfect descriptors, for radio was more electric than electronic for the first forty years or more of its life, and the designations obscure as much as illumine the present debates about such things as virtual reality, digital media, and bit-streaming. But as general designations or signposts of change, these divisions have worked. However, even while they have marked some of the important shifts in consciousness enabled by technological change, they have also contributed to the hyper-reality that makes the changes occurring now through the application of digital media more difficult to discern.

We may profitably begin thinking about digital media by asking what its relationship is to the broader and somewhat illusive concept of postmodernism. Postmodern philosophy (or at least its more common variants in everyday life) has elevated the particular over the general. That is, since every interpretation has equal validity, any single interpretation has the same status as 'common' understanding, thus reducing the value of the general culture in favor of the more specific small group or individual interpretation of culture. Thus, it has engendered or legitimized cultural fragmentation to give voice to the voiceless. It has thereby multiplied the voices to be heard and created new possibilities for both the construction of human identity and definitions of community life. Kenneth Gergen has asserted that:

> As a result of advances in radio, telephone, transportation, television, satellite transmission, computers, and more, we are exposed to an enormous barrage of social stimulation. Small and enduring communities, with a limited cast of significant others, are being replaced by a vast and ever-expanding array of relationships . . . .
>
> [T]his massive increment in social stimulation—moving toward a state of saturation—sets the stage both for radical changes in our daily experiences of self and others and for an unbridled relativism within the academic sphere. Beliefs in the true and the good depend on a reliable and homogeneous group of supporters, who define what is reliably "there," plain and simple. With social saturation, the coherent circles of accord are demolished, and all beliefs thrown into question by one's own exposure to multiple points of view . . . .
>
> In effect I argue that what is generally characterized as the postmodern condition within the culture is largely a by-product of the century's technologies of social saturation. (xi)

He grounds his assessment of the postmodern condition in the multiplicity of voices to which we are now subject as a result of developments in communications technologies. These technologies have expanded our worlds to that outside the immediate or existential, reoriented our sense of time by providing constant and instantaneous access to media, and replaced the linear or diachronic time of our ancestors (which was governed by the immutable laws of celestial motion and biological clocks) with a new synchronic sense of repeating cycles. New television programs, for instance, compete against yesterday's programs, which are still being broadcast. *I Love Lucy* and *Leave it to Beaver* compete on cable or satellite delivery systems head-to-head against *Friends* and *The Drew Carey Show*. The fifties and the new century single digit decade are jumbled together on our television screens. The Internet only exacerbates this situation by providing state-of-the-art graphic design, streaming media, animation, and pseudo-interactivity to the wired (and the newly emerging wireless) generation. The Internet delivers the musty history of the

Library of Congress or the Louvre, along with the latest in pornographic, personal, and peripatetic perusal.

Like the chicken and egg, which came first—the postmodern sensibility or digital media? The obvious answer is that postmodernism arrived first. After all, it traces its history either to the 1930s or in some histories to the late nineteenth century. This was long before the development of the digital age. But this is too facile. Both of these phenomena had roots. And despite the sophisticated philosophizing of early post-modernists prior to digital media, their treatises can hardly be said to have seeped into the collective consciousness of society before cable or satellite-delivered TV, or before the early age of the Internet.

We might trace the roots of postmodernism, for instance, to existentialism, or earlier to skepticism, or even earlier to the Enlightenment. Existentialism argued that what was most significant in our sense of self was our personal or individual experience. Skepticism questioned the prevailing orthodoxies. The Enlightenment broke the church's monopoly on knowledge.

Likewise, digital media were preceded by the electronic, which introduced the idea that what any of us watch or hear should be governed by the market—the will of the majority—and thus we accepted the myth of choice promulgated by those who would profit from it (echoes of Adam Smith). And prior to these developments were those associated with the printing press, which legitimated the use of vernacular expression in publication, beginning with the Bible itself and leading to the idea of the "priesthood of all believers." Elizabeth Eisenstein argues that

> Protestantism was surely the first [religious movement] fully to exploit [the printing press's] potential as a mass medium. It was also the first movement of any kind, religious or secular, to use the new presses for overt propaganda and agitation against an established institution. By pamphleteering directed at arousing popular support and aimed at readers who were unversed in Latin, the reformers unwittingly pioneered as revolutionaries and rabble rousers. (303–304)

Perhaps even more to the point were remarks of Arthur G. Dickens:

> Lutheranism was from the first the child of the printed book, and through this vehicle Luther was able to make exact, standardized and ineradicable impressions on the mind of Europe. For the first time in human history a great reading public judged the validity of revolutionary ideas through a mass-medium which used the vernacular languages together with the arts of the journalist and the cartoonist. (quoted in Eisenstein: 303)

There is a significant difference between these two remarks: where-as Eisenstein credits the Protestant movement with exploiting the print-ing press, Dickens calls the Reformation—or at least its Lutheran vari-ant—a child of this technology. Which came first, the chicken or the egg?

Lewis Mumford takes the question even further back in time. "At the beginning," he writes, "ritual and language were the chief means of maintaining order and establishing human identity: an increase of cultur-al continuity and predictability, the basis for further creativity, were the proofs of their success." But, he continues,

> by means of language, each group progressively organized its imme-diate impressions, its memories, its anticipations into a highly indi-vidualized and articulated design, which continued to embrace and absorb new experiences while giving them its own idiomatic stamp. It was mainly by creating these elaborate structures of significance that man eventually mastered—though still imperfectly—the art of becoming human. (78)

In Mumford's understanding of the question, language itself is a technology, and through use of that technology communities both con-structed differential sensibilities (sets of meanings and significance, or culture) that separated one group from another and provided themselves with a mechanism to change or to absorb and use what was encountered in others. Furthermore, in his interpretation, this step provided the means for humankind to understand itself as human. Was this a philosophy or a technology, then?

We might even argue that the differentiation or individualization that we now take for granted as an aspect of everyday technological and philosophical life was set into motion by God himself in his decision to scatter the people at Babel, both physically and linguistically. The rela-tionship is not one-sided (philosophy preceding technology or technolo-gy preceding philosophy), but rather there is what I call a set of enabling conditions that are provided by change (social, political, economic, tech-nological, cultural, environmental, intellectual, etc.) that allow or encour-age other changes to occur. It is a symbiotic reality in which one change—exploited by human beings—engenders others. This is what makes it so difficult to get to root causes, or for those (such as Marxists, technological determinists, and sociobiologists) who distill the human experience into unidimensional cause-effect relationships to make their claims without challenge.

Focusing on the area of technology and presuming the position staked out above, I would like to suggest that technological change can

Communication Technology

culture	oral	writing	print
	"In the beginning"	3000 BC	AD 1455 - 1605
time span	unknown	4,500 years	225 years
technology	lore totems signaling spoken word drama dance music pictography	hieroglyphics written language illumination wood block printing literacy	printing press photography photogravure written vernacular
developments	arts rhetoric drama poetry	devotionals scientific observations aesthetic criticism musical scores experimental method apologetics authorship	novels advertising tracts news journalism comics catechisms systematic theology insurance/banking/ commerce
bias	time over space	transitional	space over time
focus	tradition spirituality "nation" ritual & rites	monastic orders division of labor orthodoxy/heresy linear thought rationality	public education literacy political ideology capitalism commodity
authority	hierarchical tribal elders	hierarchical monarchy	hierarchical/ democratic revolution Reformation
inclusion	blood lineage tribe		language state orthodoxy
concepts	unrecorded	ego individualism	nationalism imperialism Reformation legitimation bureaucratization circulation evolution institutionalization
	maintenance of culture		

& Cultural Change

electric	electronic	digital/cybernetic
1840 - 1905	1919 - 1975	1980 –
	15 years	5 years
telegraph	radio	personal computer
wireless	television	cellular telephony
telephone	magnetic recording	videogame systems
mechanical recording	cable TV	DBS
cinema	satellite TV distribution	optical recording
phonograph	VCR	Internet
	laser disk	ISDN
		GPS
"objective" reports	on-the-spot news	CD-ROM
feature length films	talk shows	database retrieval
newsreels	soap operas	game cartridges
animation (cartoons)	situation comedies	arcades
recorded music	rock 'n' roll	electronic chat
Tin Pan Alley		cybersmut
jazz		virtual reality
	analog	digital
space over time	space over time	space over time
public objectivity	demagogy	capacity
timeliness	iconography	control
progress	entertainment	competitiveness
monopolization	choice/variety	profit
speed	mythos	deregulation
democratic/populist	populist	anarchical
	rebellion	none
	life style	technological sophistication
	music	income
	anti-authority	"ex-communication"
	pro-symbolic	irrelevance of authority
		irreverence to symbols
eliminate obstacles	centralization	authenticity
connectivity	fragmentation of art	continuity
subscribers	persona	convenience
mythos	fidelity	interactive
information	propaganda	access
mass entertainment	audiences	user-friendly
cultural hierarchy	systems	markets
possibility	point of view/bias	haves/have nots
		production of commodity

establish a new enabling condition that encourages or engenders change in other areas. But clearly I am not, therefore, claiming technology as a first cause or arguing a technological determinist position, for I could just as well argue that cultural or environmental change establishes a new enabling condition that encourages or engenders change in other areas. We must consider change as multi-faceted, multi-causative, and multi-consequential. Any change has multiple results, some anticipated, some not. Change likewise 'causes' (engenders, encourages, and enables) other changes to occur, and it is itself a consequence of multiple changes that preceded it.

To facilitate discussion of this point, I provide the chart on pages 44-45. It is an expansion of the traditional divisions of communication cultures mentioned earlier (oral, print, and electronic) and provides more precision for the purposes of this discussion.

This chart divides communication cultures into six, rather than three, ages: oral, writing (or chirographic), print, electric, electronic, and digital/cybernetic culture. These are useful distinctions because of the different sensibilities of each of the ages. These sensibilities are captured in this chart in the terms listed under developments, focus, authority, inclusion, and concepts. In each of the six ages these differ. Those that exist in the left-most column are carried over, to be sure, as the new age takes hold, but those aspects of sensibility in each column are less salient in those that precede it. No new sensibility arrives immediately in the wake of a new means of communication either, but it gradually takes hold within the culture that begins to be shaped in response to the new enabling conditions offered by that new means of capturing and expressing human experience. Seeing the chart in this way helps us to recognize that technology is not a singular causative agent, but borrows from ideas developed prior to its introduction, recasts those ideas in new forms, and provides a new impetus for cultural expression and understanding than what had existed before. Since my focus in this essay is on digital media as cultural metaphor, let me provide a couple of linguistic examples of how this alteration in consciousness occurs. In 1900 there was no word for "radio" in the English-language dictionary. The only assisted or amplified means of communication (and I use "amplified" here in the acoustic sense of the term—as in louder voice—rather than in the sense that a newspaper might be said to amplify a voice) was the wireless. Around 1905, when voices began to be carried through the air rather than the dits and dots of telegraphy, people referred to the receivers used to pick these voices from the air as wireless sets. By 1920, however, over 1,000 new words had been added to the English language by the phenomenon of radio—all necessary as a means to understand what this new form of communication provided. The same thing has occurred in the new digital age: language takes a quantum leap forward as people attempt to grasp what it is that has been introduced into our society. But we still use terms from the older culture to grasp what we are encountering. For example, Phil Cooke criticizes thinking within the Christian community for using Internet sites merely to provide "video and audio clips of sermons." And we already know, he says, that "Christian television has largely been a depository for video-taped sermons" (12). What Cooke criticizes is the usual kind of thinking that happens when a new culture begins to replace an older one—we think in the old categories in the effort to wrap our mind around the changes we encounter. And since the church is one of the most conservative institutions in society—slow to change, cleaving to tradition—it has more difficulty than most in accomplishing that wrapping. It continues to use the old wineskins because they are familiar and safe.

If we pay attention to the linguistic changes that accompany technological changes, we can begin to recognize their significance in how we think about the human condition at any point in time. Jesus, for instance, used pastoral or agricultural images in his stories because they were closest to his listeners' experiences and understanding. So we should not merely think that technological change provides a new set of tools to proclaim the gospel, but it provides a context within which the Christian message will have to be made new again using the new metaphors, allusions, definitions, and vocabularies afforded by such change.

What, then, should we understand about this new digital/cybernetic age, if we are to proclaim God's truth within it fruitfully? We should begin by recognizing that this new age does not merely provide a different means to deliver a message. The Internet is not merely a wired equivalent of the airwaves that carry radio and television signals. Neither is the World Wide Web merely an electronic equivalent of the newspaper or a new form of library, nor is email only paperless exchange. The new communications system that has been constructed using the creation and storage capabilities of the computer and the delivery capabilities of networking are far more interesting than previous practices, for they enable the redefinition of experience, identity, community, values, and the nature of faith itself.

To discuss this I want to concentrate on a particular portion of the chart, especially the two rightmost columns (labeled electronic and digital/cybernetic), and particularly the portions of those columns labeled focus, authority, inclusion, and concepts. It is in this portion of the chart that the idea of digital media as metaphor emerges and where the consequences of this new metaphor for human experience and relationship can best be understood. Since the Bible is the story of God's efforts to establish and maintain relationship with His people—even to save them from their own folly in rejecting Him—the establishment of a new metaphor by which such concepts may be understood has profound consequences for both Scripture and faith.

Digital culture is not merely an extension of the electronic culture that has prevailed since radio was introduced in 1919. This is difficult to grasp because the digital age has been developing since the early 1980s, when personal computers began to achieve significant home penetration. But, as with any new technology, it took some time for the new consciousness engendered by these machines to develop. So most of us today still define our consciousness in electronic rather than digital terms. And serious consideration of the consequences of this shift has only been developing since around 1995.

In 1998 Neal Gabler, referring to works by Philip Roth and Daniel Boorstin, wrote:

> What they recognized was that life itself was gradually becoming a medium of its own, like television, radio, print and film, and that all of us were becoming at once performance artists in and audiences for a grand, ongoing show—a show that was, as Roth noted, often far richer, more complex and more compelling than anything conceived for the more conventional media. In short, life was becoming a movie. (4)

Even as Gabler wrote this comment, however, people were already arguing that society had moved beyond life as movie into virtual life. In my opinion, even the cinema had difficulty trying to capture what this new "reality" was until *The Matrix* was released in 1999, although Wim Wenders's *Until the End of the World*, released in 1991, portrayed some of the consequences much earlier. But few people saw that film. David Nicholson, a *Washington Post* staff writer, wrote in that publication's *Weekly Edition* in 1995 a comment that recognized the profound difference between the digital life that people were living by that time and the disjunction with the realities of everyday life:

> It's too late, of course, to turn back and retreat to pre-digital times. But it isn't too late to think about what kind of future we want to live in and how we might affect things from here on out . . . . The more technology invades our lives, the more it obscures the real issues— the fact that our lives are really about love and work and death, about creating and maintaining relationships that sustain us, about finding

meaningful vocations, and about living with the knowledge that, alone among all creatures, we know one day we're going to die. Technology may affect the material conditions of our lives, but it hasn't done much yet for our souls.

Perhaps our souls were still living life as a movie, even while our consciousness had begun to enter this new, disembodied, parallel universe. We continue to struggle with this shift. M. Chayko wrote as early as 1993 that

> in modern everyday life, it is difficult (and becoming impossible) to definitively classify experience as 'real' or 'not real'; it is more helpful to determine the degree or 'accent' of reality in an event. The frames we once used, conceptually, to set the real apart from the unreal are not as useful as they once were; they are not as sturdy; they betray us. As they become ever more fragile, we require new concepts and understandings. (178)

This struggle is basic. It is about what defines the human condition, about what is significant in human history and consciousness, about those issues that Nicholson raises and that Christians resonate with, and about the sort of world that Scripture must somehow address in terms that are understandable and compelling within this new evanescent context. My own conclusion in 1999 was that

> we are undergoing profound changes—in those very cultural values that served as the foundation for the development of this technology. The nature of communication, relationship, value-formation, self-identity, are all being redefined in our consciousness in profoundly new ways. We participate in that redefinition just as we are being socialized into acquiescing to it or being forced into accepting some of its more disturbing qualities (e.g, redefinitions of privacy, appropriate surveillance and connection to others) (see Fortner, 1989). (1999:32)

During the electronic era, the concerns expressed about media—and especially television—have decried its impact on behavior, its encouragement of passivity, its quick fixes to problems, its mindless promotion of materialism, and its tendency to isolate people from one another. The television was referred to as the "boob tube," the "ethereal hearth," and the "flickering blue flame," terms that evoked either its simplistic content (its lowest common denominator programming) or its visual magnetism—like moths to the flame. Neil Postman tells us that "the symbolic form of political information has been radically changed. In the television age, political judgment is transformed from an intellectual assessment of propositions to an intuitive and emotional response to the totality of an image" (101). Joshua Meyrowitz tells us that "electronic media destroy the specialness of place and time. Television, radio, and the telephone turn once private places into public ones by making them more accessible to the outside world. And car stereos, wristwatch televisions, and personal sound systems such as the Sony 'Walkman' make public spaces particular." Gene Youngblood claims that while we question all sorts of traditional authority in the electronic age, we do not question our entertainment. And it is this entertainment, he says, that leads us into unthinking responses to its formulas: thus "the commercial entertainer encourages an unthinking response to daily life, inhibiting self–awareness. . . . He offers nothing we haven't already conceived, nothing we don't already expect" (225-226) And P. David Marshall explains that in our mass-mediated culture,

> audiences are constructed and defined by the type of programming that is offered. The goal behind the construction of audiences through programs is their 'sellability' to advertisers. The defining of each audience in terms of a specific configuration of consumer needs is an objective of both the program and the advertisements; program and advertisement are complementary rhetorical devices in the construction of audiences as consumers. (63)

These remarks are disparate, but they share a common characteristic. Each is concerned about the relationship of people to a medium or cluster of media. People respond viscerally, we are told, to a medium that evokes emotion through the manipulation of images and the deconstruction (and confusion) of the idea of place and that treats us not as thinking individuals or human beings committed to the common good, but as those who would consume goods and services and who would, in turn, be "consumed" by advertisers to which we are sold. This, of course, is a definition of the human condition that differs in various respects from that of the Bible. This definition has a sense of nihilism about it, a gerbil-wheel feel to it, that Scripture—even when recognizing our sinfulness—does not share.

What happens, then, when we move from this electronic cultural world—with its symbolic worlds and rituals organized around the passive consumption of film, radio, and television—to the so-called "interactive" world of digital media? It is not a simple question for, as has happened several times before in the development of new means of communication, much of what has preceded the innovation has remained in place. There are fragments of the oral age still in our new culture. For example, we still carry on conversations, teach our children to talk, take public speaking classes, and listen to presidential debates. We still read newspapers (although not like we used to) and books; in the United States the magazine industry has exploded with innovation over the past twenty years. And of course block-buster films (such as *Titanic*) still tantalize us, television programs still draw our attention (an estimated 43 million people watched the last episode of *Survivor* in August 2000, normally a dead month for television viewing), and popular music groups (aimed for the most part at young teenagers) still sell out stadiums and arenas without difficulty (but so does Bruce Springsteen, who is not exactly a young pop act).

So while much of what is familiar will remain familiar for decades to come, the move from analog to digital media may mean everything. It is a technology whose time has come—not only technologically but also culturally. As our culture has fragmented with the loss of the certainties of a simpler age (we might think of the film *Pleasantville*, for instance, as a marker of that shift), as the traditional American commitment to indi-vidualism and self-sufficiency has continued to develop, and as our philo-sophical deconstruction of society and its institutions has led our thinking ever more deeply into postmodern consciousness, our communications technologies have enabled us to become so "saturated" (to use Kenneth Gergen's term) that we struggle to keep up with the plethora of relation-ships we have developed in our families, communities, and even with dis-tant figures only encountered in mediated form (whether as celebrities, politicians, or chat room denizens).

Digital media actually encompasses two distinct but integrally relat-ed elements. The first of these is the use of digital code (1s and 0s in spec-ified word lengths—8 bit, 16 bit, etc.) to represent graphic designs, fonts, images, and sound. The second is in the delivery of this digital content. What is significant about digital coding is that it breaks with the tradition of representation as an "analogy" of that which is represented. Let me illustrate this change. Many of the paintings and frescoes so revered in our age were created several hundred years ago. Leonardo da Vinci paint-ed the *Mona Lisa* in the 1500s; Michaelangelo painted the Sistine Chapel ceiling between 1508 and 1512 and the *Last Judgment* over the altar between 1535 and 1541. The frescoes in the Basilica of St. Francis in Assisi were created in the thirteenth century. Over time these works of art have discolored or been damaged (5 millimeters of varnish buildup on the Mona Lisa, centuries of candle soot and lampblack on the Sistine Chapel, and an earthquake in 1997 that shattered the Basilica of St. Francis fres-coes into thousands of pieces), and questions of how (or if) to restore them have been hotly debated. In 1994, for instance, Sylvia Hochfield wrote in *ARTnews* that the "Louvre was considering restoring the *Mona Lisa* 'but is unwilling to endure the venomous attack that would inevitably result if it were touched'" (quoted by the "Science Observer"). The 1997 earthquake that struck Umbria, Italy, was called by Robert Hughes, *Time* magazine's art critic, the "worst catastrophe of Italian art history since the 1966 flood in Florence" and it created grave damage to "unquestionably one of the pivotal artistic, architectural and spiritual achievements of mankind" (quoted by Covington, 1999: 78).

The question of restoration or reconstruction of artworks—whether they are destroyed by natural causes or human intervention—is an analogous question. Is it better that the artwork be seen, as restorers claim, as it was originally intended to be seen (the argument for the restoration of the ceiling of the Sistine Chapel or the *Mona Lisa*) or in the state in which we have become accustomed to seeing it (as critics of the Louvre argued)? Art interacts with time, and some artworks destroyed by acts of desecration, the elements, or various catastrophes take on a patina that becomes a part of what they are (such as the *Statue of Liberty*). In some cases the passage of time has made it difficult even to know with certainty what an artist originally intended, as new layers of pigment have been laid on top of old, sometimes by the original artist himself as he tinkered with a painting or corrected a "mistake," and sometimes by later restorations. Questions of intent, integrity, originality, artistic value, and technique are historical questions, intimately tied together by their appeal to an original state of being.

New translations of Scripture have had similar connections to the past. One of the justifications for retranslating Scripture is that past translations were inadequate, that new discoveries (for example, the Dead Sea Scrolls) have revealed previously lost aspects of Scripture, that vocabularies are now better understood than before, or that the people of today would find the wisdom and truth of the past more compelling in their own language. In each case the justification for moving ahead has been a new discovery of the old. The past is intimately linked to the present, forming a continuity of perspective in which the new is legitimized by the old. Even when digital technologies have been put to work in the service of such activities (as when 3-D virtual imaging helped restorers recompose and replace the Basilica frescoes in their original locations, through comparisons made with master photographs taken before the disaster), the justification was found in the past. Paola Passalacqua, coordinator of the restoration, said that such an action was not merely an artistic opinion but "a moral necessity" (quoted by Covington, 1999: 84).

These actions are not the imperatives of digital culture, however. To return to the chart, the focus of digital culture is capacity (storage), control, competitiveness (e–commerce), profit, and deregulation (or unbridled activity). The authority structure is anarchy. The concepts raised by the culture are authenticity, continuity, convenience, interactivity, access, and so on. The questions of inclusion are made problematic by the irrelevance of authority and the irreverence to symbols (or past collective meanings).

While this is quite a laundry list of complaint, which one may see as overly negative, it need not be taken that way. For one thing, the roots of this change are still located in analog culture. Competitiveness has been a hallmark of consumer capitalism since at least the time of Adam Smith's 1776 treatise, *The Wealth of Nations*. Since the turn of the nineteenth century, control has been a focus of technological development, as James R. Beninger points out (6). For another thing, some of the characteristics of digital culture have both positive and negative consequences. The explosive growth of the Internet, for instance, has been credited to the fact that there is no central control over its development and that various software programs have made the World Wide Web's most engaging features (integration of sound, video, photography and graphics, animated gif files, etc.) extraordinarily easy to use. At the same time this non-control (or "democratic" tendency) has enabled wholesale pirating of intellectual property, both in the notorious cases of Sony vs. MP3.com and Napster vs. the Recording Industry Association of America, as well as in the more mundane activity of purloining text, gif, or jpeg files from one site to integrate into another. Some sites even suggest that you copy their information rather than link to their graphics, because linking merely clogs their servers without generating more desirable traffic (that is, visitors who want to see the site in its entirety rather than make a brief visit).

There is little doubt that digital culture is irreverent to symbols or to the traditional meanings meant to be provoked by them. The Christian cross has become a ubiquitous fashion accessory. Darwinists and evangelicals spar over the use of the Christian fish—who is gobbling whom? Even in the realm of popular culture, the distinction between "good guys" and 'bad guys' has blurred since the days of Gary Cooper and John Wayne. Dark comedy is increasingly the norm (*Fargo*, *There's Something about Mary*, *Analyze This*); 'good guys' can be legitimately responsible for the most gruesome deaths (Nicholas Cage in *ConAir* or John Cusack in *Grosse Point Blank*) or cruel indignities (Jack Nicholson in *As Good as It Gets*). Such examples are indicators of the fragmentation of meaning in the digital age. Others would be the hype about a 1,000 channel television universe, increasingly specialized magazine content and radio formats, the use of samplers by rap music artists, and the unorganized and largely uncatalogued World Wide Web.

In this digital age, art is changed by sweeping away pixels or morphing photographs, the fragile barrier between reality and representation having been broken by the change in palette from paint-based to digit-based systems. This may not seem like such a radical shift, but pixels are, by their nature, evanescent, non-corporeal, and understood collectively. They are not an attempt to recreate emotion, belief, or events through the capture of flesh and bone on canvas. They are flickering dots on a screen, occupying "space" according to number of colors used, the word length of the codes used to excite the pixels, and the compression scheme employed. They are a technological creation that can be made and unmade at will—not only by their original creator, but also by anyone with the appropriate skill and technology.

This new technology, of course, emerged from the values animating the earlier electronic culture, and it from the electric culture that preceded it, back on to print and chirographic cultures. Each new culture was constructed by exploiting the capabilities for expression created by new technologies within the social framework of its predecessor. As Donald MacKenzie and Judy Wajcman suggest, the characteristics of any society "play a major part in deciding which technologies are adopted" (6), and as Trevor J. Pinch and Wiebe E. Bijker put it, "both science and technology are socially constructed cultures and bring to bear whatever cultural resources are appropriate for the purposes at hand" (21).

Nonetheless, the new digital culture is one based in five essential new capabilities: (1) storage capacity, (2) random search routines, (3) combinability, (4) networking or connectivity, and (5) speed. These capabilities—to store enormous quantities of data, search this information at high speed, retrieve a portion of it, and combine it with other similarly ordered data through connectivity—provide the foundation for all the hopes and fears of this new age. As Michael Riordan and Lillian Hoddeson put it:

> In half a century's time, the transistor, whose modest role is to amplify electrical signals, has redefined the meaning of power, which today is based as much upon the control and exchange of information as it is on iron or oil. The throbbing heart of these sweeping global transformations is the tiny solid-state amplifier invented by Bardeen, Brattain, and Shockley. The crystal fire they ignited during those anxious postwar years has radically reshaped the world and the way its inhabitants now go about their daily lives. (10)

While the physics of this new digital age is difficult to grasp in all of its complexity, what it is capable of doing is understandable. Even if we cannot explain the electronics theory behind the operation of a transistor, a central processing unit, or a network protocol, we can see them in operation and have a sense of what lies below the surface. And the popular media hype their capabilities enough for us to gradually have at least a superficial grasp of how they function.

Regardless of what Christian magazines may suggest, it is not high-tech physics that impacts Christian witness or the relevance of Scripture. It is the metaphysics of this digital age that matters most to the relevance of Scripture, or at least to our understanding and application of it in this new culture. What we need to grasp the most is the idea of digital as metaphor.

If we take the characteristics of this digital culture and combine them with one of the facets of connectivity most promoted by those who most breathlessly embrace its possibilities—such as Howard Rheingold or Esther Dyson—we can begin to grapple with this idea. Dyson, for instance, says that

> the Net gives awesome power to individuals—the ability to be heard across the world, the ability to find information about almost anything . . . along with the ability to spread lies worldwide, to discover secrets about friends and strangers, and to find potential victims of fraud, child abuse, or other harassment. With greater ability to exercise their rights or to abuse them, individuals will need to assume greater responsibility for their own actions and for the world they are creating. (6, her ellipsis)

Don Tapscott elaborates on this point by arguing that children control "much of their world on the Net," making it

> fundamentally different from previous communications innovations because . . . [all previous technologies] are unidirectional and controlled by adults. They are hierarchical, inflexible, and centralized.... By contrast, the new media is interactive, malleable, and distributed in control. As such it cherishes much greater neutrality. . . . For the first time ever, children are taking control of critical elements of a communications revolution. (25-26)

What is significant here is not an emphasis on awesome power, neutrality, interactivity, malleability, or distributed control, but the alteration in what Barrington Nevitt called the "communication ecology." It is, on the one hand, a confirmation of Harold A. Innis's argument (117) that any fundamental alteration in the monopoly of knowledge will occur on its outer fringes, in this case the monopoly of knowledge controlled by infor-mation-based corporations and adults. It is an illustration of what Jürgen Habermas called the "structural transformation of the public sphere" (Habermas, 1991, especially Chapter 2). What it means fundamentally is that the public sphere—as defined by the values and meanings of this new digitally coded culture—has been democratized. And not only democra-tized in its most revered American sense of the word, but also democra-tized in the sense that authority has been vanquished and hierarchies based on education, age, position, title, control, responsibility, and income have crumbled. Children are as much in charge as adults, high schoolers as much as college graduates, the mail room clerk as much as the CEO.

This turns all the traditional ideas about culture on their head. And, to the extent that the legitimacy of any institution (such as the church) or any authoritative text (such as the Bible) is founded in older traditions (print, electronic, etc.), this legitimacy is beginning to erode. Tom Beaudoin, for instance, talks about the "virtual faith" of Gen-Xers, which is based in the "'deconstruction' of religious institutions" and their "reconstruction of religious alternatives" (52). "It is the sense," he says, "that 'no one is in control' that makes cyberspace hostile to the hegemo-ny of religious institutions" (55). And on the question of Scripture, Beaudoin, after perusing a set of hypertext Scripture (or Scripture verses linked to other verses, as well as to commentaries, dictionaries, etc., on the Web) asks:

> When Scripture appears in hypertext format, where does 'real' Scripture begin and end? What if *every* scriptural word were 'hot'? Is it possible, I wondered, to read Scripture in the form of its more familiar technology (the clothbound book) as hypertext. Just when I thought I had a firm theological foundation, I found this one as slip-pery as the old orthodoxies that my culture's music videos skewered. When a generation (Xers and everyone after us) grows up with access to Scripture as hypertext, what happens to the authority of Scripture, and what happens to Scripture itself? (125-126)

Beaudoin goes on to say that in such a world people are reading Scripture "errantly" or in a wandering fashion.

Beaudoin argues that we have always had to do this (126), since each of us has had to make sense of the Scripture ourselves, but in this conclusion he errs. Although we have had to deal with the truths of Scripture ourselves—particularly after it became vernacular—and have constituted the "priesthood of all believers" by interpreting a Scripture that is "clear on its face," we have done so within the confines of theologically and institutionally defined orthodoxy, with debates over the issue of meaning and application argued in everything from lengthy tomes to simple devotional materials, from pulpits to ecclesiastical assemblies. There have been communities of the ordained, of elders in the church, of years of Sunday school, all pointing us in a largely singular direction. And although the hypertext that Beaudoin describes may be seen as merely another manifestation of that, an addition to the older panoply of tools, it is (metaphorically speaking) more than that because its foundation is in democratization, irreverence, and irrelevance of authority. So the message of the meaning that emerges from the digital system is, in the sixties vernacular, "roll your own." Create what you will, for all is equally plausible, useful, and legitimate. Steven Johnson, taking a look at the "Palace" online environment (a kind of souped-up chat-room), says that some

> online denizens make the case for [its] language as a kind of digital-age free verse, a verbal stew of disconnected phrases and libidinal outbursts. . . . It reminds me of graffiti, and graffiti of the worst kind: isolated declarations of selfhood, failed conversations, slogans, tag lines. You don't really see a community in these exchanges; you see a group of individuals all talking past one another, and talking in an abbreviated, almost unintelligible code. (69)

The reason for this unintelligible code is not the 1s and 0s of the digital world per se, but its speed, multi-point (or democratized) access, and its nonlinear linearity. Speed contributes to it because it creates the system for instantaneous posting of messages (such as online chat with Instant Messenger). The fact that several people may all be in a chatroom together and posting messages to one another in a kind of virtual cocktail party means that the messages that appear are almost never consecutive, requiring people rapidly to sort, discard, or juggle multiple threads simultaneously. But unlike a cocktail party, where the surrounding conversations may appear as an indecipherable din surrounding one's own intimate conversation, in the chatroom all conversations appear line by line as though part of the same ongoing exchange. Such an effect is called nonlinear linearity, which refers to the quality whereby each message appears in sequence as though following the preceding posting, when in reality it may be responding to a posting several lines earlier, with messages that arrived between question and answer intervening in the exchange. So while the participants see the postings linearly, in actuality conversations jump one another in a kind of virtual leapfrog.

Imagining the consequences of the shifts in the relationship of people to Scripture would thus suggest the following changes:

- Scripture was at first inscribed in the consciousness of God's people by both their own existential understanding (what they had experienced first-hand) and by the mnemonic devices of oral culture. God provided a brief list of his expectations (the Ten Commandments) and a priesthood whose task was, among other things, to remind the people of how God would have them be holy (through circumcision, ritual cleansing, sacrifices, etc.). After the advent of Christianity, this pattern continued, with Christians' understanding of Scripture filtered by clergy using the rhetorical devices appropriate to liturgy (Eucharist, sermons, etc.).

- After literacy became more commonplace and vernacular Bibles available, people were able to interpret and apply Scripture to their own situation and judge the orthodoxy or connectedness of sermons to their existential reality according to their own reading of Scripture. The Word of God, which had been Christ (John 1:14) and then the preached word, had become captured in text on a page. Written Scripture, interpretable by a literate and increasingly well-educated laity, became the immutable Word (despite controversies over the language, meaning, and elegance of translations). Oral argument was judged by its congruence with written text (essentially the orthodoxy—or right opinion—of the spoken word compared with the orthography—or right writing—of the written word).

- The electronic age added to these concerns those of persona, fidelity, and iconography. Those who had powerful mediated presence (in other words, those who learned the iconography of television) were celebrated as superior mediators of scriptural truth. This celebration might apply equally to those who arguably had "earned" such accolades by their search for the holy (such as Mother Teresa, Pope John Paul, or Billy Graham) and to those who could exploit the possibilities of television for personal gain or empire building (such as many American televangelists).

- The significance of the advent of the digital age has been obscured by understandings grounded in these earlier cultures—especially the electronic. The possibilities offered by digital media seemed to accomplish two desired results. First, because of its quasi-textual nature, digital media might enhance the remnants of legitimacy that clung to the written word. Second, through the interactivity and plethora of channels offered, digital media offered the possibility of neutralizing the most objectionable characteristics of electronic media (passivity, persona/celebrity, excessive commercialism, and the negative behavioral consequences of watching television). But in the rush to embrace these results, the question of how the digital age might alter the relationship between people and Scripture, perhaps undermining the legitimacy and authority of Scripture in people's lives, has been insufficiently considered.

Warnings have emerged from some thoughtful critics of the shift to the digital, even if some of them have been overstated. Sven Birkerts, for instance, contrasts print media, which, he says, "exalts the word, fixing it into permanence," with electronic forms that reduce the word "to a signal, a means to an end" (123). He argues that the shift will have the following consequences: (1) the erosion of language through a cyclical impoverishment; (2) a flattening of historical perspective through the expunging of a sense of chronology; and (3) the waning of the private self (128-29). "We will soon be navigating with ease among cataracts of organized pulsations," he says, "putting out and taking in signals. We will bring our terminals, our modems, and menus further and further into our former privacies; we will implicate ourselves by degrees in the unitary life, and there may come a day when we no longer remember that there was any other life" (131). What is most intriguing to me about this last statement is how my own undergraduate students have confirmed it. When I try to discuss such comments in media classes, the students not only do not deny this consequence, they do not even understand the shift. They do not remember any other life, so they have no baseline to examine the truth or falsity of Birkerts's claim.

A less apocalyptic vision of the future of communication and the nature of text come from Vickie Abrahamson, Mary Meehan, and Larry Samuel, even while supporting the direction of Birkerts's prose.

> The very concept of language is in flux as writing gets a faceful of *technomorphing.* As e-mail eclipses paper correspondence across Corporate America to save cost and time, E-speak is the latest branch to bloom on the English tree. . . . E-mail symbolism (emoticons) and its chatty, often rambling writing style are changing the very nature of how we communicate at the office and, in turn, making corporate culture less formal [read loss of authority]. . . . Read any good screens lately? With more and more literature available online and on CD-ROM, there's a revolution going on in publishing not seen since Gutenberg cranked up his press. (234)

Paul Levinson, in a book that is largely supportive of the changes occurring as digital culture opens new possibilities for "reading," also suggests some of the implications of this shift:

> In the truly global, multiplex-of-multiplex movie theater that is the World Wide Web, not only is an endless series or simultaneity of productions showing—depending on whether we look at the links as sequences chosen by individuals, or as a collection of ever-changing links flashing in and out of being at any one time—but the productions vary radically in the texture, degree of original author expression, and internal-link possibilities within the constituent parts. To return to the montage analogy, we might say that in hypertext mounted on the Web there is no individual image, anywhere. Rather, we are dealing with images—texts—which at their smallest linked component, by very virtue of that link, are themselves an image connected to another, a process already in motion.
>
> This view of the Web as implicate aggregate—to borrow David Bohm's (1980) use of 'implicate' order, another accurate take on the holographic nature of reality, or its provision of complete recipes for the pie in each of its slices, regardless of how thin they are cut—further complicates the issue of enjoyment of text. To the question of whether I prefer being told or telling myself a story—and, if both are possible, in what ratio—we have the additional challenge of, if I choose to tell the story myself and go the link route, at what juncture will these linkages, the story itself under my construction, end? (145)

What, then, is happening to the Word in this developing world, and what are the implications of that world for the continuing legitimacy, authenticity, and centrality of the Word? If digital culture is not merely another way to deliver text physically, to argue cases, or to connect with a world without the Gospel, but is rather an entirely new and complex reorientation of sensibility, and a new metaphor that is redefining people's relationship with the texts that have constituted our Christian foundation, what does it mean to our ability to share this Word with the real or virtual world?

The significance of Scripture (or at least the claims of the Gospels) has been questioned from the very beginning. Islam developed from a denial of those claims. Enlightenment philosophers questioned them. Darwinism (at least in its most radical forms) threatened them. Marxism belittled them. So it is not as though Christian understandings of Scripture are suddenly and unexpectedly encountering a threat never before seen. But this newly developing culture does not set out to discount faith or Scripture. As a matter of fact, its proponents argue that it enhances the possibilities for evangelism and pursuit of the lost.

The problems created for Scripture by digital thinking are more subtle. Hypertext Bibles, Christian commentaries, Bible dictionaries, and historiographies are available online. Those who want to use them may do so without molestation. In digital culture, however, the strengths are also the weaknesses, the possibilities also the problems. One way to see this comes from Bill Joy, Chief Scientist for Sun Microsystems:

> Perhaps it is always hard to see the bigger impact while you are in the vortex of change. Failing to understand the consequences of our inventions while we are in the rapture of discovery and innovation seems to be a common fault of scientists and technologists; we have long been driven by the overarching desire to know that is the nature of science's quest, not stopping to notice that the progress to newer and more powerful technologies can take on a life of its own. (243)

More immediate perhaps than the dangers that spawned Joy's comments are the digital realities already upon us: that every image, text, and sound delivered via the Internet is now a component in a great stew of possibilities in which no single ingredient is any more significant or crucial to the whole than any other. Perhaps an example will make this point clearer.

My pastor often uses the insights from novels, films, or scholarly books to illumine a passage of Scripture. These external texts help him provide insights that can relate, explain, or connect a particular passage to the life of his congregation. Through these non-biblical texts he can make the experience of the Israelites or the apostles common with that of the congregation by connecting the past with the present. This is an analogical form of exposition. In the digital world, however, the prevailing ethos is one of fragmentation and reconnection. "Surfers" will travel from site to site, viewing disparate but equal fragments, each one illuminating the other and including not only the sorts of texts used in church, but also newspapers, e-zines, personal sites, both government and anarchist locations, libraries, etc. Depending on the whim of the surfer (who might use a search engine, subscribe to a listserv, read email, use another search engine, click on links, or check out an advertisement) the results are nearly infinite in possibility. Each search can be as valid or invalid as the next. Each tidbit of information is encountered in the same framework, often with little or no context by which to judge its truthfulness, bias, or factuality.

In the same way digitally produced photographs, sound files, loops, video clips, and graphic arts can be recombined in nearly infinite variety to create and recreate a pastiche of art, pulling bits and pieces from the cultural history of the planet and combining them with newly created artifacts. Such pastiche echoes the "sampling" done in hip-hop music and raises issues of intellectual property, fair use, attribution, homage (tribute-paying) similar to those raised by this musical form.

Personal experience is thus grounded in the quicksand of ever-shifting possibilities. Links go dead as Web sites are moved. New sites pop up and await discovery. Rings are created and then abandoned. Each new film released or celebrity created causes a new set of start-up sites to appear. Libraries and government agencies go online. Commercial sponsors pay to allow "free" delivery of services to users, and multiple visits to a single site can cause different ad copy to appear, tailored to individual interests. Cookies are planted, and data are mined from online forms and are connected to create profiles of book buyers, pornography consumers, or visitors to online showrooms or financing companies. All information becomes a commodity available to those willing to pay for access to it. The bigger the database and the faster the access, the better. *Caveat emptor*. It is up to each user to police the profile created about himself—provided he knows where it resides and who controls it. All information and connections are dynamic and their truth relative. The Bible is merely one set of stories among many, perhaps useful to some but otherwise easily ignored. It is no longer the bedrock of cultural creation and discernment, except for those who choose to use it exclusively, and such exclusivity is a foreign concept in digital culture.

"It is too late," as David Nicholson put it, "to retreat to pre-digital times" (25). Digital culture is upon us and is inducing us to see our world and ourselves in new ways. It is a culture based, as Ray Kurzweil puts it, in a new form of intelligence that is of "greater import than any of the events that have shaped human history" (5). It is a context to which the church and Scripture will increasingly need to address itself, but one that is hostile to revealed and immutable truth (as Kurzweil's claim already demonstrates). In other words, people will "see" text differently. It will no longer be the stubborn black typeface on a white page that refuses to change regardless of how loudly or persuasively we address it. It will be merely an ephemeral set of electronic pixels driven by the 0s and 1s of digital logic, one type of representation among many, all streamed together in an unending parade of arbitrarily connected fragments, all calling for attention, using color, size, animation, arrangement, sound, motion, shadow, icon, image, and perhaps soon even odor, all delivered in various orders, according to the method of accessing them. It is all a conjuring act, individualized, packaged, and anarchic.

This may be the ultimate democracy, but it jars the sensibility of people who have staked their lives on the certainty of Scripture as a foundation in an otherwise chaotic world, and who have bet their lives on an unquestioned singular story of God's reaching out to his creation to help it recognize a singular truth and, in turn, to declare it so. But this is the new culture now under construction, one that—through its metaphorical redefinition of reality—will reconfigure the symbolic world of humankind and the methodology for recognizing truth. Yet it is this new symbolic world that Scripture and those who believe it must address if we are to make the Word of God relevant to humankind. It is a new Babel.

Works Consulted

Abrahamson, Vickie, Mary Meehan, and Larry Samuel
    1998   *The Future Ain't What It Used to Be.* New York: Riverhead Books.

Beaudoin, Tom
    1998   *Virtual Faith: The Irreverent Spiritual Quest of Generation X.* San Francisco: Jossey-Bass Publishers.

Beninger, James R.
    1986   *The Control Revolution: Technological and Economic Origins of the Information Society.* Cambridge, MA: Harvard University Press.

Birkerts, Sven
    1994   *The Gutenberg Elegies: The Fate of Reading in an Electronic Age.* Boston: Faber & Faber.

Butterfield, Herbert
    1965   *The Whig Interpretation of History.* New York: W. W. Norton.

Chadwick, Henry
    1992   "The Early Christian Community." Pp. 21-61 in *The Oxford Illustrated History of Christianity.* Ed. John McManners. Oxford: Oxford University Press.

Chayko, M.
    1993   "What is Real in the Age of Virtual Reality? 'Reframing' Frame Analysis for a Technological World." *Symbolic Interaction* 16:171-181.

Cooke, Phil
    2000   "The Keys to Convergence: The Next Step in the Digital Age." *Technologies for Worship* 9 (July/August):8-14.

Covington, Richard
    1999   "An Act of Faith and the Restorer's Art." *Smithsonian* (November):76-85.

Dyson, Esther
    1997   *Release 2.0: A Design for Living in the Digital Age.* New York: Broadway Books.

Eisenstein, Elizabeth L.
    1979   *The Printing Press as an Agent of Change.* Vol. 1. Cambridge: Cambridge University Press.

Fortner, Robert S.
  1989 "Privacy is Not Enough: Personhood and High Technology." *The Conrad Grebel Review* 7 (Spring):159-177.
  1999 "The Gospel in a Digital Age." Pp. 26-38 in *Confident Witness–Changing World*. Ed. Craig Van Gelder. Grand Rapids, MI: William B. Eerdmans.

Gabler, Neal
  1998 *Life the Movie: How Entertainment Conquered Reality.* New York: Alfred A. Knopf.

Gergen, Kenneth
  1991 *The Saturated Self: Dilemmas of Identity in Contemporary Life.* New York: Basic Books.

Habermas, Jürgen
  1991 *The Structural Transformation of the Public Sphere: An Inquiry into a Category of Bourgeois Society.* Trans. Thomas Burger & Frederick Lawrence. Cambridge, MA: The MIT Press.

Innis, Harold A.
  1972 *Empire and Communications.* Rev. Mary Q. Innis. Toronto: University of Toronto Press.

Johnson, Steven
  1997 *Interface Culture: How New Technology Transforms the Way We Create and Communicate.* New York: HarperEdge.

Joy, Bill
  2000 "Why the Future Doesn't Need us." *Wired* 8 (April):238-262.

Kurzweil, Ray
  1999 *The Age of Spiritual Machines: When Computers Exceed Human Intelligence.* New York: Viking.

Levinson, Paul
  1997 *Soft Edge: A Natural History and Future of the Information Revolution.* London: Routledge.

MacKenzie, Donald, and Judy Wajcman
  1988 "Introductory Essay." Pp. 2-25 in *The Social Shaping of Technology*. Ed. Donald MacKenzie and Judy Wajcman. Milton Keynes, England: Open University Press, 1988.

Marshall, P. David
  1997 *Celebrity and Power: Fame in Contemporary Culture.* Minneapolis: University of Minnesota Press.

McManners, John
  1992 "Introduction." Pp. 1-18 in *The Oxford Illustrated History of Christianity.* Ed. John McManners. Oxford: Oxford University Press.

Meyrowitz, Joshua
  1985 *No Sense of Place: The Impact of Electronic Media on Social Behavior.* New York: Oxford University Press.

Mumford, Lewis
  1967 *The Myth of the Machine: Technics and Human Development.* New York: Harcourt Brace Jovanovich.
Nevitt, Barrington
  1982 *The Communication Ecology: Re-presentation Versus Replica.* Toronto: Butterworths.
Nicholson, David
  1995 "The Pitfalls of a Brave New Cyberworld." *The Washington Post National Weekly Edition* (October 9-15):25.
Pinch, Trevor, and Wiebe E. Bijker
  1987 "The Social Construction of Facts and Artifacts: Or How the Sociology of Science and the Sociology of Technology Might Benefit Each Other." Pp. 17-50 in *The Social Construction of Technological Systems: New Directions in the Sociology and History of Technology.* Ed. Wiebe E. Bijker, Thomas P. Hughes, and Trevor Pinch. Cambridge, MA: The MIT Press, 1987.
Postman, Neil
  1994 *The Disappearance of Childhood.* New York: Vintage Books.
Tapscott, Don
  1998 *Growing Up Digital: The Rise of the Net Generation.* New York: McGraw-Hill.
Riordan, Michael, and Lillian Hoddeson
  1997 *Crystal Fire: The Birth of the Information Age.* New York: W. W. Norton.
"Science Observer"
  1995 *American Scientist* (July-August). <http://www.sigmaxi.org/amsci/issues>.
Youngblood, Gene
  1986 "Art, Entertainment, Entropy." Pp. 225-231 in *Video Culture: A Critical Examination.* Ed. John G. Hanhardt. New York: Visual Studies Workshop Press.

3

Entering Sacred Digital Space
Seeking to Distinguish the Dreamer and the Dream

Richard Thieme

Defining the Challenge
The "Study" of "Sacred Texts" in the Digital Era

The quotation marks around "study" and "sacred texts" signify that the words inside them no longer mean what they used to mean. The symbols and images of religious experience are no longer fixed in print but are now flowing. They feel less like objective artifacts "out there" and more like pieces of thin ice in a moving river, dissolving and forming again and again. The context that defines our thoughts and actions is itself being redefined by the distribution of digital information through networks, and we humans too are being transformed into nodes in that network. As Marvin Minsky said, individual human beings are brains in bottles, like stand-alone desktop computers disconnected from the network.

The study of a sacred text is analogous to a community of people gathering around a fire, drawing on the energies of the flames. The words of the sacred text turn to flame, becoming fire and light that define a community and disclose possibilities for the future. The sacred text is a transformational engine that discloses, discovers, and creates an image of who we are now in relationship to a potential state, the discovery of which is simultaneously the discovery that we are not in that state. Thus, our interaction with the sacred text immediately creates a bridge of images and symbols that span from our present state to that future state. Of course, there is no "future" state; both states are always present here and now.

The encounter of individuals in a community with a sacred text is analogous to space shuttles docking at a space station. We come together in momentary groups, exchange energy and information, and then move on. In a digital world, however, the space station is made up of pixels (light, energy, or information), and is given form by our collective will and intention. To think of the morphing forms of communities in this way

49

makes sense in the current context of frequent, rapid transitions. We live between images that made sense in the past (the mental artifacts of formerly shared consensus realities) and those arriving faster and faster from the horizon of the future. We used to derive our liveliest metaphors from books, printing, and publishing—metaphors such as "turning over a new leaf," "her life is only a footnote," and "beginning a new chapter." Now we derive our liveliest metaphors from life in the network, distributed computing, and technologies of information and communication. To speak of morphing, interfacing, rebooting, multi-tasking, or crashing is to articulate our shared life with metaphors derived from a shared experience of networked computing.

That is happening to the study of sacred texts as well. The study of sacred texts is a specialized subset of the study of all texts, with its own vocabulary and goals. But the word "study" is not adequate to describe what we do when we read linked documents on a monitor and explore them hypertextually. "Text" does not describe very well what we experience when we interact with an iconic flow of information in an immersive virtual experience. Those are last year's words for last year's experience. We virtual voyagers, exploring dimensions of the human soul that did not previously exist, need to invent new words to describe our new experiences.

A More Literal Description of the Problem

The process of interacting with hyperlinked sacred symbols changes who we think we were before we left the shore and began our voyage of discovery. The digital world, in conjunction with other technologies, is recontextualizing what it means to be a human being. Inevitably the quest for a sacred dimension of life, and how we articulate that quest, will be redefined as well.

The energy of transformation always derives from a perception of difference, from a critical distinction that discloses a new possibility. The difference is defined metaphorically as a future state that will never be attained; if wholeness or completion were achieved, we would disappear and become something else entirely. Hence, images of ourselves as perfected at the climax of time are carrots after which we always trot. Because Judeo-Christian belief defines spiritual growth as a spiral rather than a circle, these images are not exactly Sisyphus rolling his boulder uphill, but they resemble Sisyphus once we admit that within the constrained domain of human civilization and its inadequate measures of time (in mere centuries rather than billions of years), there is no measurable moral progress.

To speak of "sacred text" is to identify ourselves as Print People, post-Gutenberg pilgrims voyaging through vast typographic seas. The sphere of consciousness inhabited by our collective field of subjectivity is bounded by the way printed text has taught us to see and perceive. Our brains and the symbols it manipulates seem to have co-evolved, hands and tools together, so to speak, and we cannot escape that feedback loop. Our field of subjectivity, then, is a horizon defined by our genetic heritage, but we can see clearly that we were formed in the image of language that was spoken, then written, then printed, only because we can now manipulate symbols digitally. We do not speak language so much as language speaks us, and today the language speaking us is digital. So we have left the shores of Print Culture forever and can return to that now-imaginary world only through a digital simulation of print culture, just as Print People could enter into oral cultures only in and through their experience as Print People, understanding oral cultures in ways that people in them could not.

Here is an analogy: When I moved to Hawaii I believed there was such a thing as Hawaiian culture. But I learned that Hawaiian culture ended in 1779 when Captain Cook sailed into Kealakekua Bay. Over the next century, the invaders did everything they could to dismantle that culture, in particular using Christianity to replace the framework for thinking, feeling, and being of the indigenous people. With the birth of various consciousness movements in the sixties (among African-Americans, women, etc.), Hawaiian culture was also reborn, but in the only way it could be reborn—in images of itself generated by the invaders over several generations and given back to remnants of the Hawaiian people who reconstructed themselves and their culture as seen by the Other. The taxonomic manner of understanding other cultures axiomatic to anthropology, although alien to Hawaiian oral culture, became the means of Hawaiians appropriating their own transformed identity from texts of the invaders that their ancestors could never have read.

It is not necessary to attend a staged luau as a tourist to witness "Hawaiians" acting as the now-dominant culture expects and teaches them to act. Hawaiians who refuse to act like "Hawaiians" for tourists and insist on thinking of themselves as "real Hawaiians" are playing roles in another's script to just as great a degree. The prisoners and the guards are the same people. Touristic space is a nested set of images of self and identity, images in a hall of mirrors. But it always begins with an image in the eye or mind of the Other.

In the same way, the Digital World is an ongoing voyage into seas of transformation (Print People becoming Digital People), which we see as a process because the digital world teaches us that processes are primary. We see now that the sense of fixity derived from texts was temporary. The Digital World is characterized by verbs, not nouns. Instead of determining a single objective and heading for it in a straight line, we see multiple possible outcomes because computers organize options into multiple outcomes fanned like playing cards in our hands. Quantum reality is replacing Newtonian physics as "common sense."

What Came Before and What's Coming Now

After this process has continued for a while, Digital People will no longer interact with images of (i.e., "worship") gods-in-Print or follow print-text religious founders, such as Martin Luther or Joseph Smith. Digital People will interact with digital images of gods-in-Pixels and with whatever animatrons, bots, simulants, or replicants represent religious founders or leaders in a world in which all information is dynamic and distributed, gathered and integrated on the fly. "Digital beings" will emerge from chaotic waters just as textual beings such as Luther emerged in the historical memory of a textual people. (I intentionally use the word "god" with a small "g" to mean the hundreds of images of Christian, Jewish, Muslim, and other "gods" to which we still refer anachronistically as "God." The gods we can name never mean the God we cannot name.)

Luther and Joseph Smith are not the only ones to exist in the labyrinthine verbal structure of historical memory. Jesus, Muhammad, Moses, Buddha, Confucius, and Lao Tzu are also "textual beings" who were translated from flesh-and-blood historical beings into mythical beings, first through stories, then through writing. Every major religious founder emerged in historical time when writing was redefining the field of subjectivity of humanity. The names of the gods worshiped for thousands of years in oral cultures either vanished or were translated into writing, just as written manuscripts were translated into printed text to remain viable. Handwritten texts might exist in museums as objects of aesthetic or historical interest, but they no longer gather adherents around them. The words on those beautiful archaic pages no longer turn to flame.

All gods being worshiped today, such as all the founders of today's major religions, emerged in history as "textual beings," known in and through text. They "mean" for us the way text means. Inevitably, transfigured, digitized images of those former gods, as well as new, exclusively digital gods, will be born. For the moment, however, we do not know their names. Or if we do, we do not yet know the significance of their names. None has yet emerged as a frontrunner in the twenty-first century religious marketplace.

The study of "sacred texts," then, will evolve into interaction with digital images aggregated in flexible groupings (hypertext rather than text) according to (1) the design of the enabling technology itself and (2) the design of the symbol-manipulating minds that engage with the technology. The exact contours of those interactions are difficult for us to define, given our predominant experience with, for example, Bible study groups in which individuals hold cheap portable books in their hands that are defined by the boundaries of their covers and that are read aloud together or silently to oneself. Such groups would have been as unthinkable to denizens of oral cultures or writing cultures in which literacy was closely held by priests and aristocrats as dynamic Internet culture was only a few years ago.

Hackers as Paradigms of Digital Humanity

My work with several generations of technophiles (what we used to call "hackers" before the word was hijacked by the media and used to mean criminal hackers only) has revealed how a generation now in their thirties engaged in a reflexive dialogue with the computer technology that created them as they created it. But the next hacker generation, now in its teens, has always known a digital world, and has always lived inside a network of distributed information and processes. The electronic games they play are more "real" than the games they replaced. Their online gaming communities are more "real" than town-hall meetings. Their digital selves are more "real" than the print-text selves they displaced. For example, a father and his young son often visited an online dinosaur museum that was physically located only a few miles from their home. One day they were disappointed after visiting the actual museum. As they left, the son told his father he had enjoyed the visit, but "I like the real one better."

In the study of sacred text, which is the "real one"? The one that emerged when we developed the capacity to live inside the domain of speech and convinced ourselves that it was reality itself? The one that emerged when writing became ubiquitous, an event that Plato believed meant the end of civilization? Or the one that emerged during the Renaissance and Reformation, after movable type was invented?

Those periods define nested levels of identity and self, and the self is once again transcending itself and spawning new ways of being human. As digital symbols, icons, and glyphs replace printed images, everything—including our deepest experience of religious truth, our modalities of spirituality, and our religious community life—is being transformed.

Naturally the meaning of processes like "redemption" and "salvation" will be transformed, too. We see that the gods we worshiped were conceived in the image of written symbols. We see that when the introduction of the printing press translated the names of those gods into print, Christianity, for example, experienced the widespread division of its several gods (Greek Orthodox, Roman Catholic, Lutheran, Calvinist, etc.) into hundreds of gods, each at the center of a community that defined itself by subtle distinctions from neighboring communities. These differences did not and could not exist before the medium of print enabled them to be created or discovered.

Deliverables

Identity, a coherent self, images of ongoing transformation of self or community (spirituality) and world (historical/mythic narrative), and processes and tools for transformation are some of the "deliverables" of religions. They are delivered in and through communities defined by their sacred symbols. These deliverables are not delivered once and for all, however. Those religions that claim to do so are whistling in the dark. New identities are difficult to sustain, or else the community would not need to meet so frequently to reinforce them. Transformation is a hoop that hands must keep rolling.

The study of "sacred text" is the willing participation in the process by which identity, self, and templates for future possibilities are created and discovered for individuals and communities. Words like "free individual with rights" and "intellectual property" designate concepts that emerged post-print. Something of those notions will likely persist in the digital era, but who we are and, more importantly, who we think we are, will never be the same. A collective sense of religious identity, like that which is axiomatic to the Hebrew Scriptures, will likely be reborn, but this time through symbols that will be moving targets.

Reflecting on the study of sacred text in a digital era is like entering the mirror-world of Lewis Carroll's *Through the Looking Glass*, in which the dreamer dreamed of a dreamer dreaming the dream. Which one dreamed it? Which was the dreamed? The symbol-using brain that believed itself to be an "I"? Or the symbols of that "I" in the brain? Or the symbols in the larger brain of the hive mind? Deliverables presume an identity determined by boundaries around giver and receiver. But how do we play chess when the board itself is disappearing?

Interactive, Modular, and Fluid

In contrast to the field of subjectivity that we shared in the past, the digital world is more highly interactive, modular, and fluid. Because our lives are shaped and changed by the technologies with which we inter-act—context creating content or perhaps context becoming content—our lives and how we think of ourselves are also becoming highly interactive, modular, and fluid.

Let us not underestimate the extent of the changes we are facing. The advent of a digital era will turn currently established religions on their col-lective ears. It has happened before, and it will again. The critical question is, will the collective identities of those religions persist in a recognizable form that includes and transcends the forms that came before, or will there be such a disconnect that when we look into the digital mirror, the face we see does not even resemble who or what we used to see?

That question confronts individuals as well as religions, societies, and civilizations. Our longer life spans are segmented into a greater num-ber of identifiable developmental phases. The word "adolescence" did not exist prior to the invention of the printing press; adolescence has come to mean the postponement of adulthood into another decade while individ-uals are socialized as literate adults. As recently as Daniel J. Levinson's 1978 book, *The Season's of a Man's Lives* (which identified developmen-tal stages of American males into their fifties), the author could only sketch vaguely the stages beyond the sixties, which he called "old age." As longevity is extended, we will have to learn how to integrate a dozen stages of adult life in a modular fashion, using a memory storage device that augments our biological memory in a way that does not violate the sense of a unified, persistent self that integrates all the stages—if, that is, we decide that the continuity and persistence of a seemingly single self is still valuable. Some biological models picture complex organisms like ourselves as colonies or hives. Perhaps that model will be deemed more appropriate when people live two hundred years or more and the pieces of memory that persist are mix-and-match, plug-and-play modules.

That our lives have already become modular in every department testifies to the impact of multiple technologies. Only a few decades ago, people had a single stable religious identity, a single career, a single mar-riage. Today we change careers, religions, marriages, and even identities, by design and intention, and we try to teach our children skills that will help them manage modular lives rather than pick a single course and stick with it.

It is not uncommon when one changes one of these modules—a religion, a career, a spouse—that one also changes communities and "starts over." That way we can create the new persona appropriate to our new self-construct without interference from people who cling to memories of our other stages. We dock, as it were, at different space stations, according to our needs, often ones with different sets of values. That is why so many religions are so highly competitive, offering constructions of reality and templates of sanctioned behavior (both secular and religious) in a fiercely contested marketplace. In this context, the study of sacred text means the use of sacred texts to reinforce the subset of religious life that each institution is offering its members. In the future digital world, these religious contexts may well evolve in simulated form first, like complex models of spacecraft or weather systems, and we will try on digital religions for size and see how our personas during particular life stages fit them. (Today we call that "shopping for a church.") If we feel "at home" and the religion fits our current stage of life, we call it "true."

One way of studying scripture is to choose stories which archetypally illuminate a critical passage or transitional episode in the lives of the faithful. The passages of scripture typically chosen by a lectionary in liturgical churches are images of healing, deliverance, and transformation. The preacher "reads the space" of the congregation in light of his or her deeper intuitive knowledge of the body and illuminates possibilities using those passages much like a Tarot deck reader uses archetypal images to illuminate an insight into the life of the person for whom they are doing a reading. The lectionary does the shuffling, and the word-pictures of deliverance, healing, and transformation provide the images.

Extrapolating on the distributed interactivity enabled by the Internet, sermons will likely be more interactive and fluid. Because the online conversation continues 24/7 and can deliver insight, consolation, or encouragement when it is most needed, the choice of when to offer access to sacred space will be customer driven, just as Roman Catholics now have the option of attending a Saturday service. The socioeconomic context has always determined the fit of sacred time and space with societal time and space. The choice of a one-day-in-seven kind of Sabbath was equally determined by the technologies of the time and the nature of work and community life.

The fragmentation and relativism of "truth" itself in a distributed postmodern world, the difficulty in reaching consensus, and the toleration of multiple thought-worlds will stretch the capacity of religious structures to tolerate ambiguity and complexity. What it means to be redeemed or saved will be transformed in both the from- and to- sides of the equation.

The human condition of sinfulness will be understood differently, as will transfigured or redeemed humanity, individually and collectively. Doctrine always follows facts the way ethics follows the power to act that is liberated by new technologies (e.g., in sexuality and child-bearing).

This will test all religions, but Christianity will be the hardest hit. Christianity claims to be exclusively true, and however that claim is nuanced to take into account the sensitivities of others in a pluralistic world, it still comes down to this: Either Jesus is the ONLY way, truth, and life, or Jesus is ONE way, ONE dimension of a larger Truth, and ONE path to life—one that works well enough for Christians but is still one path among many. The pressures of the digital world will continue to transform formerly exclusive paths into preferences. Those who need to be right and define being right by others being wrong will be flummoxed.

This means that the transformational energies of this period will turn into a real fire storm when they encounter formerly inviolable core proclamations. If Christianity is to embrace and be transformed by those energies, it will necessarily become something other than what it has been or at least what it has been thought to be. (We always save ourselves by saying that Truth is eternal and that we were merely mistaken about what it was). Either Jesus of Nazareth will take his place as an image of possibility among other viable images, or he will be the King of the Universe without peers.

The history of Judaism is instructive for Christians pondering options. Jews today are either Jews by identity, behavior, or both. Some Jews believe themselves to be Jews and live their lives from core Jewish identities but are not observant. Still, their destiny is to live life as a Jew, because identity *is* destiny. But when identity itself is in question and is no longer correlated with observable behaviors, the primary mode of social control is absent from the community. When claimed identities and explicit behaviors that proclaim identities are intentional choices, how will we know who or what we are?

American Jews today feel a threat of annihilation not so much from marching jackboots as from radical assimilation. That threat faces Christians and others as well, but many are not aware of it yet. They live inside the Kafkaesque world of "The Great Wall of China," a narrative that describes how the word has gone out from the emperor to the entire kingdom, but has not been heard by those who live on the edges. That word today is that the God fashioned in the image of the structures of prior minds, cultures, and civilization is, as Nietzsche said, dead. Of course, Nietzsche was not talking about the Creator of everything when he claimed that "God is dead." As a linguist, he knew that to speak of

"God" was to be a prisoner of linguistic structures. He meant the social construction of God, the glass house in which Christendom lived while it threw stones.

It is difficult to remember that the God of our sacred texts is not the glass but the stones. In order to be transformed, one must move through a zone of annihilation in which everything one believes oneself to be is called into question. This is as true for individuals losing the fact of individuality to an electronic collective as it is for societal structures and nation states, the boundaries of which are dissolving into a single global political and economic system.

To talk about the study of sacred text, then, raises important questions. What is the nature of humanity in the digital era? How will the symbols constitutive of human and cultural identity be different in the digital era? Who will we think we are?

Identity

In the first Christian communities, first Jews and then Gentiles brought their current identities to the scriptures and to the Christian community to be transformed. But all we can know at the outset of the journey of transformation is a possibility, glimpsed dimly from inside our current way of thinking and perceiving. From within the old paradigm, we can never predict the new paradigm. The genuinely new is predictable only after it has appeared.

The six seasons of the Christian year are six segments of a spiral of ongoing transformation, derived from the extended Christian narrative and transformed into time-calibrated rituals. The segments also define the transformational journeys of non-Christian spiritualities, but in those other contexts they are correlated with other stories, other symbols. In all cases, however, the rituals are mnemonic devices used by the community as portable bridges, easily carried and always at hand when we need them. Then we are tutored by the community in how to turn those memories into useful spiritual tools. The calendar of the Christian year is derived from a sacred text, then translated into other media based on drama and ritual. That process will happen too in the digital world.

Our identities derive from a complex interplay of genetic and cultural factors. We can only become what we can potentially become by virtue of our genetic heritage, which offers up possibilities of selfhood and identity to be framed in cultural forms. Genetic engineering is an opportunity to self-direct human evolution so that the genetic determination is itself turned into a cultural decision.

One interesting discovery of genetic research is that qualities we thought to be subjective, such as the capacity to feel awe and wonder, a tendency toward mysticism, or a generosity of spirit, all seem to cluster around certain genes. Not to oversimplify, but it is likely that the genetic and chemical basis of religious experience and emotions such as awe and wonder will be identified and pre-set or manufactured. Then we will have to answer difficult questions about how many mystics we really want to have in the population.

Given the fact that in our society so many people use chemicals to adjust levels of well-being, anxiety, and depression, this trend of genetic engineering will advance a few more steps. We may be able to determine who and how many people we will want to interact with sacred symbols at all. We may want to retain a select group of sociopaths to fill occupational niches like Army Rangers, intelligence agents, or corporate lawyers. We may also want to make available religious experience in a modular fashion, letting someone "jack in" to the symbols and use processes or chemicals to enhance their capacity to have a meaningful experience and alter their subjective states.

Of course, that's pretty much what we do now, isn't it? Religious experience in an organizational context is designed as a mood-altering experience, often using primordial rituals, music, and drama to enhance our feeling of having a meaningful experience and to bind us to one another and the institution. The difference in how that process is conducted in the digital world will be one of degree, not kind.

Historical Antecedents

In the 1470s William Caxton introduced the printing press to England. Questions of identity were immediately raised. One needed to choose a dialect in which to print, which then imprinted that dialect's way of thinking on a people who, Caxton realized, were no longer certain who they were. Walter Ong identified one religious consequence of the printing press: the process of self-examination prior to confession during which the self examines itself in scrupulous detail, then says what it sees to another person, did not widely exist prior to the printing press. All technologies of information and communication, Ong said, initially distance the self from itself and from others. The printing press helped the English language explode from thousands to more than a million words, just as the colors on an artist's palette increase exponentially the artist's ability to express subtleties that did not previously exist. The newly created self feels isolated for a time as the technology creates appropriate ways for that self to connect once again with itself and other selves.

No one thought the telephone was a device for personal communi-cation when it was invented. The telephone reproduced a simulation of the human voice so imperfectly and unnaturally that people did not want to use it except as a form of telegraph. A few generations later, we say, "Don't send an email—call me. I want to talk to a real person."

Once the technology and the simulations it delivers have been so internalized that we experience the simulation as a "real person," we become like fish in water, unaware of the water in which we are always swimming. New technologies are noticeable only by contrast with the world to which we have grown accustomed. Then the technology itself becomes the means for bridging the greater distance and creating genuine communion among those more subtle, more complex selves that subse-quently emerge.

One cannot fly a stealth fighter with a propeller or run Windows 98 on an IBM XT. We also cannot put new wine into old wineskins, only no one knows what that means anymore. We do know what it means to use an obsolete operating system, though. When spiritual leaders insist on clinging to old metaphors that are no longer understood, they are binding the people to themselves by mystification, the keys of the kingdom safe-ly tucked into their privileged pockets. However, when we use current metaphors, drawn from the everyday language of the people (as Jesus himself once did with the wineskins metaphor), we subvert the monopoly power of an organizational framework that has become synonymous with archaic images and behaviors. As digital technologies transform Print People into new kinds of human beings, sacred text will become sacred digital interaction and the study of the scriptures will become a distrib-uted process, blurring the distinction between humans and their wearable and implanted information machines. The dreamer and the dream will exist in a new relationship to one another. Genetic engineering and phar-maceutical advances will help us breed those new beings.

Cyborg Time

The dilemma of whether or not a single unified self can persist over an increasing number of segments of life is a problem that will be solved by humans who will be enhanced by augmented memory and cognition and new kinds of sensory extensions. And we cannot discuss the impact of technologies of communication and information without at least mention-ing the impact of genetic engineering on identity, self, and community. Like the replicants in the movie *Bladerunner*, whose manufacture blurred the distinction between manufacturing and breeding, we will see increased ambivalence toward memory-based identity. Our expertise in genetic engineering will enable us to be fitted with wearables and implants that make communication instantaneous, multi-level, and unconscious. The boundaries between us will at times be nearly invisible. Just as replicants were given manufactured memories borrowed from others' lives, the real memories of individuals will be indistinguishable from false ones. Of course, memory is creative, not a passive recording of what passes, and our biographies are personal mythic histories, how we want our lives to have been rather than how they were. Biography, like history, is a symbolic narrative designed to sustain the chosen identity of the present. Religions too are based on mythic memories and symbolic narratives.

The Christian world has split into those who can stand knowing that the memory of the Christ-event is a symbolic event and those who insist that the scriptures are a historical record. The latter viewpoint supports a rigid structure which admits neither dialogue nor flexibility. Whichever viewpoint comes to dominate the Christian future, the nature of the memory at the heart of Christian proclamation will be revised, because, as *Bladerunner* reminds us, memory is malleable and therefore never wholly trustworthy.

Cyborgs are blends of humans and machines. We are already cyborgs in rudimentary ways, with our pacemakers, implants of chemical catalysts for essential biological processes, transdermal patches, synthetic hips and hands and hearts, contact lenses, vision scopes that bypass the eyes of the blind and plug directly into the brain, and neural avionics that socket the optic nerve with fiber optic cables so that fighter pilots can fire weapons merely by thinking. Indeed, it's already cyborg time, and as we engineer ourselves to accept more readily transplants and artificial devices, we will become more and more cyborg. Our cyborg selves will exist embedded in ubiquitous wireless real time networks, with chips in everything—furniture and appliances, automobiles and airplanes, houses and offices—and above all, chips in us. We do not merely use computers; we are becoming computers, nodes in a ubiquitous network.

Try making a large purchase for cash and see what happens. Only your digital self with its digital markers for identity and authentication can trade in the digital marketplace. "Real" currency in the digital economy is digital. In the same way, only the digital self that uses the right metaphors for, say, inclusion in or exclusion from a redemptive religious network will have constant and immediate access to the energizing, mood-altering scenarios of renewal and transformation made available by the network. Online passwords to the communities that mediate religious experience will resemble "recommends" by Mormon bishops permitting adherents to enter a temple. This is analogous to the delivery systems of medicines, drugs, and chemicals used to enhance emotional well-being and cognitive ability available through the network. The network, in other words, will be self-referential and will maintain equilibrium, not only of individual bodies, but of the network itself, of which we will be but a part. We will interact with sacred digital scenarios as online gamers today participate in communities of tens of thousands in real time. Those scenarios will be an important part of the self-regulating mechanisms of the entire network, i.e., the trans-planetary society into which we are evolving.

Religious rituals have always used dramatic techniques. Once they become virtual simulations, using scent, sound, images, and tactile feedback to integrate distributed individuals into a unified experience, we can "run" those rituals whenever we need them. Those who control the technology will be high priests. 'Services' will be available anytime online, and because we will participate in them through complex and sophisticated avatars or online personas, which may well evolve independent and intelligent behaviors of their own, our "spiritual companions" will always be available. We will "call them" whenever we want to experience "real people" and they will always show up.

The technology world calls them "early adopters," those people out on the edge who make first use of new applications. Nietzsche called "original thinkers" those who see new realities just moments before others do and give them names. The nose of the snake gets to the mouse first, but the whole snake eats the mouse. If we are part of human society, participation in this digital transformation into cyborg humanity is unavoidable.

We will still have simulated experiences of prior times, of course, the equivalent of reading historical novels today or visiting a recreated nineteenth-century village, but we will know that the actors are in costume and that we, too, are actors in costume. But then, what else are Christmas oratorios, Purim pageants, or liturgical dramas, but historical simulations?

Religious claims to universal truth will both intensify and diminish. They will diminish as we are recontextualized in a situation that continuously reminds us that the finger pointing to the moon is not the moon. But they will intensify because those with their hands on the levers of power in organized religion often use anxiety and fear as glue for communities. Those communities use rigid rules to maintain order. The more rigid the structures, the more obvious the pathology for both individuals and organizations.

Every age picks and chooses the "books of the Bible" or the scenarios that speak most powerfully to it. The potency of the stories is a function of their relevance to our current context. The Gospels were written, redacted, and juxtaposed with each other (which changed their meaning by placing them in new contexts) by communities articulating comprehensive visions. Which stories will lend themselves to digital interaction and which will diminish?

More Questions than Answers

The history of the study of sacred text is also a history of control over the interpretation of the text, the maintenance of boundaries as a safeguard of power. That control requires a stable environment, so that the decisions of the elders will matter and so that social and psychological escape hatches are not available to individuals who choose to contradict traditional teachings. Otherwise shunning has no effect. That control is lost in distributed networks. Who can enforce rulings when alternative communities are readily available, and anyone can invent another by going online, sowing seeds, and pruning what grows, while plowing under what withers? What kinds of consensus will establish canonical texts, or will there be any consensus, just as today we draw our own conclusions about sacred texts? The person in the street does not care what a hierarchy says if it cannot enforce its decisions with physical coercion. In the absence of an invisible fence, the dogs run wild.

Digital Mystics

The imaginative reader may by now have begun to ponder the meaning of mysticism in the climate I am describing. The distributed network is a concrete manifestation of the unity of all things, the connectedness perceived in the past as a transcendent vision seen by those whose genetics inclined them to dream dreams and see visions.

Mystics do not see a different reality, but they see the wiring inside the wireless circuits. Mystics see structures of information and energy as it flows, a self-luminous tangle that can only be described using metaphors and symbols. Paradox is the language of the unconscious, which is why, like riddles or jokes, either we get what mystics say or we do not. Either mystical insights make all the difference in the world, enabling us to recontextualize everything, or they sound like snake oil.

Digital mystics are everywhere these days, searching for the words to give voice to their experience. Those who live life as nodes in a network cannot help but notice that they are enmeshed in a complex system of energy and information. The computer network becomes an image of the larger network, the planetary civilization, and even the galaxy, all the way out to the edges of the universe. We see that everything is part of one vast system of energy and information. Information is the form of energy. Information and energy, which look like two things, are aspects of a single thing, the way light is both particle and wave. The words "Let there be light!" give form to the potential of energy or perhaps make energy intelligible.

The digital world is a projection that lets us see ourselves seeing ourselves. For example, the other day I made a speech during which I moved in front of a huge video screen on the platform. The audience watched the "real" me through the camera as I pointed to an image of myself pointing to an image of myself pointing to an image of myself, ad infinitum. "That," I said, "is the digital world." When I moved to the front of the platform, the audience divided—half looking at my digital image to the right, half to the left. This division changed my job description from a speaker engaging with an audience to a wizard creating a digital image with which the audience could engage. In fact, I am doing much the same thing now, whether you read these words in digital-made print or in pixels.

Now, these sentiments clearly tend more toward the tenor of the Gospel of John than to the hard truth of crucifixion at the end of the Gospel of Mark. The balance between the two ends of the spectrum will be as important to preserve in the digital world as it was when narratives were interlaced in leaves of printed text. But the aesthetics of the online experience will not be the aesthetics that have characterized our experience of reading. We do not yet have a vocabulary to speak about the aesthetic experience of online interaction. The narratives that report online mystical experience (e.g., the sudden socketing of minds through telepathic portals as they feel each other through the wires, answered prayers or healings, or synchronous flows of words of deeply felt feelings) are scattered now in diverse Web servers and email archives. They are not yet filtered through a digitally informed imagination into the momentary stasis of a "sacred text," nor are they collected into edifying cycles of music, words, and images for a digital generation.

The Twilight Zone

Let's add to this rudimentary sketch the fact of trans-planetary culture and the inevitable encounter with multiple civilizations. It is not a question of whether "they" come here or "we" go there. Once the interface of our species with others becomes more conscious, we will see that there is no here or there to come from or go to. The distinction between "alien" and "earthling" will blur as the distinction between, say, Albanian and Greek, has blurred, and for similar reasons. Identity is a function of boundaries, and when boundaries dissolve, a new identity emerges that includes and transcends the identity that is then seen to have been the politically and economically determined structure of a prior time. When we first encounter other societies or civilizations, our initial shock at the differences of others pushes us into a self-transcendent space and forces us to realize that consciousness in its many forms is just one thing, one dimension of space and time in a universe that is becoming self-conscious. On the other side of the annihilation of an earth-bound identity, we will locate ourselves in a more complex matrix of universal self-awareness.

Throughout world history, the encounter of one people with another has often resulted in the assimilation of the technologically inferior society into the technologically superior one, but that has been in part because of the massive physical presence the superior civilization has been able to muster. A scout ship or an expedition, like Lewis and Clark's, can absorb another civilization only if a massive presence follows. But contact can nevertheless radically impact the way the impacted society sees itself in the universal scheme of things, including how it uses selected sacred texts. Hawaiian society, for example, began to dissolve the minute the explorers came off the ships. Their sacred stories were discovered to be interlaced with the entire fabric of their society, and when that began to unravel, the sacred stories dimmed and lost their numinous glow.

During times of radical transition, such as encounters between different civilizations, we tend to favor apocalyptic texts that provide symbols and images that can mediate our anxieties and that can make sense on a cosmic scale out of what we previously believed to be nonsensical. Only open-ended symbols (like the cross) that insist that the dissolution of our structures of meaning is itself a meaningful event can help us through the darkness of seeming meaninglessness that attends the end of our illusions. As we voyage to distant planets and come to terms with our status in the universe as toddlers coming down the steps of their house for the first time, rather than as Alpha Primates at the top of the food chain, images of the end-time will help earth civilizations keep their sanity and balance. Sooner or later things will stabilize again at a different level of equilibrium. We will then become aware of ourselves (or OurSelf) as an extended network or system of self-conscious nodes in a more conscious matrix, self-invented in ways we can only dimly glimpse now. How will we recontextualize images of a swarthy, uncompromising, street-smart rabbi, who several thousand years earlier lent his life to the creative memory of an emergent civilization, and who was fixed in archetypal images of self-transcendence just when that civilization could frame those memories in written words? Will we still value Bronze Age images of humanity as existentially relevant to our quest?

The Future is Behind Us

Any discussion of the future is speculative, of course, particularly since the future is a choice of one of several possibilities that we have constructed from the way information flows and organizes itself in distributed systems. Science fiction writer, Bruce Sterling, acknowledged in a private conversation that his own horizon for the future has come down to five years, more or less, as science fiction as a genre has shifted from technological speculation about the distant future to near-term issues of identity and self. The right-brain dreaming of a left-brain society dreams less of the physical landscapes of the fortieth century and more of sociological, even epistemological, contours of current interior landscapes.

Still, some likely scenarios do emerge, based on this cursory discussion of genetic engineering, the realization that we are becoming a trans-planetary civilization, and the emergence of a ubiquitous, embedded network with augmented cognition, memory, and senses. Cyborg humankind, in this imaginary scenario, is indistinguishable from its augmentations and machinery, except to the degree that the seeing self retains a feeling of autonomy and self-will, still feeling itself to be a self. That capacity will be an intentional choice, as we take the reins of evolution into our own hands. We may choose to retain the illusion of freedom because it serves our species so well. The field of human subjectivity that animates the human species will experience itself as selecting and directing its own evolution, even if the laboratory evidence indicates that this also is an illusion, a necessary fiction embedded in genetic code.

Cyborg humanity will be indistinguishable from its inventions and replicants. The power of projection will be used to glue feelings of respect, even affection, onto our own creations, much as we value dogs as companions and breed them for that purpose. The distinctions between property and persons will blur. Parts of humans, including memory modules and chemically catalyzed and activated behaviors, will be interchangeable, as well as our "artificial" parts, a distinction that will also blur until it disappears. Not only will we grow hearts, lungs, and kidneys in laboratories and in other animals, we will grow memory banks and neural functions using processes that will come to us first through war, entertainment and child's play, and sexual fantasy.

This field of subjectivity will be a network of extended self-consciousness, aware of itself as a collective with a collective memory and multiple modes of nodal operation. Long-term memory storage devices will augment innate memories. and, once we master the creation of memory clusters to cushion the impact of longevity, what we call "repression" or "forgetting" will be a conscious decision, the way societies remember or choose to forget historical experiences now. Disciplines that have already converged (such as public relations, advertising, and marketing; intelligence, counter-intelligence, and disinformation; mass media and entertainment) will cycle down from the top level (images, symbols, and media) to the level of perception. Percepts as well as concepts will be manufactured and delivered in support of a previously chosen consensus. That is, not only how we think about what we see but what we think we see in the first place will be designed. The quest for truth and justice in a designed world will itself be a simulation of the quest for truth and justice.

We will choose which memory modules are valuable as distractions (an extended romantic narrative can neutralize people as effectively as professional sports) or as useful tools (if a 150-year-old man were alive today, what memories from the Civil War or the spread of the railroads would be of survival value?). We will answer these questions as we answer all questions, through trial and error, which will of course raise ethical questions as to what to do with our mistakes.

The nodes in the network will be discrete human beings who have lost much of the notion of being an "individual" and will look upon our time (when they visit virtual memory museums) as an era of lonely isolation in which the illusion of individuality enabled some successes but at the high cost of the security, community, and stability that, as in *Brave New World*, they will value more highly. Because the interchangeability of parts and processes as one ages through a century or two of modular life will erode the sense of the "I" that Christians believe is saved or redeemed, planetary consciousness might skew toward Buddhism, which is a good default choice during times of radical transition. Why? Because Buddhism purports to describe "what is so" without reference to teleology or ultimate purposes, i.e., to what Christians call "God." So Buddhism provides a convenient receptacle for dealing with prolonged transitioning by relating what are obviously the passing scenes of a moving narrative to a non-self that survives the extinction of the illusory self. When it becomes obvious that the contents of mentation are illusory, it helps that one of those concepts is the notion that all is illusion, including the self that thinks about such things. Perhaps that metaphorical framework will further recontextualize Christianity in Buddhist terms. Perhaps the ancient Jewish and Christian belief in reincarnation, always a best-seller, will turn Buddhist/Christians toward the scriptural assertions ("Some say Elijah...") that reinforce such a contextual shift.

The boundaries around what twentieth-century humans call "the Canon" will continue to dissolve, accelerating a process already begun by print publishing over the last several hundred years. The rapid evolution of interactive scenarios with spiritual content will push more power to decide toward the nodes. People will pick and choose which paths to follow and will use archetypal symbols that correlate best with the needs of the moment. But then, this is merely extrapolating the present into the future, isn't it?

The "study of sacred text" will look like a collective consciousness choosing to distribute aspects of itself around archetypal symbols, themselves in flux, that resonate in terms of then-contemporary experience. We will step into or out of the virtual immersive experience at will or what will seem like "at will." We will accept being conditioned to choose those moments of renewal and experience them as we have bred and manufactured ourselves to experience them, much as *Brave New World* suggests. Deltas will be glad they are Deltas. Alphas will be glad they are Alphas.

A Digital Parable

All great truth, said George Bernard Shaw, begins as blasphemy. And here are my words in a different poetic form, a parable that searches for that great truth.

Islands in the Clickstream

A sacred canopy of shared belief used to soar above our heads like a large umbrella, keeping us warm and dry as the contradictory data of real life beat down.

A canopy doesn't have to be sacred—any canopy will do—but because our understanding of the cosmos and our place in it is such an important part of our stance toward life, a canopy always has a sacred component. What we believe determines how we act.

No model of reality contains everything. Life is larger than our models of it. All we need is an umbrella that is "good enough" to manage the odd drops by keeping them irrelevant. As long as our model of reality makes enough sense of the world to let us act, we hold to our beliefs.

But there is an awful lot of rain these days, forty days of rain, more than forty days, and it keeps on raining.

Our trans-planetary network of computers is a rain-making machine that—finally!—works. There is no snake oil this time, no flim-flam man. It's really coming down out there. More and more data just doesn't fit. Our umbrella has more than a few holes in it, and the water is trickling through.

At first we act as if we don't notice. The real experience of our lives contradicts what we say about life. When we hear ourselves speak, we sometimes sound like someone else, someone we used to be or someone we're overhearing. If we refuse to believe our experience and believe our beliefs instead, we get a headache, a very, very bad headache. We crawl into bed or pop a Prozac, but we keep getting wetter and wetter.

Alas! we're all too human—stubborn, blind as umbrellas, frightened out of our shivering skins—so we still insist that we're not wet. We hold the handle of the umbrella more and more tightly, telling ourselves and everyone else how dry we are and what an excellent umbrella we have found. Others politely suppress giggles and move on.

It's so easy to see holes in someone else's umbrella.

Finally the umbrella is so battered that we can no longer deny what everyone else has seen for a long time, that we're holding nothing but shreds of wet black cloth on a skeletal metal frame and we're soaked to the skin.

We all want to stay dry, but one legacy of living in the twentieth century is that no canopy spans us all. We join organizations to experience the momentary consolation of agreement, but we can't live there. Life today is like living in a village of grass huts in which everyone has a radio tuned to a different station. However high we turn the volume, we can't shut out the other songs.

I recently spoke about "The Stock Market, UFOs, and Religious Experience" to an investment conference. The speech distinguished between things we think we see out there and things we really see. It was about the psychology of projection and the psychology of investment.

I noted that in the United States and, increasingly, in the world, an attitude of respect for other religious traditions creates a good deal of tension. We both have to believe in our own belief system and acknowledge that others are entitled to contrary views. Entertaining mutually exclusive truths simultaneously in our minds is difficult. We're not even always sure which is the umbrella and which is the rain.

We will try to surrender our freedom to those selling cheap umbrellas, but we cannot avoid our destiny: we are each responsible for inventing ourselves, for creating our own lives. There is no high ground on which to hide.

Our calling is made more difficult by the digital world. The digital world consists of simulations, models so compelling that we mistake them for reality. Sometimes the digital symbols refer only to other symbols, what Baudrillard called simulacra, simulations of simulations, copies with no originals. All those simulations are umbrellas, and all those simulations are rain.

Nietzsche saw it coming at the end of the last century. It's what he meant when he said "God is dead." He wasn't talking about the creator of the universe, but about the gods in our heads, the cultural artifacts that we invent. He saw that our sacred canopy had shredded and the rains were pouring down.

Prophets are people who get wet and start sneezing before everybody else. We try to quarantine them, but reality is a cold it is impossible not to catch.

As did speech, writing, and printed text, electronic media are transforming what it means to be human and what kinds of gods we are likely to worship. "Gods," that was, not God. God is always God, and God is with us, out here in the rain, getting wet.

In the digital world, Nietzsche's questions are more urgent than ever. Never mind that he asked them long ago. Civilizations take lots of bullets and walk dead for a long time before they fall.

Some treat the digital world as if it is an umbrella, as if simulations can be more than an umbrella, as if they can be stitched together into an ark. And who can blame them? Who does not want to be warm and dry? But the words "warm and dry" will not keep us warm and dry, nor will digital simulations of 3-D umbrellas dancing and singing on the screen. The digital world is water, a rising tide, a tsunami impacting our consciousness with revolutionary force, leveling our villages, sweeping away our shrines and altars, sweeping everything out to sea.

What games, asked Nietzsche, what festivals shall we now invent? Indeed, my friends. And what games shall we simulate? What games shall we play? What games shall we dare to believe?

Works Cited

Levinson, Daniel J.
    1978   *The Seasons of a Man's Life*. New York: Ballentine Books.
Minsky, Marvin.
    1985   *The Society of Mind*. New York: Simon and Schuster.
Ong, Walter J.
    1982   *Orality and Literacy: The Technologizing of the Word*. London: Methuen.
Thieme, Richard
    1997   *Islands in the Clickstream*. November 14.
           <www.thiemeworks.com>

4

The Second Coming of Holy Writ
Niche Bibles and the Manufacture of Market Segments

Mark Fackler

Niche Bible publishing has transformed the way people read and regard the sacred text. Hand copyists of the medieval era could produce no more Bibles than needed by church hierarchy and scholars. To see and handle such a book no doubt counted as a lifetime privilege, an unforgettable event. Gutenberg opened Bible distribution to the laity. The book, eventually available to masses of people, was still a volume of divine majesty and mystery. Always the book held the key to truth. In whatever language bound by whatever technology, the reader approached the book with awe and expectation. With niche Bibles, the book approaches the reader, and neither remains the same.

Niche Bible refers to the phenomenon begun in the late 1980s, and still underway, in which a Bible translation is packaged with notes, study aids, and graphics designed to appeal to a fraction of the Bible-buying public. Its subsequent marketing is based on demographics such as gender, age, interests, memberships, or self-nominated social roles. The niche Bible surrenders the mass market while its symbols and content focus sharply on a targeted fraction of the market. For the consumer, niche Bibles have become a personalized version of the Divine Word that addresses the needs, concerns, and aspirations of a particular time or passage of life. Whereas Bibles were once lifetime possessions, clearly now most Bibles are used for a season and then traded for another, not unlike a vehicle or style of shoe.

Specialized versions of the Bible appeared with the Thompson Chain Reference (1908) and the Scofield Bible (1909), but the modern niche Bible was introduced in 1990 when the Zondervan Corporation published the *Women's Devotional Bible* (WDB). The idea of titling the Book something other than "Holy Bible" was a stroke of marketing genius not original to niche products. *Good News for Modern Man* appeared in 1966 and *The Way* in 1972. Each was an effort to refocus attention to what the book had to offer—the reason why a buyer might pick it up. But these were contemporary translations, not niche products. By marketing a version of the Bible to a limited number of potential buyers, the Bible became a book for the individual. In the case of WDB, not surprisingly, it was a product created specifically for the nation's largest group of Bible purchasers. Its success has spawned hundreds of similar products, with more on the drawing boards.

Women and Children to the Front (Cash Register)

While more women than men buy Bibles, most niche Bibles lean strongly toward male interests and instincts. On credits pages for popular study Bibles and niche Bibles produced for boomers and Gen-Xers, not a single woman is named as general editor. Features within these Bibles are, on the whole, directed toward the lives and needs of men. *The Leadership Bible* (Zondervan, 1998), for instance, profiles five men for every one woman, and reprints selections from the writings of thirteen men for every one woman. One cannot be surprised, then, that the market is currently ripe for products exclusively for women, written by women, addressed to the needs of women. As we shall see, this important market niche is becoming even more specific as publishers hunt for demographic categories with felt needs for spiritual development which are yet without their own Bible version.

The *Women's Devotional Bible*—the mother of all niche Bibles— wraps into the text of the New International Version (NIV) 918 devotionals by 98 women, past and present, mostly American. Among the contributors are hymn writer Fanny Crosby and author Catherine Marshall. Name-recognition contributors include Dale Evans Rogers and Ruth Bell Graham. The roll-call of this Bible's assembled contributors could read as a generation of evangelical women whose star has crested and whose reputation is now set: Elisabeth Elliott, Debby Boone, Ann Kiemel, Gloria Gaither, and Rosalind Rinker. Indeed, Mother Teresa is represented with devotional statements on poverty, prayer, and small acts of love. Only one male author made the cut into the WDB: evangelist Luis Palau, who lends a piece on Clara Barton, founder of the Red Cross.

This first successful niche Bible makes no effort to interrupt the text with apparatuses now common to these products. Rather, the devotionals are windows in the text, bordered with flowers, so that roughly every three pages a reader can step from the Bible world into the modern world, although the metaphors and analogies contained in the notes often seem to want to transport the reader to a more serene, pastoral, and thus stable setting than modernity permits. Take, for example, the note opposite

Matthew's record of Jesus' Great Commission (28:18), which rises to a crescendo unlike any other Gospel. The WDB's devotional window speaks of dandelions and perseverance: "Our sunny yellow faces should be a reminder that simple faith has deep roots that are impossible to dislodge." And themes which were to emerge with the sound of trumpets in the 1990s are sounded with tinkling cymbal here. Author Marlene Obie's three devotionals on balancing career and home have a distinctly apologetic tone, though she persists in believing that work outside the home is both a woman's privilege and burden.

Thomas Nelson Publishers actually beat Zondervan to the women's breakfast table by one year, although the results of *The Businesswoman's Bible* (1989) were so lackluster that this product is nearly forgotten in niche lore. The BWB used the King James Version (one must always reckon with a significant number of conservative Christians who still confuse high English with accurate translation), and collected 57 "Priority Profiles" written by Charles F. Stanley, the distinguished Southern Baptist preacher. Stanley and Nelson, presumably, were inspired to produce the Bible by a 1983 Gallup Poll on American values which showed as much "secular" thinking among people who claimed church affiliation as among those who did not. Troubled by the apparent domination of values from the outside, Stanley sought to redirect Christians toward biblical values in twin volumes, this one and its brother, *The Businessman's Bible,* published the same year.

The WDB was revised and reissued in 1994. Then came 1998, the year of niche products for women. Nelson, discontent to be merely first out of the gate, needed a revival in that segment of its market and joined with Christianity Today Inc. (CTI), a publisher of evangelical magazines, to produce *The Bible for Today's Christian Woman* (TCW). Carolyn Nystrom, a veteran editor and established evangelical author, was hired to write a large share of the notes and to recruit and direct a team of exclusively women writers who were, oddly, not credited in the book for their work. Nonetheless, this product was by women and for women all the way. Nelson/CTI abandoned the KJV in favor of the American Bible Society's Contemporary English Version, much easier on the mind and clearer on the meaning. Instead of a focus on business or cultural values, this product goes right to the heart with meditations on matters such as: "My husband doesn't share my passion for spiritual things. How can I deal with my frustration and sadness?" Intra-family concerns are balanced with similar questions addressing other areas of human responsibility, but all of these meditations are grouped under a general heading of "Hope and Encouragement." The tie-in with CTI's popular evangelical magazine *Today's Christian Woman* would be obvious to most Bible bookstore customers. Indeed, CTI's in-house editor, Ramona Tucker, fashioned the entire project around the style and voice of the magazine. Thus, a Bible was born to augment a magazine for a well-defined market segment.

Honor Books in Tulsa, Oklahoma, jumped into this promising niche with *God's Little Devotional Bible for Women* (1998), produced by the Livingstone Corporation, and combining in one volume the text of the New King James Version and the popular *God's Little Devotional Book,* a presumptuous title that has helped sell more than a million copies in a variety of editions. The GLDB-W is a year-long read-through-the-Bible product with daily meditations, indices, and topical tables. At 1600 pages, it is anything but little.

World Publishers completed the 1998 trifecta with *Voices of Faith: A Woman's Personal Study Bible.* The book used all the customary apparatuses and special features but took a distinctive approach: in this product modern readers can establish friendship—"come to know these women intimately"—with women whose stories are told in the Bible. General editor Doris Rikkers makes her appeal to readers, as they open the book, to recover the voices of women from the past and thereby enlarge the family of faith in the present.

If 1998 glutted the market with niche Bibles for women, one group at least felt unrepresented. African-American publishing entrepreneur Mel Banks Jr. responded. In February 2000, the *Women of Color Study Bible* was introduced with contributions from 120 scholars, educators, and pastors, and 110 "Insight Essays" addressing issues on the life agenda of African-American women particularly. Remarkably, none of the contributors to this volume shows up anywhere else on the lists of other Bible products. The WCB offers a completely new group of Bible writers, many of them pastors, all women. How is it possible that at this late stage in the niche Bible phenomenon, a completely new constellation suddenly appears in the sky? The answer is simple and devastating. Mainstream evangelicalism, which produced and buys almost all niche Bibles, has very little crossover with the African-American community. Two cultures operate around the same core beliefs, without common rhetorical space and little culturally shared ground.

Banks owns and operates Nia Publications (*nia* is Swahili for purpose). His Children of Color series of Bible story books has been a market success (over 250,000 sold to date), and his first press run of 40,000 WCB's was already sold out four months after it appeared. Banks teamed on this product with World Publishers of Iowa Falls, Iowa, a company that capitalized on American popular culture's discovery of angels in the mid-1990s. World brought out *The Angel Bible,* most successfully sold through major retail outlets such as Walmart.

Niche Bible tie-ins to established products (which CTI and others have used to great advantage) may find their dean, mentor, and chief strategist in Mel Banks. Almost certainly it will not take the mainstream long to see this collaborative potential. In the meantime, Banks is planning several product tie-ins, forcing Bible bookstores to open more shelf space to a group of customers heretofore largely unknown and untapped.

All Bibles written for children are niche Bibles, but all niche Bibles aimed at child readers are also heavily marketed to adults.

The *New Adventure Bible* (NAB) appeared in late 1989, published by Zondervan with the NIV text and written by Lawrence O. Richards, a writer so well known to evangelical book buyers that the NAB never identifies him beyond name. Perhaps following the intuition that ancient data is the most difficult part of the Bible to make relevant to adolescents, the NAB uses four colors to highlight names (the list of kings, for instance) and once-memorized portions that rarely come up for drill in most churches today: the Ten Commandments and the list of books in Old and New Testaments.

Clearly the NAB has adopted a dynamic equivalent standard for its paraphrasing of Bible texts, and yet today's children, nearly 15 years after the appearance of the NAB, may need even more interpretive help if traditional meanings are to hold. For instance, in a Ten Commandments feature, the first commandment is rendered: "You may not love anyone or anything more than you love God." To the ancient Hebrews, "love" evoked awe, respect, reverence, and silence before the majesty of the other. To a modern generation raised on the virtues of equality and mutual affirmation, not to mention rampant sensuality, "love" must have a much less reverential, more familiar, even possibly illicit sense. So the question, "What is love?," must be addressed if the meaning of the first commandment, as rendered by the NAB, is to help children understand the starting-point of a relationship to the divine.

Commandment seven in the NAB reads: "Keep your thoughts and actions pure. Sex is a gift of God to married couples." This highly modernized version of the Old Testament rule raises one important question: What is a married couple? Former meanings once widely understood can no longer be assumed.

The NAB mixes contemporary narrative with biblical story. As Nehemiah and Sanballat threaten and insult each other, preparing for a battle, the NAB poses another story in its apparatus, fighting words between Tim and Bruce and an after-school confrontation in which books are set down and a punch-out is about to begin. To young readers the question is posed: What to do?

And the NAB appeals to childhood curiosity with its explanation of locusts, yokes, treasure, and jewelry; and to childhood expressiveness with "to do" recommendations of crafts and games. Tagged "A Study Bible for Kids," the NAB includes an index, dictionary, maps, and inter-textual features. This product has become the standard against which competitors in this lucrative niche weigh in.

And weigh in they do. It is impossible to review in any depth the array of Bibles available to children and teens. Each seeks a market share and each tries to establish a personality. Nelson's *Spirit Filled Life Bible for Students* (1995) is edited by Jack Hayford and uses the New King James Version. This conservative approach to the Bible text is linked to a breezy and populist appeal in the book's introduction: "God is alive and well—*BIG TIME!!!*"

Zondervan's *Teen Devotional Bible* (1999) uses stories by named teens (Chris, Anna, etc.) to bring readers into the Bible text through the door of all the stress-points in modern white America: peer relationships, parents, money, work, sports, cars, clothes, self concept, and jobs. The "What About You?" application feature still advises, however, time-tested devotional basics such as personal prayer and relational transparency as solutions to those recurrent problems.

Kirkbride, known throughout Christianity as the publisher of the ponderous Thompson Chain Reference Bible (once the symbol of serious spirituality), moved into the children's market in 1998 with *The Treasure Study Bible,* assembled by the Livingstone Corporation, which also produced the *New Thompson Student Bible* (1999), a product which promises the same integrity and biblical sensitivity as Kirkbride's weighty original.

The graphically wonderful *Adventures in Odyssey Bible* (1994, Word), also a Livingstone project, uses for its text the International Children's Bible, New Century Version (a translation owned by Word).

A note on Bible translations is needed here. The Preface to the *Odyssey Bible* heralds the International Children's Bible as the first full translation created especially for children. The market value of such translations cannot be overstated. Indeed, much of the recent debate concerning the popular New International Version has been market driven. Now that the NIV is fixed forever by these same market forces, the TIV (Today's International Version)—on the horizon—will become the corrective to the NIV's mistakes. Market pressure prevented the NIV from correcting itself, but new niche translations will prevent the NIV from monopolizing the Bible market. To some degree, the strong copyright exercised over the NIV text has also driven competing publishers to do their own in-house translations.

Tyndale House, famous for Kenneth Taylor's *Living Bible,* has the *Kid's Activity Bible* (1998), again produced by the Livingstone team. It includes 150 puzzles that become the book's teaching tool and best marketing device for parent-buyers. The book's back-cover blurb artlessly reads: "Your child will have a tough time putting [this book] down. Begin your child's journey through God's Word today." In the same year, it was hardly remarkable that the Tyndale-Livingstone team produced a tie-in to the extremely successful *Life Application Bible* (LAB), called, for obvious reasons, the *Kid's Life Application Bible.* It follows LAB notes and recasts LAB advice on godly living to the vocabulary, life, and world of pre-adolescents.

Among the many serious efforts to get non-reading teenagers to pick up the Bible is the hyper-niched *True Love Waits Youth Bible* (1996), published by Broadman and Holman. The book uses dramatic graphics to articulate the theme of the True Love Waits movement of Nashville, Tennessee. Here is a sub-niche product which broadens an effective national effort in promoting teenage chastity into an interpretive lens for the entire Scripture. The product uses many famous evangelical writers to broaden its appeal: Oswald Chambers, James Dobson, Josh McDowell, and even one author who has a niche Bible of his own, San Antonio pastor Max Lucado. (See the Max Lucado Inspirational Study Bible produced, once again, by the Livingstone Corporation, whose editorial team on that project was headed—full and complete disclosure is a virtue—by the author of this essay.)

Is the children's niche Bible market saturated? No one thinks so. Several new products with a specialized focus are in process. This market niche will be recreated for as long as new readers enter the tidal basins of popular entertainment, moral pluralism, and material culture that characterize American Christianity and for as long as parents seek a way to put their values into the heads and hearts of their children.

New Directions

Yet spiritual formation is not only the need of the young. Two relatively new products testify to the attraction of spiritual renewal that serves as counterpoint to materialist-frenzy in contemporary American life.

The *Knowing Jesus Study Bible* (Zondervan, 1999) and *The Leadership Bible* (Zondervan, 1999) seem remarkably similar in design, with the first graphically directed toward a person seeking an intimate relationship and the latter, less personal and more leather toned, appealing to a reader's quest for meaningfulness and impact. Both motivations may be found in the same Bible reader obviously, but they appeal to differing spiritual sensitivities, and a Bible for each makes good sense in today's meet-my-needs marketplace.

The *Knowing Jesus Bible* (KJB) features a cover photo of Jesus, soft and slightly out of focus, interrupted with an eye-catching sticker which points buyers to the book's "bargain": an introduction by author Philip Yancey (who has written highly successful books for Zondervan and other firms) on "My Top Ten Surprises About Jesus." Yancey's work precedes the Bible text itself and constitutes an apologia for faith. Throughout the text, adding to its unique graphic design, are close-up stills of traditional Christian symbols (such as a cross, dove, and olive branch) over well-known Bible texts, all reflecting an aspect of Jesus' character or mission.

By this time in the development of niche Bibles, the apparatuses are a sophisticated blend of theological explanation and personal application. The KJB team of writers was led by Ed Hindson, a Baptist preacher from Atlanta, and Ed Dobson, pastor of Calvary Church in Grand Rapids, Michigan. Each editor's signature appears on the Bible's first page, for a personal touch. The plan of the KJB is a year-long (365 one-a-days) series of "Discoveries" and 200 text notes, including quotations by recognized evangelical leaders (such as Joni Eareckson Tada and Jack Hayford), and a few not so well known (such as Athanasius, I. Howard Marshall, and Augustine, who is curiously identified as a "Catholic theologian"). The 365 Discoveries are unsigned page-length devotionals that conclude with a question for self-reflection. Certain of these devotionals will likely stretch the reader's imagination. For instance, Discovery 29 on the Old Testament's sin offering asks readers to imagine what deficits of peace and joy would afflict their lives were they to be living during Old Testament times—hardly a question that busy Gen-Xers will ponder for long. Nonetheless, the book has a distinctive two-color design and its consistent focus on Jesus is unique to niche Bibles.

The Leadership Bible (TLB)—outwardly a masculine counterpart to the quietly pietistic KJB—follows a similar strategy in its apparatuses, but takes a different approach in its execution and editorial breadth. The heart of TLB is a five-day, 52-week series of devotional notes on themes related to leadership in the home, church, and workplace. Week One, located at Genesis 3, offers five lessons on "Long Range Planning." Eventually this plan leads to Week 52, at Hebrews 11, on "Rewards." The five-day lessons for each of these weeks direct the reader to roam throughout the Bible, sometimes using quoted material from one of the fifty-two books and articles used to expand on the notes provided by the lean (by niche production team standards) editorial team of Sid Buzzell, Kenneth Boa, and Bill Perkins. All of the editorial team and all but three or four of the quoted authors in TLB are male, making this book one that reflects a decidedly masculine orientation to leadership. For example, at 2 Thessalonians 1:4, the short note advises: "Have you ever worked with so much purpose and passion that your supervisor couldn't help but brag about you to his or her peers? Consider making that your personal goal for the week." Purpose, energy, productivity, and peer approval are common themes in male leadership literature.

TLB profiles seventy-eight Bible characters, only twelve of whom are women leaders, both good ones and not so good. Jezebel makes the list, but so do Naomi and Esther. Negative examples of leadership include Ahab and Pontius Pilate, making this a book about leadership virtues and pitfalls. Jesus is included among the profiles, with his distinctive leadership philosophy pulled from Matthew 20:20-28 and reduced to a simple command: serve others.

The TLB editorial team obviously did not want to restrict its sources to any narrowly Christian circle. Its bibliography cites well-known evangelicals (such as Howard Hendricks and Charles Swindoll), a few authors that evangelicals admire (such as Martin Luther King Jr. and Peter Drucker), and then some a bit further from the fold (such as Pat Riley and several scholars whose religious commitments are not widely known).

Leadership is a large and flexible term. Surveying the topics of the 52 Weeks, one could conclude that this is actually the Successful Living Bible or the Well-Directed Life Bible. But the term *leadership* itself carries stronger rhetorical freight. Any responsible Christian view of leadership, however, includes the radical turnabout that makes leaders first and foremost servants of all. Clarifying what Jesus meant by this about-face has led to hundreds of titles and studies. Of course, the Christian view (namely that the first shall be last, the last shall be first) is often ridiculed as weak and ineffective, as nice poetry but impractical. Great military generals and corporate leaders are rarely set apart from the masses by their intense humility or their eagerness to wash the feet of anyone. Thus, Viking Books recently released the Nietzsche-inspired *48 Laws of Power*, which sneers at the Christian mode and, were it possible, advises readers to turn the appearance of niceness into the disguise that leads to the coup d'grace.

Jesus' radical about-face on leadership was bewildering when he delivered it in the context of Roman expansionism and growing imperial idolatry. It is no less breathtaking today. In this book, the devotional lessons and Bible notes regularly highlight Jesus' side, while the practical application notes often seek at least a convergence with the needs and aspirations of the worldly side. The note previously cited (at 2 Thessalonians 1:4) advises readers toward passion, productivity, and peer approval—all vital components of every corporate scheme ever devised. Hard workers careless toward non-professional obligations usually produce the best short-term profit.

The problem for Christian leadership theorists is that Jesus himself simply defies any such simplistic scheme. At the apex of his popularity in Capernaum, he leaves to pray and preach elsewhere. When people seek his best thinking on the key to a happy life and scribes prepare to record his most important sermon, he says: "Blessed are the poor in spirit" (Matthew 5:1). When an adroit self-defense could have set a bad record straight, he is silent (Luke 23:9). No contemporary leadership manual knows what to do with these seeming contradictions. The advantage of this book above the others is that the Bible text itself is ever-present, disturbing theories and upsetting strategies with its Spirit-directed alternative consistently dethroning the powerful and enfranchising the destitute. "Leadership is an art," corporate leader Max DePree writes. That may be the most helpful metaphor in which to address the problem of Christian leadership and its cultural contradictions. The TLB provides a canvas, a montage, a direction, but not an air-tight argument with enumerated steps to successful enactment. The TLB is best regarded as a bridge between two competing worlds—one driven by acquisition and conquest, and the other by restoration and shalom.

Gentlemen, Open Your Books

The gendered counterpart to the women's niche preceded the TLB by several years. Here we examine two products, the *Men's Devotional Bible* (Zondervan, 1993) and the *Promise Keepers Men's Study Bible* (Zondervan, 1997). The plan of the MDB is quite simple: Mondays through Fridays, readers are invited to learn from half-page devotionals inserted near key verses in the text of the New International Version. The regimen varies slightly on Saturday and Sunday with a feature called "Weekending" (which could have been called Weekstarting)—slightly less reading and a less structured lesson for those hectic Saturdays and busy Sundays. Unlike niche products soon to follow, this Bible has no varied apparatuses, no shorter notes to contrast with the devotional lessons, no complicated system of symbols to master, and no graphics imitative of a webpage on a screen. Indeed, at points this Bible even has no need of copyright permissions, as the list of 107 contributors goes back to Christian leaders as old as St. Francis of Assisi. Most contributors, however, are names that men tuned to the popular culture will recognize handily: sports figures Tom Landry and Reggie White (football professionals only here, no one from basketball, baseball, or hockey); church leaders Billy Graham and Bill Hybels (no one outside of evangelicalism in this group); a few theologians, scholars, and literary figures; singer Michael Card; sundry other leaders, some of whom have carved a terrain of popular expertise, such as Larry Burkett in money management.

Not surprisingly, the first devotional in the MDB relates to work and toil, and the last, a Weekending, to heaven and rest. Perhaps the organizers of this product took their cues from Ecclesiastes—a time to work, a time to cease working—or perhaps from the focus groups that are now standard for all such products. Either way, the multi-faceted job of living in the late twentieth century and new millennium as a man of faith, energy, and compassion is given aid and encouragement through stories and insights from other places and epochs. At times poignant (one father relates the death of his nine-year-old) and at times pedantic—"a real man will follow through"—the MDB carries an outdoors graphic theme and offers a variety of authors' wisdom to chew upon and digest.

The *Promise Keepers Men's Study Bible* (PKB), which issues from the organization founded in 1993 with a then little-known name, strikes a much different graphic note. By 1997 this name had bolted to stardom and was among the most marketable in the Christian Booksellers Association (CBA). The PKB is all about machines and coordination. The cover photo is a series of gears probably meant to convey the impression that this book works well, that a spiritually coordinated life is preferable to brokenness, or that one gear needs another to do successful work. The symbolism of the PKB is ambiguous, worldly, and plainly evocative.

Due in part to the early conceptual plans of the Livingstone Corporation, the PKB shows the sophisticated and complex evolution of niche Bibles in the four-year gap between the MDB and the PKB. However, organizational reshuffling within Promise Keepers (PK) coincided with its early partnership with Livingstone, and the result was an abruptly cancelled contract and a turn toward Zondervan. In the process, PK gave a start to the writing team that would produce another niche Bible oriented toward men—the aforementioned *Leadership Bible*. Kenneth Boa, Sid Buzzell, and Bill Perkins, with Gene Getz (not part of the Leadership Bible team), used a Promise Keepers' template to assemble and write the PKB. That template was presented even before the reader could approach the Bible text itself, as well it should be. The interpretive grid used to understand the Bible ought to be forthright and plain, and

PK makes no apology concerning its positions and policies. In one sense, this Bible preaches its sermon before the text is even considered. It has become a reference text for men attracted to PK, and the controlling beliefs of the organization are up-front and "man to man" (as the introductory material is called). To insure breadth and orthodoxy, a "review board" is acknowledged by name only.

The plan of the PKB follows the Seven Promises of a Promise Keeper, which, in short form, pledge fidelity to Jesus Christ, other men, moral purity, wives and children, churches, and commitment to racial reconciliation and evangelism. In all, the book offers 1093 notes organized in fourteen chains, two for each of the seven PK promises. The notes are embedded in the Bible text, so a reader could follow the chain and move around the Bible or follow the Bible and move uncoordinatedly through the notes.

The notes themselves strike familiar themes within the PK orbit: work hard, be faithful to commitments, embrace all the people who walk within your boundaries, show brotherliness without regard to color, and reserve ultimate devotion for God. With respect to those troubling New Testament passages which critics of PK often cite as evidence for the organization's narrowness or chauvinism, this book simply does not address them. No notes address a woman's role in the church or a gay individual's role in the world. On these matters, PK has apparently opted not to comment but simply to allow the Bible to speak for itself. Four of the forty-five character profiles are women, the same names included in similar profiles in the TLB. In fact, most of the Bible characters profiled in this book are also profiled in the TLB, evidence that a niche retread phenomenon may be upon us. The TLB carries, in addition, profiles of six women not in the PKB, Jesus, David, Job, and a few more, notably the bad-example quartet of Judas, Pontius Pilate, Herod, and Satan.

Perhaps the growth of voluntary religious societies has evolved to a point that requires distinctive editions of the Bible to secure a link both to the past as well as to the present organization. The PKB is a book of order and a token of identity to the thousands of American men who have attended PK stadium rallies and been advised by PK discipline and teaching. The TLB is likewise a token, not so much to an external organization, but to the need for men to identify with something grander and more influential than their own customary workaday world.

Point of Purchase Overload

The immense popularity of niche Bible products led in 1998 to publishers' worst fears: hints from neighborhood booksellers that the market was saturated and that their shelves could no longer contain the latest niche. Firms once bustling with production business were reducing the size of their writing teams, while publishing houses declared moratoriums on new proposals. In 1998 this writer attended a day-long planning meeting in which participants brainstormed on new niche and sub-niche Bible ideas, but none that the leadership considered marketable. Niche Bibles are not being produced as quickly as during the heyday of the early 1990s, but neither is the market moribund.

Now as the new millennium begins, another phase of the niche marketplace may be appearing: once popular books are being revived and updated, retread with contemporary apparatuses, and reintroduced to a market still eager for spiritual insight and succor. The Leadership Bible enlarged the scope and audience of the 1997 PKB, which is not a retread, but is certainly an example of one good idea given a new face by the same publisher and writing team. Perhaps the largest retread project currently underway involves the *Bible for Groups*, a remake of the *Serendipity Bible for Groups*.

This early *Serendipity Bible for Groups* was one of the first specialized products to appear, jointly published in 1988 by Serendipity House, a ministry of Lyman Coleman, and the Zondervan Corporation. The book's dedication is "to small groups around the world who share in the Serendipity dream," defined in the introduction as getting people together to "love each other, care for each other's needs, and celebrate koinonia." The project employed forty-eight freelance writers and a coordinating executive editor, Dietrich Gruen. Each segment of the Bible included questions for group discussion, leading groups to examine mostly personal virtues. For example, the wicked King Ahab's melancholic reaction to an unknown prophet's gloomy forecast leads to the questions "When are you moody? How do you deal with it? What role does God play in your moods?" Answering these questions cannot lead to greater theological clarity, as the typical study Bible seeks to promote, but to greater personal transparency and vulnerability in group settings. This niche Bible was for people eager to develop a closer circle of friends and to build community around common religious concerns. The notes were written in a conversational style, not as monological footnotes on a text. The intention was thoroughly dynamic and social, and because social life changes and social roles evolve, the book, now almost twenty years old, is getting a new wardrobe. The *Serendipity Bible* will be available soon for a new generation of readers still hungry for social bonding.

A Potpourri of Products

The niche Bible phenomenon, while tapering in market energy in the late 1990s, was still powerful enough to inspire an investigation by *Publisher's Weekly* (PW) as the millennium approached. Bible publishers, PW assured, "need not fear the Good Book will lose its status as the all-time best seller" (PW 11 October 1999). PW then cited a market study conducted by Zondervan on the Bible-buying habits of 1800 bookstore customers, who reported ownership of an average of eight Bibles and a desire for more. Still strong are perceived needs of teenagers for spiritual formation, an idea supported by recent tragedies of school and church shootings and by commonplace drug use and uninhibited sexual activity that attract people who are too young to understand the consequences. Every major Bible publisher is launching a Bible for teenagers, especially those in high school, PW reports.

PW's survey reveals titles destined to an extremely narrow market, but such is the trend. HarperSanFrancisco is scheduled to release the Dead Sea Scrolls Bible and Eerdmans the Dead Sea Scrolls Study Edition. Driving these books is an unclear and perhaps magical fascination with the mystery and romance associated with the discovery of the scrolls and the Jewish religious sect that hid them in caves two millennia ago.

Other world religions are producing versions of holy writ in reader-friendly translations for English speakers. New diglot editions of Jewish, Hindu, and Buddhist texts will appear soon—not as a threat to niche Bible sales but riding on their draft. The nation's oldest Bible publisher, Thomas Nelson, is beginning to reach into the Catholic youth market with *My First Catholic Bible* (2000). Catholics have always been included as potential buyers of the popular evangelical editions; they now have their own *International Student Bible for Catholics*.

Special holiday editions will take advantage of traditional gift-giving. A green leather edition of the *Come Let Us Adore Him Bible* should sell during Decembers, as should the *Daughters of God* edition, which will include a one-ounce bottle of frankincense and myrrh. As business travel increases after the holiday season, new editions of *Wow: The Bible in Seven Minutes a Day,* a condensed version of 365 readings, should be packed in thousands of carry-ons. Next year, inevitably, some enterprising publishing house will offer a six-minute-a-day counterpart or two-minutes-in-the-evening companion guide, timed for easy reading during network station breaks. Nelson will be tying Bible promotions to rock music tours soon, while Oxford University Press promotes its *Access*

Bible (targeted to readers in small church or home-based study groups) on the World Wide Web.

Publisher's Weekly is clearly impressed with the strategic positioning and graphic sophistication applied to Bible products, and it predicts continued health in this market niche with no saturation point clearly in sight. With over 3000 Bibles available on a SKU search, this essay could not even contain all the titles, but we cannot bypass a brief note on some products not previously mentioned.

Some niche Bibles are born of personal experience on the part of a Christian pilgrim who has access to the publishing world, some born from years of observation about the needs of people, and some born of opportunism and market savvy. Publishing is a vital and promising business, for it places culturally relevant notes and applications into the text of the best-selling book ever published. See what a rich harvest of spiritual guidance has been invested in these niche products:

- David Mains, Chicago-area pastor and long-time leader of the radio program "Chapel of the Air," integrated radio directly into church programming with his "50-Day Spiritual Adventure" program begun in 1980 and used by nearly two million people. In 1998 Zondervan published *The Bible for Personal Revival*, of which he was general editor. In the Introduction, he dismisses any notion that his project is "complicated"—perhaps a veiled reference to the elaborate apparatuses which must be learned in most current niche products. Rather, the BPR "distills from a lifetime of study . . . basic concepts that can be understood by everyone."

- The *Worklife Inspiration Bible*, compiled by Ronald C. Williams, answers the need for Bibles on desktops and other work-related sites. Notes in this product deal with stress, technology, emotional violence, and career management, but the gist of the project is not merely personal reading but product placement where people can see it.

- The *Positive Thinking Bible* (1998, Nelson) resurrects the popular writings of Norman Vincent Peale, whose best seller, *The Power of Positive Thinking,* appeared in 1952. Peale was the voice of liberal, optimistic, mid-twentieth-century Protestantism, and his legacy endures in the still popular *Guideposts* magazine.

- The *Prophecy Study Bible* (Nelson, 1997), edited by John C. Hagee, trades on the universal yearning to know, prepare for, and survive the future. Such a passion catapulted the *Scofield Reference Bible* in the 1920-30s and continues to be one of the best-selling topics to general and religious readers. Today's phenomenal popularity of the Tim LaHaye-Jerry Jenkins *Left Behind* series attests to the insatiable appetite for hints and helps for tomorrow.

• The *Parents Resource Bible* (Tyndale, 1995) establishes a template for the successful niche product: Bible book introductions, a variety of notes, profiles, and applications, and selections from popular authors. Appearing in this book are words by James Dobson, Bill Hybels, Max Lucado, Josh McDowell, and Joni Eareckson Tada— a veritable stable of evangelical advice counselors whose work appears in several of these products. It should also be noted that the Livingstone Corporation produced this book. Much of this Bible relates to family and home, so it is not a stretch to find biblical material to surround with notes.

Our review is truncated. This essay is not meant to be a catalog, but an overview. Some worthy products have not been mentioned, but readers may consult the websites of any publisher for the latest products available.

Will there be more? Indeed, new ideas are more difficult to come by, given the number of books currently available, but idea factories are still in business. And niche Bibles have been around long enough now to have spawned makeovers, retreads, and redesigns. They, too, compete for space on the bookstore shelf.

Agents of Change

Perhaps these niche products will save the Bible from obscurity in an era when much of its context strikes many readers as antiquated and even morally out of pace with the ethics of a new millennium. Among the surge of books and articles exploring the meaning of a millennial transition was a short and personal reflection from the Dalai Lama, who could not be expected to champion Bible distribution but whose appeal is particularly contemporary and noticeably bereft of any reliance on an enscripturated word from God. In a book titled *Ethics for a New Millennium,* he calls people of all faiths to a celebration of their distinctive traditions and, more importantly, to a convergence of attitude and action that he believes will lead to the future all nations seek. Indeed, the convergence has nothing whatever to do with refurbishing and contemporizing the Book of Judges or the Prophecy of Zephaniah. Rather, without regard to social distinctions he calls people to a new opportunity and era when compassion promotes human happiness on all fronts: environments are restored; business practice submits to human need as a first priority; media promote social well-being; political leadership shuns corruption. This new millennial effort requires nothing more than each person doing better at cultivating the innate virtues that characterize advanced civility. The text is the human self alone. The meaning of its interpretation requires reflection and common sense alone. Some holy texts, or the parts that celebrate these common themes, may be acceptable today, but none is indispensable. Against these sentiments articulated by a world-class religious leader but understood also at every PTA and corner pub, the niche Bible market keeps the ancient Word alive.

In her brilliant work on the social effects of the printing press, Elizabeth Eisenstein observed that the communications shift in fifteenth century Europe

> altered the way Western Christians viewed their sacred book and the natural world. It made the words of God appear more multiform and His handiwork more uniform. The printing press laid the basis for both literal fundamentalism and for modern science. (Eisenstein: 704)

Surely the Bible press of the late twentieth century has pushed the multiform side of that shift to its highest expression and the uniform side toward the science of marketing and audience demographics. At no time in Christian history have so many adaptations of the Bible been so readily available to such a studied market. Driven by the self-help phenomenon of the late twentieth century, Bible publishing has understood its audience in terms of life-stages, worship preferences, gendered spirituality, and social roles of all kinds. Yet a point-of-purchase decision requires that these book buyers put forward $20-$50 to add a special-interest Bible to their armory of faith. This is most likely to occur among an affluent, largely evangelical population. Members of that group presently find themselves faced with a cornucopia of choices; minority populations are not so blessed. Perhaps the community of faith of the "lessers" will finally be the more expressive of older communal virtues such as ecclesial solidarity and confessional unity, while well-Bibled people discover that life needs and social roles have fragmented the fellowship: where two or more gather together, no two texts will match.

On another extreme, the World Wide Web may one day offer to Bible readers a radically personalized version—unique, private, and fully niched. Already Broadway Books has offered what PW calls the ultimate niche Bible, titled *Create Your Own Sacred Text.* The author, a marriage counselor, has put together in sacred format a collection of song lyrics, poems, and stories that she credits with providing inspiration during her own marital crisis. If one can do this, more will surely follow.

Works Cited

Eisenstein, Elizabeth L.
    1979   *The Printing Press as an Agent of Change.* Cambridge: Cambridge University Press.

5

Packaging the Word, Peddling Holy Writ

Canongate and their Pocket-sized Bibles

R. S. Sugirtharajah

Think what would have happened to the English if they had not an authorized version of the Bible.

—M. K. Gandhi (177)

Without it [i.e. the Authorized Version] we can scarcely imagine English constitutionalism or English imperial expansion.

—A. G. Dickens (193)

Here in England everyday a chapter of Genesis and a leader of *The Times*.

—R. W. Emerson (cited in The British and Foreign Bible Society, 1933:25)

Recently, the Edinburgh-based publishing firm, Canongate, has brought out the Bible in the form of single books and in the King James Version. Each volume is introduced by a writer, not necessarily associated with the Christian tradition, who encourages the readers to approach them as literary works in their own right. For long the Christian Bible came with erudite commentaries written by prominent religious scholars. Now it looks as if the cultural totem of Western civilization needs a preamble by novelists, pop artists, scientists, and even non-Christians in order to make the once familiar texts, now widely neglected in the West, come alive again. The essayists include prominent novelists: Doris Lessing (Ecclesiastes); Ruth Rendell (Romans); P. D. James (Acts); Joanna Trollope (Ruth and Esther); Will Self (Revelation). They also include pop artist U2's Bono (The Psalms), scientist and atheist Steven Rose (Genesis), and individuals from other faith traditions. Jewish writers look at Exodus (David Grossman) and the books of Samuel (Meir Shalev). Among the non-biblical faiths, only Buddhism is represented: Charles Johnson, raised in the African Methodist Episcopal Church and now turned Buddhist, introduces Proverbs, while the exiled Tibetan Dalai Lama deals with the Epistle of James. Incidentally, the Dalai Lama is the only non-Westerner to join the disparate and, at times, contradictory group of prologue writers. Most are lay people (with the exception of Richard Holloway), thus investing the text with literary rather than religious legitimacy.

Although Christian bookstores in the United Kingdom refused to stock these single volumes, they have become a publishing sensation and have sold more than a million copies. The cover design by Angus Hyland, of Pentgram of London, won the Silver Award in the book category of the Design and Art Direct Awards. Suddenly, this chic, taut, practical, and portable Bible has become something that will not prove embarrassing to anyone reading it on the tube. Its publication has also generated a fair amount of theological storm. The disagreements have ranged from David Grossman's remark about Moses' life as a "fairy tale" (vii) to Steven Rose's claim, echoing current biblical scholarship, that the Genesis stories are "accretions of early Mesopotamian and Egyptian myths and sagas" (ix; Byng). When Alasdair Gray, in his preface to the books of Jonah, Micah, and Nahum, described Abraham and Isaac as "polygamous nomads who get cattle or revenge by prostituting a wife or cheating foreigners and relatives" (viii), Jews as well as Muslims were offended, and both the Board of Deputies of British Jews and the Muslim Council urged that the book be withdrawn (Millar).

The purpose of this essay is to examine the following set of issues: the role of the interpreter's personal voice within the process of discovering meaning in a narrative; the positive potential of this Pocket Canon; the re-iconization of the Bible through the King James Version; the colonial parallels in the investment, promotion, and dissemination of the Bible; the marketing of the Bible and the appropriation of religious themes by secular marketeers; and the challenge of personal-voice criticism to biblical studies. Put at its simplest, can this disparate group of essayists rescue the Bible, which is fast losing its grip and importance in the West, and discover fresh significance in it?

Take, Read, and Wait for Revelation

The introductions by various authors throw light on the texts to which they are appended. They do not burden the readers with complicated textual, historical, or theoretical discussion nor baffle them with unnecessary erudition such as one finds in a standard biblical commentary. They repeatedly point to the beauty, narrative power, and idealism of biblical texts. Doris Lessing waxes lyrical about Ecclesiastes containing some of the "most wonderful English prose ever written" (ix). Louis de Bernières, of *Captain Correlli's Mandolin* fame, applauds the "fair share of poetry" in the text (Job), despite the fact that the translators of the King James Version did not have the benefit of modern scholarship and got their renditions "confused and inaccurate" (viii). Bono rhapsodizes over the "poetic" truth found in the scriptures. Peter Ackroyd locates Isaiah within the tradition of oral poetry and hails it as "a river made out of many streams…fluent and harmonious" (vii). Blake Morrison declares that John is the most poetic of all the gospels and that it "opens with one of the greatest passages of poetic prose in the language, philosophically dense, metaphorically rich, and rhythmically lucid at the same time" (xi). For him the writer of the Fourth Gospel is a poet "through and through" (xvi).

Although the idea was to present the Bible as a literary text, the introductions are both spiritual and personal. The biblical books elicit a testimonial mode among the introducers. What these authors seek to do is to make the text their own. Therefore, they are not particularly interested in the different layers or deep levels of the text but want to have a personal engagement with it. With the exception of two, none of these writers is a trained biblical scholar. Most opt for a personal response, frequently drawing on memories of their first encounter with the Bible. The Canongate publishers state that for the Pocket Canon series an impressive range of writers was commissioned specifically to "provide a personal interpretation of the text and explore its contemporary relevance." Their biblical exegesis may be weak, suspect, and even cynical—Self sees it as a "perverse" activity, like squeezing toothpaste out of a tube—but they are totally in command of their personal preoccupations and histories. The prefaces are replete with anecdotes, reevaluations, and even private grouses.

It is no surprise that many of these introductions come from men and women who grew up at a time when the Bible was an unavoidable part of their childhood experience but who then lived their adult life either in a declining state of faith or with an ambivalent attitude towards the Bible and lost touch with it. Some of them fondly recall their childhood encounter with the Bible. Blake Morrison, who spent every Sunday morning in the choir stalls of an English village church and at fifteen "swapped the Apostles for another Fab Four, the Beatles," tells the readers that rereading the Fourth Gospel carried him back to the place where he had first heard it. In his journey back to the text, he finds the rhythms of St. John's Gospel "inspiring and sensuous" (xvi). Bono reveals that he was a fan of

David at the age of 12 and that he found comfort in the scriptures, despite growing up in a divided Ireland, where organized religion came through to him as the "perversion of faith." He also reveals how, as part of a white rock group, "plundering of the scriptures was taboo." He chose Psalm 40 to end one of his albums, *War*, because of its suggestion that there will be a time when "grace will replace karma, and love replace the very strict law of Moses" (xii). Read goes on to say that as a child he was greatly impressed by how King Solomon came to acquire great riches and wealth. Byatt casts her mind back to her first bewildered reading as a Western child, with the compulsory Bible on her desk (xv). Nick Cave, the Australian song writer and musician, one of the non-believing contributors, remembers, in his introduction to Mark, how in his early twenties the Old Testament spoke to that part of him which "railed and hissed and spat at the world" (vii). He goes on to recall how the gospel has informed his spiritual maturity: "The Gospel according to Mark had continued to inform my life as the root source of my spirituality, my religiousness" (xi).

Interwoven with personal anecdotes one finds personal complaints of the introducers. These essayists particularly bemoan the marked bloodthirstiness of the God of the Hebrew Scriptures; such perceptions precariously border on antisemitism. Steven Rose contends that Genesis is full of "seemingly motiveless and often unjust Godly acts" (xii). The novelist Louis de Bernières is equally unimpressed. In his preface to Job, he points out that the implicit God who emerges from the Hebrew text is one that is "an unpleasantly sarcastic megalomaniac" (xiii), a "mad, bloodthirsty, and capricious despot" (xiv). Nick Cave sees him as a "maniacal, punitive God, that dealt out to His long-suffering humanity punishments" (vii). P. D. James, too, observes that the punishment meted out to Ananias and Sapphira as typical of "a vengeful Jehovah" (1999: xii). Will Self finds Revelation a "sick text," "a guignol of tedium, a portentous horror film" (xiii, xi). The Church's presentation of Jesus also gets some stick. Nick Cave writes: "The Christ that Church offers us, the bloodless, placid 'Savior'—the man smiling benignly at a group of children, or calmly, serenely hanging from the cross— denies Christ His potent, creative sorrow or His boiling anger that confronts us so forcefully in Mark" (xi). In his introduction to the Fourth Gospel, Blake Morrison describes Jesus as self-assured, pushy, and somewhat dislikeable; he finds him "wan, frozen, and passive, too passive for his own good—someone who'd change wine to water, and not the other way about" (viii). Paul, too, is not spared. Fay Weldon sees him as "a very Mandelson" of the time, demanding a united front (viii).

The introducers often unhinge the narrative from its original environment and make it speak for universal human conditions, thus perpetuating the notion of the Bible as a timeless and contextless text. Richard Holloway notes :

> We do not know who Luke was, and it does not matter, because it is the very anonymity of this text that confirms its power....We do not need to know anything about its provenance for it to affect us. We do not really know who wrote *Genesis* or many of the other ancient writings and we need not care, because these great texts communicate truth to us at a level that goes beyond the artistry of any particular individual. They create archetypes that express the general condition of humanity, and its sorrow and loss, heroism and betrayal. This is also why the gospels go on touching us long after we have abandoned the orthodoxies that have been built upon them. We do not know who wrote them or when, but they still have power to connect with our lives today.... (x)

Joanna Trollope, introducing the widely contrasting stories of Ruth and Esther, locates them on two levels. At one level, they are simple narratives, one romantic and the other dramatic, but at another level "they are illustrations, or images, of human behavior, human attitudes, human arbitrariness, human trial and error, human failing, human (with divine assistance) triumph. We may not be able to identify with the time and place, but in some way, however small, we can identify with some aspect of the human condition" (ix). Will Self, who wrote an extraordinary introduction in which he hardly refers to the text he was supposed to introduce, Revelation, thinks "that this ancient text has survived to be the very stuff of modern, psychotic nightmare" (xiv). Fay Weldon comments thus on the magnificence of the Corinthian passage: "The timeless truth remains. Two millennia are just the twinkling of an eye in the sight of God, and/or the writer" (xii). In Louis de Bernières's view, Job 14 stands out as a moving lament for the human condition: "Man that is born of a woman is of few days, and full of trouble. He cometh forth like a flower, and is cut down" (viii).

Although for most of the introducers the narrative world of the Bible may seem strange, they see scriptural narratives as the defining story of humanity, to which one can connect in spite of living in a different time and a different cultural space. Holloway claims, "Luke connects with us again and again by the immediacy of his art" (x). Charles Johnson goes on to state with reference to Prov 30:11-12:

> In fact, I realized that Proverbs not only speaks powerfully to our morally adrift era, but describes rather well my own often benighted rebellious-on-principle generation (the Baby-Boomers) when it says

"There is a generation that curseth their father and does not bless their mother. There is a generation that are pure in their own eyes, and yet is not washed from their filthiness." (ix)

The introductory preambles make the Bible appear as an optimistic and generous document, unapologetically holding on to the simplicity of Christian truth. They create a cultural space in which the Bible can be popularized and still retain its place, dignity, and valency. A literary presentation of the Bible may be more than an attempt to bring fresh readers to the Bible. The outcome is more evangelical than literary and more spiritual than narrative.

These introductions simultaneously free readers from the authority and mediation of critics and entrap them in the essayists' over-simplistic and often skeptical views, capitalizing on their authors' popularity and status as novelists, pop-icons, and serious scientists. What these introductions make clear is that theory and methods are not enough to help us recognize our role and place as interpreters or to make us aware of our impressions and expectations. Throughout these introductions, the hallmark of Protestantism is in evidence: the primacy of the individual reader responding to a sacred text in a manner quite unmediated by the authority of institutional readings. The aim is to rescue the text from the various ways in which it has been manacled. Lessing notes: "Thus do the living springs of knowledge, of wisdom, become captured by institutions, by churches of various kinds" (xii). The essayists' reading re-emphasizes and even increases the power attributed to the reader.

Interestingly, the by-line of each author is reduced to lower-case. Whether this has to do with the humility of the authors before Holy Writ or with the imaginative work of the designer is difficult to fathom. But the reverential attitude accorded to the text is copious. Here are a few examples of such venerable sentiments:

- "We must approach this sacred text with great respect, doubting the ability of our mind to comprehend it and of our tongue to describe it" (Ackroyd: vii).
- "We will go away sorrowful, deeply conscious of our inability either to understand the Gospel, or to live up to its precepts or to have the humility to accept Divine Grace. Yet, though we are sorrowful, and though we go away, we shall never read this text without being, in some small degree, changed" (Wilson: xiv-xv).
- "Believers and non-believers alike cannot help but be stricken with awe by its (Romans) temerity and Paul's genius" (Rendell: xvii)

Undoubtedly, the whole enterprise is aimed at Western Christians. However, whether the focus is on the lapsed or potential believer is not clear. The aim is to present the Bible as a classic of literature in order to attract a generation which has lost the sense of Holy Writ. Lessing laments the loss of biblical literacy among the present generation. She recalls the day when everyone in "Britain and for that matter everyone in the Christian world" would have heard every Sunday "the thundering magnificence of this prose" and would have been able to identify "the origin of phrases and sayings that are as much a part of our language as Shakespeare. These days, if someone hears 'There is a time to be born and a time to die...' they probably do think it is Shakespeare, since the Bible these days is the experience of so few" (vii). She goes on to say that "we are very much the poorer because the Bible is no longer a book to be found in every home, and heard every week" (ix-x).

We live in a time in which secular literature is gradually gaining sacred status and sacred literature is being read as secular fiction. Morrison calls the Hebrew Scriptures "a school boy's adventure story" (viii). In its pages one encounters a variety of characters varying from "hustlers, murderers, cowards, adulterers, mercenaries" to classic existentialist "heroes" like Job. Its narratives, in Holloway's view, contain a "catalogue of improbabilities." Such perceptions sow doubt in the reader's mind and do not impel them to believe. By treating the Bible as literature, sometimes going against its main tenets and often puncturing its pomposity, the introducers invite the readers to judge the Bible's credibility, thus overturning the long-held view of the sacred text's assertion of its believability. This is to be welcomed insofar as it dispels fanatical claims made on the text's behalf, claims that often have resulted in frenzy within religious communities.

The introducers extol the intensity of the text's vision, compliment its power and beauty, admire its once-powerful hold on Western culture, but not all of them believe in its theological efficacy. Their purpose in reading the Bible was not to learn the theology of Paul nor to listen to the universalism of the Second Isaiah, even if such was concealed in its pages. Rather, theirs was an attempt to get at the religious experiences and convictions that generated this literature and gave it shape. In effect, they admire its aesthetic beauty but neither accept nor are convinced by its religious potency. They marvel at its literary brilliance but are reluctant to seek guidance from its teaching or invest power in its message. Steven Rose is the most unambiguous in discarding the truth-claims of the text and questioning its serious claim to be a guide to morality. Rose writes: "If believers find useful ethical values to be drawn from these stories, I must leave to those who read the Bible as allegory to make their own case" (xii-xiii). As these introductions illustrate, some of the Canongate essayists participate in the project only to puncture the Bible's authority.

Sacred Text as Literature: Perils and Potentials

The current interest in the Bible for its narrative and literary quality is not a new hermeneutical phenomenon. At the turn of the last century, Thomas Arnold, Richard Green Moulton, Ernest Sutherland Bates, and James George Frazer—among others—argued for the notion of the Bible as literature and began to treat biblical narratives as novels. It was no longer possible to believe in the biblical accounts as divine oracles or in the supernatural qualities that surrounded the life and work of Jesus. Instead, biblical accounts became narratives or literary treatises, and biblical personalities like Jesus and David became characters or heroes. Some of the earlier advocates of this view went on to produce their own edited versions of the Bible. Unlike the present project, where the biblical books are left as they are to make their own impression on the readers, literary or religious, earlier advocates were daring enough to produce their own edited versions, excising passages that did not make any literary sense. Contrary to the current enterprise, they were radical enough to reorganize biblical narratives and select passages which did not, in their view, mar the aesthetic qualities of the Bible. Bates maintained that not all parts of the Bible were literary marvels. In fact, he argued that, from a literary point of view, the Bible was replete with "irredundant repetitions" and cumbersome punctuations and was courageous enough to suggest an edition which required "not the whole Bible but a coherent arrangement of the greater part" (xvii).

Even the printing of Canongate Bibles militates against reading them as literature. Sir Arthur Quiller-Couch, who was keen to promote the Bible as literature, questioned the traditional mode of presentation, insofar as verse numbers and arbitrary chapter divisions flattened the various literary forms contained in the Bible. He suggested in the 1920s that the printed version should reflect and retain the original narrative style of biblical writers: "Will you still go on to imagine that all the poetry is printed as prose; while all the long paragraphs of prose are broken up into short verses, so that they resemble the little passages set out for parsing or analysis in an examination paper?" (72). The Canongate publishers were not that venturesome. One does not see a comparable subversiveness in Canongate's attempt to present text as literature. Although the introducers make it abundantly clear that the Bible was designed to be read as literature, the Canongate publishers indulge in little editorial interference in the presentation of texts and retain the traditional verse and chapter divisions.

Endorsing the Bible as literature and endowing it with literary qualities proves problematic. Among the introducers only the Dalai Lama tried to do otherwise, placing the Epistle of James within the Buddhist genre of *lojong* (literally "training the mind"). As a result of the overemphasis on the literary aspects of the text, coupled with the comfortable and affluent background of the essayists, the concerns of the poor and the disadvantaged go unnoticed; their plight does not occupy a central place in these introductions. These introducers are sympathetic to and respect the needs of the disadvantaged, but their solution seems to be a politics of the transcendental kind, which simultaneously respects the state of mind of the poor and acknowledges the goodness of the oppressors too. The Dalai Lama, who finds explicit advocacy of the poor in the Epistle of James, cautions the reader that James' severe criticism of the oppressors must be seen within the historical context of the Epistle and that one should not overlook "an important spiritual principle, which is never to forget the fundamental equality of all human beings. A true spiritual practitioner appreciates what I often describe as our 'basic spirituality.' By this I am referring to the fundamental qualities of goodness, which exists naturally in all of us irrespective of our gender, race, social and religious background" (xiv-xv). The poor are not offered uplift from their misery but are admired for their detached and dispossessed status, which enables them to hear the gospel. Their state of poverty is seen as a virtue to be emulated if one wants to hear the gospel. Wilson declares that "only those who live as though there is no tomorrow, and who do not store up treasure, can enter the kingdom" (xii).

The other outcome of the eulogization of the Bible as literature is its colonization as a Western book. The narrative features of the Bible are seen as belonging rightfully to the Western literary tradition. Peter Ackroyd observes:

> Certainly the narrative devices are clear, with affiliations to western poetry and fiction. There is, for example, satire approaching an almost Swiftian vision of disgust at the flesh, in the description of women of Zion "with stretched forth necks and wanton eyes, walking and mincing as they go, and making a tinkling with their feet" (3:16), or in the depiction of the priests of Ephraim so drunk that "all tables are full of vomit and filthiness" (28:8). (xi)

The Bible, essentially an "Eastern Book," according to Adolf Deissmann, migrated from its Mediterranean context, settled on English soil, and is now being claimed as belonging to Western civilization and its literary tradition. The Bible is now being freed from Hebraic and Hellenistic discourse practices and seen instead as the bearer and marker of English literary tradition. Prickett's observation is worth pursuing: "[a]stonishingly little critical attention has been paid to the way in which western Europe, with its cool temperate climate and abundant rainfall, was able to assimilate and successfully make use of the everyday imagery of a semi-nomadic Near-Eastern desert people as part of its own cultural and poetic heritage" (68-69).

One uneasy thought keeps cropping up. Is a literary approach really an important hermeneutical device, or has it become a counterpart of the heritage industry, an escapist activity which replaces an historical and praxilogical engagement with nostalgia? It may serve as a stimulus not for critical engagement but for luring the readers into dreaming for a long-lost imaginary and idyllic past.

Authorized Bible: The Version on Which the Sun Never Sets

The publisher's textual choice of the King James Version is an interesting and intriguing one. James I, by all accounts, was not particularly an attractive personality nor a progressive monarch, yet it was during his rule that the two most significant books in the English language emerged—the authorized version of the Holy Bible in 1611 and the first folio of the collected works of William Shakespeare in 1623. The former was initiated by royal authority; the latter had royal backing. The objective of Canongate was to present the Authorized King James Bible, not as a religious text, but as a work of literature with a profound and long-lasting impact on English literature and life. P. D. James, herself a contributor to and reviewer of the first series of the Pocket Canon, wrote: "No single book has had more influence on our national identity, our literature and the development of the English language than has the Authorised King James Version of the Bible" (1998:21).

The preeminent place of the Authorized Version as the supreme literary production needs demythicizing. The King James Bible is often portrayed as a definitive version, without rival since the date of publication. However, English translations of the Bible were undertaken at a time when English as a language had no literary status. It was only much later that the Authorized Version came to be praised for its literary quality. In seventeenth-century England it was the Geneva Bible that was seen as the people's Bible. It had the twofold advantage of an attractive printing and a convenient size for private use. David Norton, in charting the eventual triumph of the King James Version, points out that it was commercial considerations and political influences, not literary merits, that played a crucial role in its elevation. It is his contention that the ascendancy of the King James Version owed nothing to its scholarly or literary rendering of the original texts. Rather, the King's printer and Cambridge University Press, which had a monopoly on the Authorized Version, secured the suppression of the Geneva Bible in spite of its superior printing and rendition. More significantly, the anti-monarchical notes in the Geneva Bible did not find favor in the court of James I (1-2).

In their introduction to the Oxford World Classic Bible, Carroll and Prickett note that the "Authorised Version was not, as is sometimes argued, simply the product of the English language at a peculiarly rich stage of its evolution, but of a deliberate piece of social and linguistic engineering" (xxviii). Furthermore, they point out that "it was designed to control the language of salvation, and to occupy the linguistic high ground in such a way as to allow its rivals whether the puritan Geneva or the Catholic Rheims and Douai Bibles, less verbal space, less legitimacy, less power" (xxix). It was thus a political as well as a religious undertaking. As Peter Levi aptly puts it, "if ever successful establishment prose existed, this is it" (35).

For many in countries with a history of colonialism, the King James Version was not "the noblest monument of English prose," as claimed by John Livingstone Lowes (16), but an intruding text deeply implicated in the colonizing enterprise. Surveying the territorial spread of the British Empire from Hobart to Ottawa, Christopher Anderson, who wrote a two-volume history of the English Bible, claimed that the Authorized Version was "at present in the act of being pursued from the *rising to the setting sun*" and went on to claim that it was "the *only* version in existence on which *the sun never sets*" (italics original) (xi). The Authorized Version was first encountered in the colonies, particularly in India, as part of colonial education. It was part of the civilizing process aimed at the moral improvement of the natives.

Two uncomfortable questions keep emerging. At a time of what J. R. Watson calls a "seemingly endless series of piddling translations" (15), one wonders whether the Authorized Version has been offered as a work of literature and a Holy Writ that has magisterially held its own in the face of numerous upstart versions, such as the New English Bible, the Jerusalem Bible, the Revised Standard Version, the Good News Bible, the New International Bible, and the Revised English Bible. Is the use of the King James Version for the Canongate series a kind of nostalgia, throwing the clock back to a time when the English had one main version? The concluding paragraph of P. D. James' review of the first series of the Pocket Canon Bibles is indicative of such a wish:

> Is it too much to hope that the day may actually come when, even if the Church of England continues to neglect the Authorized Version in its worship, the King James Bible will at least be part of the reading syllabus of students of English Language and Literature? Or, in this timid, media-obsessed age of all faiths and none, would that be regarded as politically incorrect? (1998:21)

Reclamation of the Authorized Version could be seen as a ploy to placate the traditionalist. Or it could be a ruse to woo impressionable youth, who would not dream of buying a copy of the Psalms written in an unfamiliar prose were it not introduced by Bono, who professes an affinity with David as a fellow pop-star, whom he calls the "Elvis of the Bible."

The other uncomfortable question arises from the fact that Britain and most of the Western world are becoming more multicultural and that a new version of national belonging is emerging, due to immigration and unprecedented social and geographical mobility. Might the reintroduction of the King James Version encourage a pining for an imaginary single culture and an old homogeneous glory? The Authorized Version was seen as a common bond holding together a divergent group of people who were part of the British Empire. The popular report of the British and Foreign Bible Society, *In the Mother Tongue*, recorded that a large number of copies of the Authorized Version were being sent to the colonies to keep together the disparate nations of the British Commonwealth; it claimed that "devotion to the ideals of the Holy Scriptures is at once the sign and instrument of that unity" (42). Now that the Empire is gone, is the use of the Authorized Version the Canongate's way of recovering a singular sense of English identity?

Colonial Parallels

One notices certain parallels between Canongate's marketing of the Bible in the West at the end of the twentieth century and the journeys of the Bible into non-Western cultures with the missionaries a hundred years ago. Unlike the missionaries of the colonial period, who set out to bring culture and morality to a primitive proletariat, Canongate and its introducers appear to want to humanize a Western population seen as decadent, secular, individualistic, materialistic, and theologically illiterate. As a way of introducing the Bible, most missionaries painted the colonies as morally and spiritually degenerate and in need of salvation. Hence the

Bible was made to participate in the colonial project of "improving" the natives, in the process destabilizing peoples and cultures. The Authorized Version has become the quintessence of Englishness and the measurement of humanity. Now, however, in an ironic twist, the West is seen as needing salvation. These introductions emerge from a context that is naturally Western and variously described as a "secular age" (Morrison: xvi), a "post-Christian" age (Wilson: vii), "a time of religious transition" (Armstrong: vii), a world of investigative journalism and science (Wilson: vii). Karen Armstrong, in her introduction to Hebrews, writes: "In many of the countries of Western Europe, atheism is on the increase, and the churches are emptying, being converted into art galleries, restaurants, and warehouses" (vii). She could have added that they have also been turned into Hindu temples and Sikh Gurdwaras, as has been the case in England. In such a context, the Bible, the sacred text, is advocated primarily as a literary text, to be read like any other book.

The opposite was at work in colonial India. In the colonies, the Bible as literature became a pretext for the moral improvement of the natives and a source for biblicizing activities. Colonial educators envisaged a double project for the Bible: to act simultaneously as literature and as a religious text. Having pronounced that the literary or scientific or historical information contained in vernacular literature proved no match to Western learning and literature, and that the indigenous writings lacked the moral and mental power to equip the Indians (as in the famous/notorious 1835 Minute of Lord Macaulay: "single shelf of a good European library was worth the whole of native literature"), colonial administrators and educators decided that carefully selected English texts infused with biblical references could shape the minds of the Indians to appreciate and recognize the authority of British rule and, more specifically, lead them to read the Bible without any compulsion from missionaries. With this view in mind, English writings suffused with biblical and Christian references were introduced into the Indian university curriculum. Shakespeare, Locke, and Bacon were seen as texts that could supply and uphold Christian faith and inculcate morality and civility. Lengthy extracts from the Bible were also incorporated into textbooks prescribed for the Bachelor's degree course at Calcutta University. The literary techniques employed in the Bible—narrative, plots, events, and characters— were seen as more effective in attracting the attention of the students than preaching or doctrinal teachings. The Bible may be the word of God, but religious truth was conveyed through literary images and analogies. The power of the Bible was seen as lying in its powerful imagery. The objective was a personal awakening and conversion through an appeal to imagery. Gauri Viswanathan, who studied the inextricable link between English literature and the politics of the Empire, observes:

> The horrors of sin and damnation were not to be understood through reason but through images that give the reader a "shocking spectre of his own deformity and haunt him, even in his sleep"…To read the Bible well, to be moved by its imagery, to be instructed by its "dark and ambiguous style, figurative and hyperbolical manner," the imagination first had to be fully trained and equipped. (55)

The concern was not immediate conversion but rather realization of their degenerate spiritual state. However, colonial educators were very particular about not subjecting the Bible to "parsing or syntactical and other grammatical exercises of linguistic acquisition—practices that necessarily reduced the Bible from its deserved status as 'the Book of Books' to merely one among many books" (53). Whereas currently the Bible as literature is viewed skeptically with regard to its religious potency, in the colonies the secular use of the Bible in the university syllabus was seen as a source of religious belief and moral improvement.

In the marketing of the books, there are similarities as well. The chief instrument of evangelistic distribution during the height of the missionary activity was the single gospel or book of the Bible. The British and Foreign Bible Society used to publish and circulate scriptural portions; their annual reports often boasted about the amount of literature thus disseminated. The distribution figures for the so-called portions were very much greater than those for the full New Testament.[1] These portions were mainly gospels and were sold chiefly to non-Christians at a cheaper rate. In changed circumstances, single biblical books are now aimed at a generation whose attention span may not extend more than fifteen minutes, as television schedulers have discovered, and who may find the tome in its entirety too demanding to handle. The hermeneutical aim remains the same. Just as in the case of the colonized, the prospective Western reader is emotionally, aesthetically, intellectually, spiritually to be liberated (Morrison: xvi)

Secular Advertising and Religious Values

Quite ironically, at a time when the Christian churches are in decline and struggling to reconfigure their message, identity, and role in the West, it is the secular advertising agencies that have more effective-

---

[1] For instance, 1930 publication figures were as follows: Bible, 24,078; New Testament, 58,640; biblical portions, 5,306,027. (British and Foreign Bible Society, 1930: 50).

ly appropriated and given a wider exposure to the traditional religious images of the Christian Churches. Individuals with commercial and marketing savvy are quick to recognize the potency of such motifs. For example, Benetton, the clothes manufacturers, has for some time now successfully run controversial advertisements which have wittingly invoked religious ideas and themes to convey the firm's mission statement, "united colors of Benetton." The pictures in their commercials are noticeably simple: they explore subjects which are the common concern of all people—peace, reconciliation, life, and death. The message they convey is a moral one, attracting the attention of consumers and inviting them to reflect, and eventually to buy their products. Whereas Benetton uses no text, Canongate depends entirely on the written word for its marketing purposes.

Christian churches may frown upon the misappropriation of such images and texts. The very fact that secular commercial advertisers and publishers have been able to recoup and utilize these religious images and texts is a pointer to the effect that religion is still a powerful form of currency in a world which has almost wholly become secular and dominated by consumer values. Secular advertisers such as Benetton that rely on the visual have been willing to exploit religious images and utilize them to sell their products. Secular publishers such as Canongate have been able to exploit a reading public which is unlimited, heterogeneous, and whose reading tastes vary from the secular to the specialist to the spiritual.

Biblical books are presented in a new format as self-contained, separate booklets, clearly disengaged from other books of the Bible, thus dislodging the unitary status of the Bible. In their new form the biblical books are able to reach wider audiences, far removed from the circle of the initiated circle—the Christian faithful, the readers for whom it was originally intended. By giving them a different, portable, physical guise, the publishers have put the texts within the reach of new readers who do not read them in the same way as did the original readers. These are seen as handy books that one could take to read while lazing on a deck chair in the summer and that could act as a portable means of escape from problems of all sorts. As McKenzie has put it, "new readers of course make new texts, and their meanings are a function of their new forms" (20). The traditional prerequisites for reading the Bible—an unwavering faith, seeking for the most original text, the wholeness of the Scripture—have now given way to literary pleasure, contending with the translated text in an old prose and being satisfied with single books and separate volumes.

Personal Testimonies as Reading Practices

The most illuminating attitude towards the Bible is to be found not in direct exegesis but in coupling the narratives with people's lives. Most of the biblical commentaries under the influence of biblical criticism have made the Bible nothing more than a subject for linguistic, historical, and theological analysis, quite divorced from issues related to life. In contrast, these introducers have appropriated the Bible for what it is—a story, or stories, resonating and in some cases not resonating with their own. In a climate obsessed with theories, it is tempting to slot these subjective reflections into the newly emerging and theoretically underdeveloped category of autobiographical or personal-voice criticism (Staley, 1995a, 1995b; Kitzberger). This reading practice is an undertaking in which interpreters write self-consciously out of their social and cultural location. There is a kind of a confessional and liberal feel about these readings— "I felt it, therefore it was true." Personal-voice criticism may give the impression that it is an interpretation without texts, and its interpretative ventures may not have any bearing on the biblical books. The whole enterprise may sound like the end of the Bible and critical biblical scholarship. However, what such criticism further reinforces is how complex is our appropriation of the Bible.

The Canongate project is reflective of both modern and postmodern tendencies. The introductions are symptomatic of the modernist thinking which has polarized and housed simultaneously two conflicting but correlative Protestant attitudes to the Bible. One is the pietistic and subjective instinct which turns inward and wallows in the text, unconcerned with the affairs of the world, and which encourages personal reading and a personal response to the Bible. The other is a rationalistic and objective instinct which wants to seize the text and subject it to severe historical and critical scrutiny. Both instincts have a common assumption: real meaning lurks within the texts and the text is the bearer of meanings. The project is postmodern in its underscoring of the fractured, fragmented, and disjointed nature of our reality. The Bible, a collection of books which came to be seen as "a book" with a sense of unity, is now reduced to a miscellany of books. The very printing mechanism which brought order, compactness, and integrity to the Bible has, with an ironic twist, fractured the Bible's manufactured coherence.

The reading of the individual essayist reinforces the idea of closeted reading as opposed to communitarian form of reading. The principal location of this reading continues to be the urban and private domain. Thus, reading has come to be seen as a solitary and private occupation rather than a social activity. It offers a moment in which one can be free from the pressures of everyday life and yet be in receipt of wisdom, consolation, and, in some cases, discomfort. The reader remains the master or mistress, free to interact with and manage the text without being overpowered by it. Such private readings risk encouraging readers to internalize their spiritual and political vision and withdraw into the realm of imagination.

What we are witnessing is not only the emergence of a plurality of reading practices but also the recognition that no one mode of reading is privileged. The once supreme reign of historical criticism which made "disinterested," "objective," "scientific" and "apolitical" reading the main virtues for engaging with the text is now being severely challenged by context-based and ideologically-committed readings of various subaltern groups—women, indigenous people, dalits, burakumin. We need to treat these different approaches—the established and the emerging voices—not as competing practices, branding some as superior and virtuous and others as exotic and marginal. Rather, we need to recognize that in different ways the practitioners of these reading modes are active participants in a shared textual and critical tradition and that in their usage of methods and application of theories they are interrelated. The art of reading, then, is to see connection between these reading practices. In this way one can overcome the dangers of prooftexting, obtuse academic reductionism, and ideologically closed reading. The explosion of methods for investigation of the Bible has made it imperative that biblical study be a cooperative enterprise between professionally trained scholars and those who read the Bible as dictated by experience and culture. What these introductions indicate is the need for what Edward Said advocated in an another kindred discipline, literary studies—secular criticism. For Said such criticism frees criticism from the "priestly caste of acolytes and dogmatic metaphysicians" (5) and academic specialization. Furthermore, it alerts critics to see their connection with the social and political realities in which they operate and practice their discipline. These introductions acknowledge the Bible's emotional and spiritual place in the individual's life. What is needed is a connection between academic criticism, private feeling, and critical politics, so that hermeneutics can engage in radical work, thereby overcoming the distance and working for a collective desire for change.

Two examples from the introductions make it clear how vital this hermeneutical exchange is. For instance, the Israeli novelist and commentator, David Grossman, sees the Exodus, and rightly so, as a redemptive autobiographical story of the Jews. He refers to it as a "grand story of the childhood of the Jewish people, sketches the primordial face of that people as it is being formed, and, as we now know, describes what will be its fate throughout the thousands of years of history" (xvi). While generations of Jews have derived both legitimation and identity from the retelling of the Exodus, indigenous people whose lands have been plundered—such as Palestinians, Native Americans, Aborigines, and Tribals—find the Exodus paradigm troublesome and are less likely to be optimistic about its hermeneutical purchase.

The other case in point is the claim of A. N. Wilson, novelist and biographer. In his opening paragraph he makes the following claim for Matthew's gospel: "You are holding in your hands a tiny book which has changed more human lives than *The Communist Manifesto* or Freud's *Interpretation of Dreams*: a book which has shaped whole civilizations: a book which, for many people, has been not a gospel but The Gospel" (vii). True, a host of people including Gandhi were enthused by Matthew's Sermon on the Mount, but the Gospel also contains a crucial verse, Matt 28:19, the reactivation of which provided scriptural sanction for and legitimization of colonial enterprises resulting in the despoiling of other peoples' cultures (Sugirtharajah: 95-100). What is increasingly clear is how important it is not to finalize meaning and restrict its interpretation to one context. It may be profitable to think of narratives as exiles, always on the move, to be appropriated in manifold forms. What this act of exchange does is to enable people not to domesticate the text and overpower it but to recognize that they have the ability to transfer it from context to context, thus shattering any attempt to finalize their meaning. Texts throw up new meanings as they meet up with new readers and contexts, and that is a good enough reason to consult all players concerned in the task of interpretation.

Reading practices are ultimately an ongoing struggle for control over texts and the monitoring of meanings. Biblical reading has been largely controlled by the producers of texts, and latterly by various Christian Church authorities or professional interpreters whose readings are not only compromised by their denominational and institutional agendas but also by their authority to regulate the production and distribution of meanings. These Canongate essayists are like poachers who move across a hermeneutical territory belonging to someone else, abduct the texts and meanings, and then deliver them to ordinary readers.

New reading practices are not necessarily created anew, but they do always exploit those practices already existing. Reading practices do not stand alone but are built up upon previous attempts. In the end, reading has to do with the choosing of an appropriate paradigm, either within the Bible itself or outside its framework. The important thing for those who choose to work within the biblical vision is to expose the reader to a range of textual paradigms embedded within the biblical texts. Biblical writers themselves adopted this method. For example, in the time of Paul, when it was a question of Maccabean-style armed struggle against Rome or subversive submission à la Jeremiah, Paul chose the latter. The history of interpretation is littered with such hermeneutical recycling.

Biblical hermeneutics alone cannot provide answers for life's pressing questions or effect changes that people look for. Nonetheless, people turn to sacred texts not so much for the answers to hypothetical questions as for the narratives themselves, which recreate a sense of living in a different time and place and which remind them about the tremendous diversity of human beliefs and experiences. Perhaps it is through these narratives that they try to reconfigure who they are and where they are going. There is a danger, however, that the Bible as literature may end up as an idol which Piers Paul Read rightfully identifies as the God that failed (xiv). Holloway himself provides a timely and apt warning. To paraphrase him: Often we treat words about God as though they were equivalent to God; this can trap us in the language *about* mysteries rather than opening us to the mysteries themselves (vii).

Finally, in reading these introductions it is difficult to say whether one has come closer to a better grasp of the biblical truth, whether one has come to learn a great deal about the Bible, or even whether one has been introduced to a new mode of reading practice. What we hear loudly and clearly is the authors and their often complicated lives and their well-worn concerns. This does not make these introducers as inherently appealing as the texts themselves, nor does it relieve us of our obligation to read and to continue to draw pleasure out of texts. Those who are in the business of interpretation have long realized that the act of interpretation often reveals more about the interpreter than the texts which he or she tries to unravel. The "philosopher" Madonna was spot on, and articulated for many, when she responded to the question, "What do people see when they look at you?" She replied simply, "They see themselves."[2]

Works Consulted

Ackroyd, Peter
    1999   *The Book of Isaiah with an Introduction.* Edinburgh: Canongate Books.

---

[2] See *Life: The Observer Magazine,* September 26, 1999:5.

Anderson, Christopher
　1845　*The Annals of the English Bible. Volume I.* London: William Pickering.
Armstrong, Karen
　1999　*The Epistle of Paul the Apostle to the Hebrews with an Introduction.* Edinburgh: Canongate Books.
Bates, Ernest Sutherland
　1937　*The Bible Designed to Be Read as Literature.* London: William Heinemann.
Bono
　1999　*The Book of Psalms with an Introduction.* Edinburgh: Canongate Books.
British and Foreign Bible Society, The
　1930　*In the Mother Tongue.* London: The British and Foreign Bible Society.
　1933　*Tell the World.* London: The British and Foreign Bible Society.
Byatt, A. S.
　1998　*The Song of Solomon with an Introduction.* Edinburgh: Canongate Books.
Byng, J.
　1998　"God, give me Strength." *The Observer* 4 October:30.
Carroll, Robert and Stephen Prickett
　1998　"Introduction." Pp. xi-xlvi in *The Bible: Authorized King James Version.* Ed. R. Carroll and S. Prickett. Oxford: Oxford University Press.
Cave, Nick
　1998　*The Gospel According to Mark with an Introduction.* Edinburgh: Canongate Books.
Dalai Lama
　2000　*The Epistle of James with an Introduction.* Edinburgh: Canongate Books.
De Bernières, Louis
　1998　*The Book of Job with an Introduction.* Edinburgh: Canongate Books.
Dickens, A. G.
　1964　*The English Reformation.* Glasgow: Fontana Paperbacks.
Gandhi, M. K.
　1977　*India of My Dreams.* Compiled by R. K. Prabhu. Ahmedabad: Navjivan Publishing House.
Gray, Alasdair
　1999　*Jonah, Micah and Nahum with an Introduction.* Edinburgh: Canongate Books.
Grossman, David
　1998　*The Second Book of Moses Called Exodus with an Introduction.* Edinburgh: Canongate Books.

Holloway, Richard
  1998   *The Gospel According to Luke with an Introduction*. Edinburgh: Canongate Books.
James, P. D.
  1998   "Canons of Authorship." *The Times Literary Supplement* (December 25):21.
  1999   *The Acts of the Apostles with an Introduction*. Edinburgh: Canongate Books.
Johnson, Charles
  1998   *Proverbs with an Introduction*. Edinburgh: Canongate Books.
Kitzberger, Ingrid Rosa, ed.
  1999   *The Personal Voice in Biblical Interpretation*. London: Routledge.
Lessing, Doris
  1998   *Ecclesiastes or, the Preacher with an Introduction*. Edinburgh: Canongate Books.
Levi, Peter
  1974   *The English Bible 1534 to 1859*. Grands Rapids, MI: Eerdmans.
Lowes. John Livingstone
  1938   "The Noblest Monument of English Prose." Pp. 16-42 in *English Bible: Essays by Various Writers*. Ed. Vernon F. Storr. London: Methuen.
McKenzie, D. F.
  1986   *Bibliography and the Sociology of Texts: The Panizzi Lectures 1985*. London: The British Library.
Millar, S.
  1999   "Bono Sings the Bible Blues." *The Guardian* (October 30):7.
Morrison, Blake
  1998   *The Gospel According to John with an Introduction*. Edinburgh: Canongate Books.
Norton, David
  1993   *A History of the Bible as Literature Volume II: From 1700 to the Present Day*. Cambridge: Cambridge University Press.
Prickett, S.
  1996   *Origins of Narrative: The Romantic Appropriation of the Bible*. Cambridge: Cambridge University Press.
Quiller-Couch, Arthur
  1944   *Cambridge Lectures*. London: J. M. Dent and Sons.
Read, Piers Paul
  1999   *The Wisdom of Solomon with an Introduction*. Edinburgh: Canongate Books.
Rendell, Ruth
  1999   *The Epistle of Paul the Apostle to the Romans with an Introduction*. Edinburgh: Canongate Books.

Rose, Steven
    1998   *The First Book of Moses Called Genesis with an Introduction.*
            Edinburgh: Canongate Books.
Said, Edward W.
    1991   *The World, The Text, and the Critic.* London: Vintage.
Self, Will
    1998   *Revelation with an Introduction.* Edinburgh: Canongate Books.
Staley, Jeffrey L.
    1995a   *Reading with a Passion: Rhetoric, Autobiography and the
            American West in the Gospel of John.* New York: Continuum.
    1995b   "Taking it Personally." *Semeia* 75. Atlanta: Scholars Press.
Sugirtharajah, R. S.
    1998   "A Postcolonial Exploration of Collusion and Construction in
            Biblical Interpretation." Pp. 91-116 in *The Postcolonial Bible.* Ed.
            R. S. Sugirtharajah. Sheffield: Sheffield Academic Press.
Trollope, Joanna
    1999   *Ruth and Esther with an Introduction.* Edinburgh: Canongate
            Books.
Viswanathan, Gauri
    1989   *Masks of Conquest: Literary Study and British Rule in India.* New
            York: Columbia University Press.
Watson, J. R.
    1993   "The Bible in English Literature: Review Article." *The Expository
            Times* 105 (October):15-16.
Weldon, Fay
    1998   *The Epistles of Paul the Apostle to the Corinthians with an
            Introduction.* Edinburgh: Canongate Books.
Wilson, A. N.
    1998   *The Gospel According to Matthew with an Introduction.* Edinburgh:
            Canongate Books.

6

"Hidden in Plain View"
Postcolonial Interrogations, a Poetics of Location, and African-American Biblical Scholarship

Abraham Smith

Every society is really governed by hidden laws, by unspoken but profound assumptions on the part of the people, and ours is no exception.
It is up to the American writer to find out what these laws and assumptions are. In a society much given to smashing taboos without thereby
managing to be liberated from them, it will be no easy matter.

—James Baldwin

This essay examines the contributions which postcolonial studies
could make to African-American biblical hermeneutics through an exposure of the "hidden texts" of traditional biblical studies and the development of a new paradigm for Bible study. An initial section depicts the
largely text-based character of traditional African-American biblical
scholarship and the ways in which a number of scholars are now deconstructing notions of text and textuality, especially through postcolonial
studies. Next, through the use of the optic of postcolonial studies, a discussion follows on three "hidden texts" which constrain the larger field of
biblical studies and the more specific focus of African-American biblical
scholarship. Finally, using the parable of the Prodigal Son as a test case,
the essay proffers a new paradigm of reading for biblical studies as
informed by postcolonial studies and the "poetics of location" of Mary
Ann Tolbert.

Interrogating Textuality: "Is There a Text in This Class?"

In recent works surveying the writings of African-American biblical scholars, Randall C. Bailey notes four types of scholarship pursued by
African-American biblical scholars: (1) the identification and function(s)
of the African presence in the Bible; (2) the exposure of racist and white

supremacist traditions of interpretation; (3) the reception of the Bible by African Americans, both historically and currently; and (4) the ideological critique of biblical texts that support class, race, and gender biases (1998:66-90; 2000:696-711). The sheer volume of material produced in the second, third, and fourth categories suggests a possible shift in biblical interpretation beyond both the text-based identification of the African presence in the Bible and the text-based singular determination of the function(s) of that presence (Wimbush).

In alignment with this shift away from strictly text-based studies, African-American biblical scholars have exploded the notion of textuality by exposing the hidden canons of authority at work in biblical hermeneutics. Thomas Hoyt, Jr., for example, connects the authority of scripture to the authority of black culture, that is, the authority of a fairly common story of black experience in the United States. This common story includes the following elements: suffering, exodus, creation, eschatology, and larger mythic constructions of what God has done and will do in the world for black people and others. Likewise, William H. Myers challenges African-American scholars to examine near-canonical sources (e.g., call narratives, conversion tales, spirituals) in their history and thereby develop a systematic and holistic accounting of African-American biblical hermeneutics. Moreover, in a recent volume of *Semeia* edited by Vincent L. Wimbush, several budding scholars, of whom some are African American, draw on James C. Scott's *Domination and the Arts of Resistance* to push past the traditional notions of textuality (Jones; Aymer). These scholars explore some of the "arts" of resistance, as they proceed to deconstruct the boundaries of traditional notions of textuality and examine other unwritten "texts" or hidden transcripts that govern thought and behavior.

In many respects this shift also positions African-American biblical scholarship toward an alignment with postcolonial criticism, a broad-based mode of analysis that critiques texts, interpreters, and the various traditions shaping texts and interpreters with the purpose of identifying and eliminating oppressive forces. From such an alignment, African-American scholarship would critique not only historical colonialism ("the political, economic, and social domination of people of less developed countries by those from more developed countries") but also discursive colonialism ("the psychological domination of people through appeals to authority, based on the asserted superiority of one race, gender, class, or culture over another") (O'Brien Wicker: 377). From such an alignment, moreover, African-American biblical scholarship would also advance a postcolonial critique or exercise in "decolonization" ("the process of

identifying assumptions and assertions of historical and discursive colonization in order to reevaluate or to reject them" [O'Brien Wicker: 377])
that would not be confined to examinations of colonialism in the modern
period. In other words, such a critique would also examine ancient cultures for acts of domination and the various rituals of domination accom-
panying such acts.

Interrogating Hidden Texts and Agendas

Broadening the meaning of "text" leads to the realization that there
may be "hidden texts" or traditions shaping the approaches with which
African Americans read the Bible. Postcolonial studies has raised questions about three such types of hidden texts.

First, there is the shadow of empire that rests over so much of biblical studies—its focus and its agenda. One such element involves the
Christianizing of those ancient religions deemed important enough to
note, *when noted at all*. The failure to acknowledge such "other religions," conveniently designated as "pagan," exposes the power of a discipline that is still Christian-centered, still dealing with the residuals if not
the real force of the missionary enterprise of modern Christianity. Put
another way, since many biblical scholars have failed to place biblical
studies within the larger contexts of modern-day imperialistic ventures,
the role of the shadow of empire on biblical criticism itself has gone
largely unnoticed. Thus, although the "biblical" texts—despite their own
bias toward the religion of Israel or Second Temple forms of Judaism and
the religion of early Christianity—actually give evidence of a variety of
religious traditions (Segovia: 58-60), few biblical scholars have found
archival research in such religious traditions appealing (Donaldson: 5).
Favoritism toward the aforementioned religious traditions reveals, in fact,
the extent to which much of the work of biblical scholars is Christian in
character, Protestant at that, and thus laden in many ways with a form of
neocolonialism.

Second, there is the neocolonialism present within the Bible itself.
While biblical texts have often been used as resources against colonialism,
as tacit overtures or explicit claims against historical and discursive forms
of colonization, many of these texts actually support the forces of oppression and repression. They run the gamut, to name but a few examples,
from the legitimization of the annihilation of whole nations (Liburd: 79),
to the depiction of "femaleness" with negative characteristics (A. Smith,
1997:121-124), to the subordination or silencing of women (Martin).
While the canonization of these texts renders them sacred to certain communities, one must not deny the oppressive or repressive nature of the

texts. So entrenched are these texts within the forces of patriarchy, more-over, that Cornel West has rightfully argued, "without the addition of mod-ern interpretations of racial and gender equality, tolerance, and democra-cy, much of the [biblical] tradition warrants rejection" (233).

Third, there is the false dichotomy posited between traditional Anglo-European biblical scholarship and more recent biblical scholar-ship, known for its explicit ideological agenda and its political interven-tionist agenda. In point of fact, traditional scholarship is no less ideolog-ical, but its ideology is often left unexposed, with no account taken of the history of Anglo-European biblical studies. Indeed, both fundamentalism and traditional Anglo-European biblical scholarship constitute responses to Anglo-European modernity ("the Anglo-European enlightenment . . . the dominance of science . . . and the increasing secularization of culture across the globe" [Tolbert, 1995b:339]). On the one hand, fundamental-ism responded with "autocratic assertions of authority from unquestion-ing acceptance to 'infallibility'" (340). On the other hand, Anglo-European biblical studies responded by taking on the "mantle of adjudi-cating biblical interpretation and religious practice earlier ages left solely in the hands of church authorities" (340).

It is also true that Anglo-European biblical scholarship has not been completely devoid of a desire to intervene in society, although the most prevalent form of this scholarship has touted itself as disinterested. As Elisabeth Schüssler Fiorenza has shown, several prominent scholars, from James Montgomery (1919) to Henry Cadbury (1937) and Leroy Waterman (1947), used their SBL presidential addresses to push biblical scholars beyond a monastic mode of responsibility and toward a rigorous use of biblical scholarship in the service of a larger public than the acad-emy or even the church (12).

Given the ideological roots of Anglo-European biblical scholarship and its sporadic interventionist agendas, any belittling of the more recent approaches in terms of their "interests" and "agendas" proves disingenu-ous at best and historically naive at worst. Indeed, if biblical scholarship of any stripe is to offer a new paradigm, honesty demands not the whole-sale dismissal of approaches that move beyond the "usual suspects" of biblical criticism but rather more self-reflective strategies that seek to reveal the role of texts in the production of subject formation. To some extent, of course, these strategies will appear unsettling and, for some, impertinent, insofar as their goal is to raise a different set of questions and not simply to continue quarrying the "textual mines." In truth, however, such strategies could not be more relevant, since they wrestle with the fundamental concerns of people—questions about identity, how identity is shaped, the role of institutions in the shaping of identity, and the exposure and elimination of those forces perceived to be detrimental to the wholesomeness of any particular community's formation.

Interrogating Webs of Subject Formation

The work of Mary Ann Tolbert on a "poetics of location" provides a helpful approach for postcolonial interrogation (Tolbert, 1995a). For Tolbert, a poetics of location is a stance toward "reading" that incorporates the analysis of power dynamics in a variety of ways and not just at the level of the text itself. Thus, a poetics of location is an analysis of "each site of writing, reading, or theorizing by carefully investigating the specific historical, cultural, political, and social matrix that grounds it" (314). More specifically, a poetics of location would include: (1) explorations of the perspectives shaping the reader; (2) established academic reconstructions of the text; and (3) an examination of the text's historical production (332). Furthermore, a poetics of location would presuppose interpretation to be a matter of rhetoric as opposed to hermeneutics (the search for an "objective" reading [333]).

Using Tolbert's grid, I should like to examine the parable of the Prodigal Son as a test case for postcolonial analysis. A word of introduction is in order. In the first part of the analysis, the exploration of perspectives shaping the readers, I shall look at several African-American readers from the period of the Harlem Renaissance. While the writer of this essay is African-American and an examination of my own social location could prove insightful, I choose to examine instead the social locations of particular African-American readers from the Harlem Renaissance for two reasons. First, it is easier to see the influence of traditions on past readers whose historical periods have received sufficient analysis and exploration. Second, even in the formation of African-American subjectivity today, the Harlem Renaissance continues to have a critical impact.

Explorations of Perspectives Shaping the Readers

The parable of the Prodigal Son may very well be the most popular of all the parables attributed to Jesus. It has left a mark on painters such as Albrecht Dürer and Rembrandt van Rijn, dramatists such as William Shakespeare and Eugene O'Neill, preachers such as C. H. Spurgeon and Alexander McClaren, and novelists such as Stephen Crane and John Steinbeck (Fitzmyer: 1083). It has "served as artistic autobiography and erotic genre; as commentary on family relationships and the preservation of property; and as inspiration for narratives of pathos, of the prodigal daughter, and of redeemed or self-exiled sons" (D'Oench: 3).

Within Afro-America, this parable has also been a favorite: from its typological use in the eighteenth-century spiritual autobiography of John Marrant (Costanzo: 101) to Frances Harper's nineteenth-century pensive poem "The Prodigal Returns" (Boyd: 88), and from the autobiographical blues song "The Prodigal Son," penned by former blues artist Robert Wilkins (Davis, 1995:114; see Spencer: 107-131) but later recorded by the Rolling Stones (D'Oench: 26), to the stirring "Prodigal Son" sermon preached by the Reverend C. L. Franklin, father of rhythm and blues singer, Aretha Franklin.

In the early twentieth century, three well-known African-Americans used the parable in their respective crafts in the period known as the Harlem Renaissance: James Weldon Johnson, in poetry; Aaron Douglas, in visual art; and Langston Hughes, in his first novel. Accordingly, an exploration of their use of this parable could reveal how the parable played a role in shaping African American subjectivity in the early twentieth century. To discuss their appropriations of the parable, however, I shall begin by highlighting some of the tendencies at work in the appropriation of the parable in the period before the Harlem Renaissance. In so doing, we will be able to see some of the possible ways in which these three artists could have used the parable in their distinctive genres. Then, I shall examine more fully their actual use of the parable to respond to the socio-historical conditions of Afro-America in the 1920s.

Tendencies of Appropriations before the Harlem Renaissance

As the subject of exegesis and commentary, or as a narrative template for conversion tales and autobiographies, prints and paintings, morality plays and novels, or as the basis for sermons and musical compositions, this parable has not ceased to pull the heartstrings of its readers over several centuries. Within this long tradition of reception, two tendencies have been evident, and an articulation of these could inform our understanding of the possibilities of reception available to Johnson, Douglas, and Hughes at the turn of the twentieth century.

First, writers and painters often amplified the narrator's terse description of the prodigal's perils: "He wasted his substance on riotous living" (Luke 15:13). That is, some writers and painters accepted and extended the elder son's rendition of the prodigal's perils as "sexual" dissipation (D'Oench: 8). Whether the motivation for the elder son's commentary was just a simple dissatisfaction with the narrator's sparsely detailed accounting of the frivolities of the "far country" or perhaps a desire to heighten the significance of the prodigal's redemption, many writers and painters placed enormous importance on sexual debauchery as the basis for the prodigal's far country failure. In some paintings, moreover, the sexual debauchery theme was enhanced through portrayals of the son as dancing with prostitutes or depictions of musical instruments associated with sexual freedom and license (D'Oench:8). Again, perhaps not satisfied with the terse description of "riotous living," many writers and painters also featured gambling paraphernalia (cards or dice) or drunkenness as possible causes of the prodigal's dissipation (D'Oench:8).

Second, writers and painters (especially in the Christian tradition) have exploited a radical contrast between the younger and elder brothers. The contrast, at times, has supported a crude dichotomy between types of Christianity, with the younger brother representing Protestantism and an emphasis on grace, on the one hand, and the elder brother representing Roman Catholicism and an emphasis on a system of merits, on the other (D'Oench:3; Baldwin, 1985:122). At times, and with more lethal potential, the contrast has supported an unsophisticated and simplistic distinction between Christianity and Judaism, as if the parable had been used (by Jesus or Luke) to contrast the Jews, represented by the elder brother, and the Christians, represented by the younger brother. Indeed, this kind of contrast appears as early as Jerome and continues in such figures as Augustine, Calvin, and Luther (Snyder:365).

As we shall see, both tendencies are problematic; for now, however, our discussion has helped us to see some of the specific ways in which this favorite parable had been used. To see whether or how these tendencies were used by Johnson, Hughes, and Douglas, however, one must first examine some of the socio-historical conditions of African Americans at the turn of the twentieth century, particularly the problem of negative and controlling images—images to which Johnson, Douglas, and Hughes all sought to provide a response.

Harlem Renaissance Appropriations of the Parable of the Prodigal Son
Although the Harlem Renaissance is often touted as a phenomenon that occurred strictly in Harlem, the designation actually represents an early twentieth-century movement of cultural affirmation throughout the major cities of the North. Accordingly, the Harlem Renaissance (aka the New Negro movement) period emerged in the 1920s and early 1930s, as African Americans in urban centers turned to their ancestral roots and celebrated the wide variety of their artistic expressions. On the one hand, the Harlem Renaissance could not have emerged without the migration of blacks into urban areas. Crop failures in the South between 1910 and 1920, beatings and lynchings at the hands of white Southerners, and the promise of jobs to service the war industries created ripe conditions for

blacks, as many as eight million by some estimates, to move to the cities of the North. On the other hand, specific organizations and events also helped to create the Harlem Renaissance. Marcus Garvey's Universal Negro Improvement Association (UNIA) laid a foundation by his stirring of race consciousness and pride in the African heritage of blacks among the masses. The National Association for the Advancement of Colored People (NAACP) and the National Urban League also played pivotal roles, with their journals (*Crisis* and *Opportunity*, respectively) providing a venue for literary and visual artists to publish their poems and art work. Most critical, moreover, was a dinner organized in 1924 by Charles S. Johnson, editor of *Opportunity*, which launched the publication of a special issue of *Survey Graphic*, dedicated to acknowledging "the progressive spirit of contemporary Negro life" (Watson: 28).

The acknowledgment of this progressive spirit was necessary, because most of the images of blacks published in the post-Reconstruction period were negative and went unchallenged. These images of blacks as thoroughly inferior, wholly exotic or even rapacious, served to support political disfranchisement, to legitimate anti-black economic riots, and to demoralize the spirit of African Americans. Thus, the Harlem Renaissance arose—flowering as it did in music as well as in the visual and literary arts—to invigorate or reinforce race pride, to present a vast array of black life, and to recreate, to the extent possible, "a distinct African-American culture" (Kirschke: 32).

Within this period, then, how did these three visual and literary artists appropriate the Prodigal Son parable? Moreover, how did they contribute to the shaping of black culture and subjectivity?

A. James Weldon Johnson

"Prodigal Son" (21-25) is one of several free-verse sermonic poems composed by James Weldon Johnson, collected in his *God's Trombones* (1927), and created over several years to capture the spirit of earlier sermons Johnson had heard from southern black preachers. While the biblical stories behind the sermon poems do not reflect the Christian Bible's canonical order, according to Johnson, the collection was inspired by "an old folk-sermon that . . . [began] . . . with the creation of the world and ... [ended] . . . with Judgment Day" (6). Thus, after an opening prayer ("Listen, Lord—A Prayer"), the collection includes the following poems: "Creation," "Prodigal Son," "Go Down Death: A Funeral Sermon," "Noah Built the Art," "Crucifixion," "Let My People Go" and "Judgment Day."

All of the poems were composed while Johnson "fought for the passage of the Dyer Anti-Lynching Bill and documented cases of countless victims who suffered the effects of racial violence" (Fleming: 103). One should expect, then, poems that speak to the suffering of black people, especially those in the urban areas who searched for better jobs only to find crowded conditions, anti-black race riots, and destitution. Such is indeed the case. "Creation" redefines "mammy" as someone who takes care of "her baby" (20), in contrast to the stereotypical construction of the mammy as "an asexual woman, a surrogate mother in blackface devoted to the development of a white family" (Hill Collins: 72). "Go Down Death: A Funeral Sermon" offers consolation (Fleming: 57), not only for those bereft of family but also for the weary-worn and tired who—unlike Sister Caroline, the deceased woman in the poem—*yet* must carry "the burden and heat of the day" (28). "Crucifixion," by virtue of its mention of the African Simon of Cyrene and its intimations of the black spiritual "Were You There?" (43), would likely remind Johnson's black audience of the innocence of their suffering. "Let My People Go" draws on the Exodus motif, long exploited by African Americans as a source of inspiration during and beyond slavery. "The Judgment" bespeaks, with its apocalyptic tenor, "a desire for retribution" that is both a part of biblical religion and a longstanding tradition in black musings on the issue of justice (Smith, 1994:223).

In the case of "Prodigal Son," Johnson paints a vivid portrait of the younger son's life in the far country, his ultimate devastation, and his return to the welcoming arms of his father. Because Johnson depicts the far country as "a city," the poem draws on images of "the city" with which Johnson's readers would have been familiar: crowdedness; the pleasures of night-life; and destitution.

First, Johnson's depiction of the city as crowded ("The streets are all crowded with people" [23]) allows him to play on the word "crowd," with the younger son becoming a part of two crowds: the one spends its money and time in lewd affairs; the other becomes the lot of those who spend money and time recklessly, the crowd of "the beggars and lepers" (24). Second, Johnson also plays on the metaphorical association between "night-time" (22-23) and uninhibited debauchery. Thus, he places the younger son's arrival in the city at night—a time when the streets are crowded, so-called friends are instantly found, and venues of vices abound. While the younger son spends his days and nights, respectively, in drinking and gambling dens, the turning point for his devastation also takes place at night ("in the evening, in the black and dark of night . . . they left him broke and ragged in the streets of Babylon [Johnson's appellation for the city]" [24]). Third, Johnson could not have drawn the destitution of the prodigal in starker terms. The young man is stripped of money and clothes, "left . . . broken and ragged" (24). His entrance into the crowd of beggars and lepers is not by choice; rather, it is the consequence of his choices. He takes on animal instincts: not only did he feed the swine, he also "got down on his belly in the mire and the mud and ate the husks with the hogs" (24). Furthermore, even the hogs do not consider themselves "too low to turn up a nose" at him (24).

It is likely, therefore, that Johnson used the "Prodigal Son" to convey the perils of the city to those who migrated from the South. This theme is found pervasively in black arts and letters—from the philosophical musings of Harlem Renaissance leader Alain Locke (47-56), to the gutsy "Far Away Blues" song of Bessie Smith and Clara Smith (Davis, 1998:84), to the semi-autobiographical novels of Langston Hughes. It is also a theme to which Johnson had turned in his *Autobiography of an Ex-Coloured Man* (1912) and one to which he would return in his *Black Manhattan* (1930).

If Johnson used the Prodigal Son parable to depict the problems of urban life for black people, his embellishment of the parable aligns him with the long history of the parable's reception. While Johnson does not use the parable to make a distinction between either Christianity and Judaism or Protestantism and Catholicism, he is not satisfied with the Lukan narrator's terse description, "he wasted his substance in riotous living." Accordingly, Johnson also provides a commentary to describe the son's "riotous living" and thus appears to have accepted the perspective of the elder brother, that is, that the younger son's devastation came at the hands of prostitutes.

How so? Johnson's intimations about the younger son's drinking and gambling (details found in the history of the parable's reception but not mentioned by the Lukan narrator) seem minuscule compared to the space he gives to the description of the women of "Babylon." Several of the senses are brought into play as Johnson describes the women: the younger son can see the women "dressed in yellow and purple and scarlet" (24); he can taste their lips, which are "like a honeycomb dripping with honey" (24); their smell is almost narcotic, "the jasmine smell of the Babylon women got in his nostrils and went to his head" (24). While the seductiveness with which Johnson describes the women does not automatically render them as prostitutes, he does describe them as "the sweet-sinning women" (25) and makes intertextual associations about prostitution with the Apocalypse of John in which "Babylon," "great whore" (19:2), and "the mother of whores" (17:5) are gendered designations for Rome. Johnson also describes Babylon as the "great city" (23), an appellation repeatedly used by the seer (17:18; 18:10,16,18). Johnson's vivid portrayal of the women as "dressed in . . . purple and scarlet" (24), moreover, appears to mimic the seer's description of Babylon: "The woman was clothed in purple and scarlet" (17:4; cf. 18:12,16).

Thus, although Johnson likely brought succor to black people through all of his poems, especially the "Prodigal Son," with its warnings about urban life for black people in the early twentieth century, his portrait of the far country as a city proffers a negative view of women as seductive and destructive (Smith, 2000).

B. Aaron Douglas

The illustrator for the "Prodigal Son" poem, as for all the other poems in Johnson's collection, was Aaron Douglas, a trained artist with a B.A. degree from the University of Kansas (1922) and a M.F.A. degree from the University of Nebraska (1923), and the premier illustrator for the Harlem Renaissance. To appreciate the contribution of his illustration of the "Prodigal Son" to the formation of black subjectivity, it is necessary to understand the style and function of his illustrations in general as well as the possible critique offered by his particular illustration of the "Prodigal Son" to Johnson's poem.

In *God's Trombones* Douglas combines modernism with African sculpture. Thus, each illustration exploits silhouettes as well as geometric arcs and wedges with "[f]aces and limbs . . . carefully drawn to reveal African features and recognizable Black poses" (Driskell: 112). For example, faces are drawn with slitted eyes or protruding lips as if resembling African masks. The prominence Douglas gives to black subjects in *God's Trombones* was unusual but highly inspirational. Black subjects were rarely used in traditional biblical art, but Douglas used them in *each* of the eight illustrations. Furthermore, while black subjects were usually restricted to servant roles on the rare occasions in which they were depicted in biblical art at all, Douglas depicts them as strong, even as central characters (Driskell: 129). Thus, Douglas's repeated use of black subjects likely brought inspiration to blacks, who faced a barrage of negative and controlling images during this period.

In many ways, Douglas's illustration for Johnson's "Prodigal Son" nicely complements the poem. First, the illustration, like the poem, does not invoke the traditional distinction between Christianity and Judaism or between Protestantism and Catholicism. Second, the illustration, like the poem as well as the tradition of reception of the parable, provides a commentary on the younger son's life in the "far country." The far country is a city, much like Harlem; the scene is a city's nightlife in a bar; and the central characters, the younger son and two women, are dressed in the fashions of the 1920s, with a flood light placed above their heads as they dance on the barroom floor. Lastly, the illustration, like the poem, conveys a sense of crowdedness as well as the pleasures of night-life. The artist covers virtually every space around the central characters with symbols from the city's nightlife: a neon light, to signify the evening hours; a dollar bill, to symbolize money; the letters GI_, presumably to indicate a type of alcohol (gin) served in the bar; brass horns, to represent jazz music; and cards and dice, to symbolize gambling.

Unlike Johnson's poem, however, Douglas' illustration does not appear to portray the women as the *cause* of the younger son's demise. The women are not "loaded with rings and earrings and bracelets" (24), as in the poem. Nothing in the illustration suggests that they are prostitutes, as the poem suggests (again, without explicitly saying so). Rather, the women and the younger son are placed at the center of the illustration, drawn to proportion and depicted as dancing partners under the blare of jazz music. The illustration does depict vices, but these are so situated as to suggest that they could destroy *all* of the central characters, the younger son *and* the women, given their placement at all corners of the illustration. In the upper lefthand corner, the letters GI_ —giving the slight impression that the letter N follows—are cast in a neon light. Furthermore, the woman to the left of the younger son has what appears to be a drink, perhaps to suggest alcohol as the proper subtext from which to discern the identity of the GI_ word. In the upper righthand corner, the artist has drawn a huge dollar bill. Just as disproportionately drawn, there are dice in the lower lefthand corner and a King of Spades card in the lower righthand corner. Thus, Douglas' description of the nightlife, with its disproportionately drawn instruments of vice, appears to show gambling, alcohol, or even greed as the possible cause for the younger son's failure and seems to indicate that the women are equally susceptible to the lures of such vices.

C. Langston Hughes

Literary reviews of Langston Hughes' *Not Without Laughter* usually lament the novel's apparently incoherent plot (Bone: 75-77; Dickinson: 53). These readings, however, fail to note the importance of the character, Harriett Williams, in integrating the novel and in recreating the unity of a family torn apart by economic racism (see Miller: 369). Thus, while racism disintegrates the family and causes several characters to seek a better standard of living in the urban centers away from the little town of Stanton, Kansas, the ultimate success of Harriett Williams as a blues singer makes it possible for her to reunite a small part of her family, to finance her nephew's education, and thereby, potentially, to provide leadership for her race.

To develop the characterization of Harriett Williams as a blues singer, however, the novel repeatedly alludes to the Prodigal Son parable. Thus, the novel draws her as a blues-singing prodigal daughter whose life followed the basic template of the plot of the Prodigal Son parable—his status as a "younger" sibling, his journeying away from home, his deprivation and return.

Like the prodigal, Harriett Williams is a younger sibling, the youngest of three (Luke 15:11). At 16, compared to 28 and 35 (the ages of her sisters), she is described as the "wildest of the three children" (45) and as one who "wants to run de streets tendin' parties an' dances" (35). However, Hughes does not fully follow the Lukan narrator in the depiction of the younger sibling's status. Although the ancient biblical tradition usually showed favoritism to the youngest son, Luke subverts the tradition, with the father rejecting neither son and caring dearly for both of them (Scott: 125). In the case of the novel, however, Harriett is the favorite child, the one loved by her father, who has passed on, and of most concern to her mother. Also like the prodigal, Harriett Williams travels away from home. Unable to abide by the strictures in her mother's home, as was the case for many blues women (Wall: 42), and unable to accept the racist caprice of Stanton whites, Harriett joins a carnival show and moves on. Hughes joins others in the history of the reception of the parable, moreover, in making associations between the journey and sexuality. For Hughes' novel, however, Harriett's journey was an escape from sexual repression (55). Finally, like the prodigal as well, Harriett Williams experiences deprivation and returns home. Her letter to her sister Anjee is telling:

> Dear Sister. I am stranded in Memphis, Tenn. And the show has gone on to New Orleans. I can't buy anything to eat because I am broke and don't know anybody in this town. Anjee, please send me my fare to come home... (146-147)

When she returns, she is received warmly, as in the case of the prodigal son: her nephew Sandy and her sister Anjee kiss and hug her, while her mother, Aunt Hager, extends her arms open and exclaims, "Done come home again! Ma baby chile come home" (164). Unlike the Prodigal Son parable, however, Harriett does not return to live *with* her mother. Indeed, the novel seeks to develop the idea of "return"—the caption for one of its chapter headings—as a shift from Harriett's "individuality" to her mother's "community-mindedness." Thus, Harriett travels away from home again and becomes wealthy in the course of her travels. At the end of the novel, however, readers can see that her "return" combines the free spirit of her blues-singing travel in the urban centers with a concern to educate a race leader.

Thus, *Not Without Laughter* uses the Prodigal Son parable as a profile for its characterization of Harriett Williams. With Harriett Williams as the integrating character in the novel, moreover, Hughes actually writes a novel about black people's search for true success in urban America. While Hughes appreciates the value of the urban centers and the plights of racism that may have driven some there, he also offers in the novel a warning that an individual black person's success must be combined with "community-mindedness," both for the integration of one's own family and the development of one's race.

D. Summary of Harlem Renaissance Inflections on the Parable

All three African-American inflections on the parable from the early twentieth century proved, in all likelihood, helpful for black people, who needed to respond to regimes of representation in the post-Reconstruction period. All three boldly mixed biblical imagery with the experiences of black people. All three treated the perils and realities of urban life, especially for those who attempted to escape racism elsewhere. Furthermore, in their artistic critiques of psychological domination, all three affirm blackness without falling into the traps of repressive and demonizing religious distinctions. Yet, in one instance, as we have seen, one of the artists seeks to move beyond the gendered constructions of another artist. In effect, Douglas affirms black subjectivity without supporting the "gendered structures of thought and feeling" that one finds in Johnson's poem (Carby: 20-21). While the misogyny of Johnson's poem may be attributed to the patriarchy of the period in general or to the black bards for which his collection of sermonic poems represents an encomium, it is extraordinary that Douglas' elaboration of the parable did not take it in this direction.

The examination of this site of reading reveals, moreover, one of the problems of the Harlem Renaissance and indeed a continuing problem in the formation of black subjectivity. The formation of black subjectivity has suffered not only because of racist stereotypes designed to dehumanize black people and render them politically and socially inert. It has also suffered and failed to reach the admirable goal of "enabling solidarity" ("the desire to promote love, friendship, and moral cooperation among black folk" [Dyson: xvii]), because it has been hamstrung by one or more quests for racial unity—quests for racial essences without the clear recognition that "[r]acial identity is not exhausted by genetic inheritance" (Dyson: xx). Indeed, the Harlem Renaissance artists' emphasis on racism, while indeed necessary, may have obscured a focus on class politics or gender politics, both of which brought disaster, destitution, and death to communities of black people for reasons other than their pigmentation. Douglas' critique of Hughes thus represents an early call for a "radical politics of identity," not a narrow one based on racial essentialism (hooks: 20).

Given the results of this study so far, two questions must be raised: (1) Would readings of the parable based on established academic interpretation curb some of these tendencies to exploit the parable in repressive ways? (2) Does the parable itself, especially within the larger context of the Gospel of Luke, actually lend itself to repressive ethics? To answer these questions, I extend Tolbert's "poetics of location" to its second and third levels.

Established Academic Reconstructions of the Parable of the Prodigal Son

Established academic scholarship, with its focus on historical, socio-cultural, and literary questions, provides basic data with which to understand the function of the parable and evaluate a variety of tendencies in its interpretation and appropriation throughout history.

In historical-critical circles, much of the scholarly focus has been on the parable's origins. On the one hand, if traceable to Jesus (Bultmann: 169), the parable is seen as yielding insight into Jesus' nature. On the other hand, if coming from the Lukan source "L" with touches of Luke's own "distinctive traces," the parable is said to provide insight into a certain period in the early development of Jesus' movement (Fitzmyer: 1084).

In sociocultural-critical circles, still largely a type of historical inquiry, questions have been raised about the social status of Jesus' audience. The results are as follows: on the one hand, Pharisees as those who represented the "religious ideal: pious and devout, and rigorous in observing both the written and oral law" (Forbes: 213; see Josephus, *War*, 1.5.2) and scribes as "lawyers and religious experts" (Culpepper: 128); on the other hand, tax collectors as a group "ritually defiled by contact with Gentiles and further despised due to their collaboration with the Romans" and "sinners" as those perceived to be "the immoral, who deliberately and consistently violated the law" (Forbes: 109). This type of investigation has also examined the ancient codes of inheritance—particularly drawing on Sirach 33:19-23, which warns against the disposal of a family's property before the father's death—to indicate the oddness of the father's decision to grant the younger son's request for an early disposition (Tannehill: 240).

In literary-critical circles, scholars have examined the function of the parable within Luke's gospel. Tannehill suggests, for example, that all three parables in Luke 15:1-32 "define the character of Jesus and the mission of Jesus" (239). For Sellew, the parable of the Prodigal Son, along with five other parables (The Foolish Farmer, 12:16-20; The Unfaithful Servant, 12:46-46; The Crafty Steward, 16:1-8a; The Unjust Judge, 18:1-5; and The Owner of the Vineyard, 20:9-1), all present a character who uses interior monologue. Moreover, all such interior monologues in Jesus' parables expose the characters' plights as well as Jesus' insight into their plights, an insight which Simeon forecasts as early as 2:34-35 (259-63).

A literary-critical orientation could also reveal that the Lukan Jesus tells a number of parables that critique acts of calculated giving for maximum return in this world. Both the parable of the Good (or better, "Merciful") Samaritan (10:30-35) and the parable of the Prodigal Son (15:11-32), for example, critique human motives. In the parable of the Good Samaritan, the Samaritan aids the fallen man not because that man can give the Samaritan a good return for the aid given; in fact, the Samaritan stands to lose both present and future (earthly) resources in aiding the man. He simply aids the man because of his compassion (*esplangnisthe*, 10:33). In the larger context of the story's application, however, the Samaritan's action becomes a model for inheriting eternal life. In the parable of the Prodigal Son, the father's response to the younger son is not based on any possible gains he can make, since the father has already suffered great loss (15:12-13, 23, 30, 32). The father runs to aid the son because of his compassion (*esplangnisthe*, 15:20). These parables, then, while always directed to a narrative audience, also guide Luke's audience in constructing images of the characters in the plot. On the one hand, those characters in the narrative who calculate earthly success as do the characters in Jesus' parables are to be viewed negatively. On the other hand, those characters in the narrative who simply act without regard for the honor they can receive or the loss they can recover on earth are identified as positive characters. Consequently, these parables provide commentary and thus function as orienting devices with which to steer Luke's audience in its assessment of the characters in the larger narrative.

More specifically, the parable of the Prodigal Son forms part of a series of three parables designed to welcome and celebrate the recovery of those persons not usually accepted by society's conventional standards. In Luke 15:1-32, the repetition of terms associated with "joy" (vv. 6, 7, 9, 10, 32) confirms a connection among the parables (or their contexts), while the repetition of "lost and found" terminology (vv. 3, 5, 6, 8, 9, 24, 32) suggests an attitude of celebration in all three parables toward those who repent. To be sure, the parable of the Prodigal Son makes two distinctive contributions. First, it gives a human touch to the theme of joy over the lost that is found. Second, it provides a contrast in attitudes toward that which was lost. Accordingly, although the parable speaks about two sons, its basic drive or goal is not a contrast between the behavior of the two sons but rather a contrast between the attitudes of father and elder son toward the younger son's return.

The parable condemns the elder son not because of his work ethic, as some commentators have asserted, for ironically the elder son envisions himself as a slave, not a son ("I have slaved" [*douleuo*]). However, the attitude "condemned" is a self-righteous, stereotypical evaluation, oblivious to any actual conversation with the younger brother. The father, like others in Luke's Gospel (7:13; 10:33), "sees" and has "compassion." The elder brother only thinks of his brother from a distance. Without going to see his brother at all—it should be noted that the news of the celebration and its cause are reported to him (15:25-27)—he imagines, while yet "in the field" (15:25), the lot of his younger brother (15:30). Furthermore, if Luke's audience were to constrain the third parable within the interpretive framework provided by the two earlier ones, the elder brother would emerge as lacking the orientation that serves as climax for each of those parables. In other words, the orientation of heaven or of the angels is not at all conventional, based on lost or achieved status or just desserts. Throughout Luke's Gospel, what God gives is based on an eschatological orientation—God's paradoxical plan that favors the inclusion of the unexpected (13:29) and the filling up of God's house (14:23). The father's insistence that "we had to celebrate" (15:32) is not based on what the younger son deserved or on any questions about his former or previous status. With words akin to the culminating statements of the previous parables, the father insists: "It is necessary to celebrate and rejoice, because this brother of yours was dead and has come back to life; he was lost and has been found" (15:31). The logic of the celebration is the same kind of imperative that breathes throughout Luke's Gospel. The expression, "It is necessary" (*edei*), points to an imperative, a force that governs what people do. For Luke, that imperative always is the will of God.

Thus, an acknowledgment of the contrast between the attitude of the father and that of the elder son could demonstrate the problem of those who too quickly want to institute a contrast between the sons in order to support a pre-interpretive perception of inherent differences between Protestantism and Roman Catholicism, on the one hand, or Judaism and Christianity, on the other. Furthermore, even if the purpose of the parable, as used by Luke, had been to attack Pharisees and scribes who did not like

Jesus' association with tax collectors and sinners, this is no reason to think that Luke was directing an attack against *all* Pharisees or against *all* Jews. Rather, one must not fail to note Luke's fairly stylized portraits of the Pharisees and scribes. Besides, elsewhere, Luke attacks the attitude of self-righteousness with broad strokes: "Whoever exalts himself will be abased; and whoever abases himself will be exalted" (Culpepper: 341; Young: 136).

In using the results of established academic scholarship, therefore, it is possible to curb some of the interpretations that support repressive regimes of representation. Yet, in the light of these findings, one can ask: Are there additional dangers in the parable itself? Are there hidden texts in Luke's culture and in the Gospel of Luke that need to be exposed? An examination of the text's historical production suggests that the text itself is problematic and potentially a re-inscription of the historical and dis-cursive colonialism that Luke seeks to reject.

Examination of the Text's Historical Production

While traditional studies are always helpful and necessary in clari-fying some of the power dynamics inherent in the interpretive act, stances of decolonization require the raising of questions about the text's histori-cal production. Such questions move us away from simplistic atomistic analyses to larger issues like the following: the socio-historical conditions under which the entire Gospel of Luke was written; the parable's function in the larger narrative against Roman imperialism; and the shadow of imperialism within the Gospel of Luke.

If Luke's Gospel was written to set Jesus' friendship network over against presumably superior power complexes in the real world, its rheto-ric appears to *compensate* for losses that people have sustained in becom-ing a part of Christianity or in staying with it (Smith, 1995:228). The nar-rative rhetoric also appears to *correct or critique* certain notions about power and prestige characteristic of other subcultures (such as the prestige found among the Pharisees, as stylized by Luke) or of the larger world. Finally, the narrative rhetoric seems to *contextualize* as well the misfortune and misunderstanding that Jesus and some of his earliest followers may have experienced (see Luke 24:13-27). At points in all of our journeys, any one of these affirmations may be necessary for life today, especially for oppressed people. However, although Luke's rhetoric may be alluring in some ways for many victims of oppression, it should be resisted. As Lennard Davis suggests, even the best "collective defenses and ideologi-cal assumptions" may be "damaging and neurotic" (15) over time.

I conclude, therefore, by raising two perils in modernizing Luke, both associated with the parable of the Prodigal Son.

First, although Luke critiques that kind of prestige that will not allow a person or group (as in the case of the Pharisees who hear the three parables of Luke 15) to associate with socially marginalized "others," he does not critique the prestige associated with verbal wit. For example, Luke, like the writer of the *Life of Aesop*, accepts the notion that outstanding wit in verbal duel is a sign of honor (Adrados: 99). Jesus bests his opponents repeatedly, reducing some to shame, leaving others in silence, and rendering others rageful and vindictive. Although it is a given that oppressed people must find some way to esteem themselves in the face of degradation, continuous verbal dueling ultimately eventuates in physical dueling, as modern groups, from gangs to whole countries, give evidence (Parks).

Second, the well-known note of universalism or cosmopolitan beneficence (to men, women, the socially marginalized [in the case of the parables of Luke 15], and even to Gentiles) in Luke's writings is not an innocent offering of God's beneficence to all people. Rather, it is a power play given sacral character as part of a divine plan and a legitimation motif for a minority struggling to exert some form of prowess before the formidable presence of the Roman imperial complex. It should not go unmentioned, moreover, that the similarities some have seen between Luke's writings and ancient novelistic literature also mark Luke's agenda as one of exertion of prowess, for the ancient Greek novels and ancient Jewish novelistic literature were all designed to "capture a sense of ethnic pride and competitiveness" (Wills: 224). All of these works then employ a hermeneutics of return to express ethnic prowess in the face of Roman power. Thus, even if the intent is to oppose the colonizers, these works do so through discursive neocolonial means. While on the one hand beneficence to all seems appealing, on the other hand Luke's emphasis on cosmopolitan beneficence appears to be in competition with the Roman Empire's claims of worldwide benefaction. In my judgment, a dangerous imperialism lurks behind cosmopolitan beneficence, which often leads those who offer such beneficence to assume that they have a responsibility to dispense it at whatever cost, even if the beneficiaries never wanted or requested the gifts.

Works Consulted

Adrados, Francisco
    1979   "The 'Life of Aesop' and the Origins of Novel in Antiquity."
            Quaderni Urbinati di Cultura Classica 30:94-102.

Aymer, Margaret P.
1997 "Hailstorms and Fireballs: Redaction, World Creation, and Resistance in the Acts of Paul and Thecla." *Semeia* 79:45-59.

Bailey, Randall C.
1998 "The Danger of Ignoring One's Own Cultural Bias In Interpreting the Text." Pp. 66-90 in *The Postcolonial Bible*. Ed. R. S. Sugirtharajah. Sheffield: Sheffield Academic Press.
2000 "The Current Status of Scholarly Black Biblical Interpretation in the US." Pp. 696-711 in *African Americans and the Bible*. Ed. Vincent L. Wimbush. New York: Continuum.

Baldwin, James
1959 "The Discovery of What It Means to be an American." *The New York Times Book Review* 64:4, 22.

Baldwin, Robert W.
1985 "On Earth We Are Beggars, as Christ Himself Was": The Protestant Background of Rembrandt's Images of Poverty, Disability, and Begging." *Konsthistorisk tidskrift* 54:122-135.

Bone, Robert
1965 *The Negro Novel in America*. New Haven: Yale University Press.

Boyd, Melba Joyce
1994 *Discarded Legacy: Politics and Poetics in the Life of Frances E. W. Harper*. Detroit: Wayne State University Press.

Bultmann, Rudolf
1963 *The History of the Synoptic Tradition*. Trans. John Marsh. Revised Edition. New York: Harper & Row.

Carby, Hazel V.
1998 *Race Men*. Cambridge: Harvard University Press.

Costanzo, Angelo
1987 *Surprising Narrative: Olaudah Equiano and the Beginnings of Black Autobiography*. New York: Greenwood Press.

Culpepper, R. Alan
1995 "The Gospel of Luke." Pp. 1-490 in *The New Interpreter's Bible: A Commentary in Twelve Volumes*. Volume 9. Nashville: Abingdon Press.

Davis, Angela Y.
1998 *Blues Legacies and Black Feminism: Gertrude "Ma" Rainey, Bessie Smith, and Billie Holiday*. New York: Pantheon.

Davis, Francis
1995 *The History of the Blues*. New York: Hyperion.

Davis, Lennard J.
1987 *Ideology and Fiction: Resisting Novels*. New York: Methuen.

Dickinson, Donald C.
1967 *A Bio-Bibliography of Langston Hughes*. Hamden, CO: Shoe String.

D'Oench, Ellen D.
1995 *Prodigal Son Narratives: 1480-1980*. New Haven: Yale University Art Gallery.

Donaldson, Laura E.
   1996   "Postcolonialism and Biblical Reading: An Introduction." *Semeia* 75:1-14.

Driskell, David
   1987   "The Flowering of the Harlem Renaissance: The Art of Aaron Douglas, Meta Warrick Fuller, Palmer Hayden, and William H. Johnson." Pp. 105-154 in *Harlem Renaissance: Art of Black America.* New York: The Studio Museum of New York.

Dyson, Michael Eric
   1993   *Reflecting   Black: African-American   Cultural   Criticism.* Minneapolis: University of Minnesota Press.

Fitzmyer, Joseph A.
   1985   *The Gospel According to Luke (I-IX).* The Anchor Bible. Garden City: Doubleday and Company.

Fleming, Robert E.
   1987   *James Weldon Johnson.* Boston: Twayne Publishers.

Forbes, Greg W.
   2000   *The God of Old: The Role of the Lukan Parables in the Purpose of Luke's Gospel.* Sheffield: Sheffield Academic Press.

Hill Collins, Patricia
   1990   *Black Feminist Thought: Knowledge, Consciousness, and the Politics of Empowerment.* Boston: Unwin and Hyman.

hooks, bell
   1990   *Yearning: Race, Gender, and Cultural Politics.* Boston: South End.

Hoyt, Thomas, Jr.
   1991   "Interpreting Biblical Scholarship for the Black Church Tradition." Pp. 17-39 in *Stony The Road We Trod: African American Biblical Interpretation.* Ed. Cain Hope Felder. Minneapolis: Fortress Press.

Hughes, Langston
   1995   *Not Without Laughter.* Introduction by Maya Angelou. New York: Scribner.

Johnson, James Weldon
   1927   *God's Trombones: Seven Negro Sermons in Verse.* New York: Viking.

Jones, Darryl L.
   1997   "The Sermon as 'Art' of Resistance: A Comparative Analysis of the Rhetorics of the African-American Slave Preacher and the Preacher to the Hebrews." *Semeia* 79:11-26.

Kirschke, Amy
   1995   *Aaron Douglas: Art, Race, and the Harlem Renaissance.* Jackson, MS: University Press of Mississippi.

Liburd, Ron
   1994   "'Like . . . a House upon the Sand': African American Biblical Hermeneutics   in   Perspective."   *The   Journal   of   the Interdenominational Theological Center* 22:71-91.

Locke, Alain
      1995   "The New Negro." Pp. 47-56 in *Voices from the Harlem Renaissance*. Ed. Nathan Irvin Huggins. New York: Oxford University Press.
Martin, Clarice J.
      1991   "The Haustafeln (Household Codes) in African American Biblical Interpretation: 'Free Slaves and Subordinate Women." Pp. 206-31 in *Stony The Road We Trod: African American Biblical Interpretation*. Ed. Cain Hope Felder. Minneapolis: Fortress Press.
Miller, R. Baxter
      1976   "'Done Made Us Leave Our Home': Langston Hughes's *Not Without Laughter*—Unifying Image and Three Dimensions." *Phylon* 37:362-69.
Myers, William H.
      1991   "The Hermeneutical Dilemma of the African American Biblical Student." Pp. 40-56 in *Stony The Road We Trod: African American Biblical Interpretation*. Ed. Cain Hope Felder. Minneapolis: Fortress Press.
O'Brien Wicker, Kathleen
      1993   "Teaching Feminist Biblical Studies in a Postcolonial Context." Pp. 367-80 in *Searching the Scriptures. Volume One: A Feminist Introduction*. Ed. Elisabeth Schüssler Fiorenza. New York: Crossroad.
Parks, Ward
      1990   *Verbal Dueling in Heroic Narrative: The Homeric and Old English Traditions*. Princeton: Princeton University Press.
Schüssler Fiorenza, Elisabeth
      1988   "The Ethics of Biblical Interpretation: Decentering Biblical Scholarship." *JBL* 107:3-17.
Scott, Bernard Brandon
      1989   *Hear Then the Parable: A Commentary on the Parables of Jesus*. Minneapolis: Fortress Press.
Segovia, Fernando F.
      1998   "Biblical Criticism and Postcolonial Studies: Toward a Postcolonial Optic." Pp. 49-65 in *The Postcolonial Bible*. Ed. R. S. Sugirtharajah. Sheffield: Sheffield Academic Press.
Sellew, Philip
      1992   "Interior Monologue as a Narrative Device in the Parables of Luke." *JBL* 11:239-53
Smith, Abraham
      1995   "A Second Step in African Biblical Interpretation: A Generic Reading Analysis of Acts 8:26-40." Pp. 213-28 in *Reading from This Place. Volume 1: Social Location and Biblical Interpretation in the United States*. Ed. Fernando Segovia and Mary Ann Tolbert. Minneapolis: Fortress Press.

1997 "I Saw the Book Talk: A Cultural Studies Approach to the Ethics of an African American Biblical Hermeneutics." *Semeia* 77:115-38.

2000 "Aaron Douglas, the Harlem Renaissance, and Biblical Art: Toward a Radical Politics of Identity." Pp. 682-95 in *African Americans and the Bible: An Interdisciplinary Project*. Ed. Vincent Wimbush. New York: Continuum.

Smith, Theophus
1994 *Conjuring Culture: Biblical Formations of Black America*. New York: Oxford University Press.

Snyder, Susan
1966 "King Lear and the Prodigal Son." *Shakespeare Quarterly* 17:361-69.

Spencer, Jon Michael
1990 *Protest and Praise: Sacred Music of Black Religion*. Minneapolis: Fortress Press.

Tannehill, Robert
1996 *Luke*. Abingdon New Testament Commentaries. Nashville: Abingdon Press.

Tolbert, Mary Ann
1995a "The Politics and Poetics of Location." Pp. 305-17 in *Reading From this Place. Volume 1: Social Location and Biblical Interpretation in the United States*. Ed. Fernando F. Segovia and Mary Ann Tolbert. Minneapolis: Fortress Press.

1995b "When Resistance Becomes Repression." Pp. 331-46 in *Reading From This Place. Volume 2: Social Location and Biblical Interpretation in Global Perspective*. Ed. Fernando F. Segovia and Mary Ann Tolbert. Minneapolis: Fortress Press.

Wall, Cheryl A.
1995 "Whose Sweet Angel Child?: Blues Women, Langston Hughes, and Writing During the Harlem Renaissance." Pp. 37-50 in *Langston Hughes: The Man, His Art and His Continuing Influence*. Ed. C. James Trotman. New York: Garland.

Watson, Steven
1995 *The Harlem Renaissance: Hub of African-American Culture, 1920-1930*. New York: Pantheon Books.

West, Cornel
1989 *The American Evasion of Philosophy: A Genealogy of Pragmatism*. Madison: University of Wisconsin Press.

Wills, Lawrence M.
1994 "The Jewish Novella." Pp. 223-38 in *Greek Fiction: The Greek Novel in Context*. Ed. J. R. Morgan and Richard Stoneman. London: Routledge.

Wimbush, Vincent
    2000   "Introduction: Reading Darkness, Reading Scriptures." Pp. 1-43 in *African Americans and the Bible*. Ed. Vincent L. Wimbush. New York: Continuum.
Young, Brad
    1998   *The Parables: Jewish Tradition and Christian Interpretation*. Peabody, MA: Hendrickson.

7

Finding a Home for Ruth
Gender, Sexuality, and the Politics of Otherness

Kwok Pui-lan

My daughter, should I not seek a home for you, that it may be well with you?

> —Ruth 3:1 (RSV)

When is the word "home" shrunk to denote the private, domestic sphere and when is the "domestic" enlarged to denote "the affairs of a nation"?

> —Rosemary Marangoly George (13)

The study of the Bible in the American churches and the academy has always been shaped by the cultural ethos and political struggles of its time. In the nineteenth century, the Bible was vigorously debated among those who supported slavery and those who worked for its abolition. In the early twentieth century, the Bible was again a focal point of contention in the cultural war between the modernists and the fundamentalists. During the past several decades, the interpretation of the Bible has been much influenced by the larger conversations regarding the politics of identity, multiculturalism, immigration, and increasing pluralism in American society. As a theologian of Chinese descent, I would like to reread the story of Ruth to understand its implications for today's discussion of foreigners, strangers, and immigrants in the larger context of identity formation in the United States.

Introduction

When we open the advertisement section of the *World Journal*, the best-selling Chinese newspaper in the United States, we can find almost everyday advertisements of women in China looking for men with American citizenship to begin a relationship or with marriage in mind. These advertisements remind us of the heart-wrenching history of the mail-order brides, involving not only women of Asian descent but women of other nationalities as well. Besides mail-order brides, women's sexuality has been used in other ways as a ticket to the U.S., such as prostitution, fake marriages, and marrying an American G.I. Some of these marriages have a happy ending, but some eventually end up in domestic violence, divorce, poverty, and neglected children.

The harsh realities of U.S. immigration history and the global displacement and dispersal of huge numbers of people challenge the cozy picture of home defined by family romance and a perfect middle-class nuclear family. In the case of the U.S., gender, sexuality, and marriage have been much tied with the powerful propaganda of the "American Dream" and the national narrative of the U.S. as an immigrant country open to all. Thus, "home" cannot be read through the myopic lens of the warmth and comfort of the private sphere without taking into consideration how the private intersects with national identity, ethnicity, citizenship, law, and women's rights. In the global scene—where war, violence, ethnic strife, political instability, and the global market combine to drive many people into homelessness, migrancy, and diaspora—home is not a fixed and stable location but a traveling adventure, which entails seeking refuge in strange lands, bargaining for survival, and negotiating for existence. Such a destabilized and contingent construction of home dislodges it from its familiar domestic territory and questions the conditions through which the cozy connotations of home have been made possible and sustained. For postcolonial and cultural critics, the home and the outside—or the home and the world—are categories that are mutually constitutive and contingent, whose content and meaning cannot be predetermined in advance, without examining how they are deployed in specific discourses (Sagar: 237; Bhabha: 1992).

In the book of Ruth, the Judahite mother-in-law Naomi wants to find a home for her Moabite daughter-in-law Ruth. The Hebrew word translated as "home" (mānôach) can also mean a place where one can find rest and a sense of security. For many readers, the word "home" connotes the private sphere of domesticity, shelter, comfort, nurture, rest, and protection. It is, therefore, not surprising that the story of Ruth has been a favorite of Christians and Jews throughout the centuries because it can be read as a romantic story with a happy ending (Sakenfeld: 1). Indeed, if taken as an idyllic tale, the book of Ruth can offer readers some comfort and respite in the midst of war, murder, violence, disloyalty, rebellion, and unfaithfulness in the scriptures.

But such a romantic reading has been demystified by biblical scholars, who have deployed a wide array of methods to illumine different parts of Ruth's story, including sociological analysis, narrative theory, feminist criticism, intertextuality, and analyses of realist fiction, the arts, and popular media. These new and divergent approaches do not emerge in a vacuum but are made possible by the change of contours in the field of biblical studies. In the past several decades scholars have challenged the hegemony of traditional methods and proposed new paradigms of interpretation such as reader-response criticism, rhetorical criticism, feminist criticism, cultural studies, postcolonial criticism, and vernacular hermeneutics. The understanding of "scripture" has shifted from the sacred word of God and a historical document of the past to a relational concept involving interaction with interpretive communities (Smith, 1993). The meaning of the Bible is no longer seen as located in the authorial voice of God, or in the intention of the author or the redactor, but increasingly in the interpretive community, whether it is the religious community or the academic guild. Collectively, these new paradigms have shifted the emphasis from the world *behind the text* (historical criticism) to the world *in the text* (literary criticism informed by critical theories) and the world *in front of the text* (reader-response). New Testament scholar Fernando Segovia traces the proliferation of new paradigms to two factors: theoretical shifts introduced into the discipline by literary and cultural criticisms and a crucial demographic shift in the discipline, namely, the increasing presence and influences of "outsiders," including Western women and non-Western critics residing in both the West and the Third World (1-2).

In this chapter I use the expression "finding a home" for Ruth as a metaphor and a heuristic device to describe and interrogate the different ways scholars have constructed meanings and mobilized data from their respective reading strategies. In the first section I group different readings of "home" under three categories: home as kinship; home as patriarchal household; and home as hospitality to strangers. My interest is not to use these categories to demonstrate three distinct modes of reading, or to classify scholars into different camps, because many scholars do talk about "home" in more than one way. For example, feminist scholars may critique the oppression of home in a patriarchal context and at the same time affirm the offering of hospitality to foreigners. My intention, rather, is to show that implicit or explicit assumptions of "home" have led scholars to pay attention to certain parts of the story and to activate certain registers of reading, even though these scholars may come from distinct academic backgrounds utilizing different methodologies. In the second section I discuss two recent readings by Regina Schwartz and Laura Donaldson that raise some new and significant questions and problematize the relation between home and identity, violence, genocide, and assimilation. In the conclusion I offer some observations on the link between finding a home for Ruth and scholars' finding a home for themselves in the academy and the religious community.

Biblical Interpretation and Home-Making for Ruth

In the beginning of her book, *The Politics of Home*, Rosemary Marangoly George discusses various ways in which "home" has been conceived:

> Today, the primary connotation of "home" is of the "private" space from which the individual travels into the larger arenas of life and to which he or she returns at the end of the day. And yet, also in circulation is the word's wider signification as the larger geographic place where one belongs: country, city, village, community. Home is also the imagined location that can be more readily fixed in a mental landscape than in actual geography. (11)

Based on different constructions of "home," the story of Ruth has been interpreted in many different ways. Read as a novella, the reader can focus on love, courtship, seduction, female subjectivity, the new home, and the birth of the child. As such, the story has no historical reference and is irrelevant to the larger picture of national destiny and political salvation. If, however, we relate the home to the broader contexts of tribe, community, people, and nation, then the short book of Ruth offers many interesting scenarios for readers to plot different interpretive trajectories. I would like to illustrate what I mean by tracing three such trajectories, which by no means exhaust all the possibilities.

Home as Kinship

For some readers, the family saga of Naomi and her Moabite daughter-in-law is included in the Bible and placed between the book of Judges and I Samuel because Ruth is supposed to build the house of Israel and establish the patrilineal genealogy of David (4:21-22). Kirsten Nielsen suggests that the original purpose of the book was to "champion the right of David's family to the throne" (29), because there were people who raised doubt about the legitimacy of David's rule on account of his Moabite ancestry. Although Nielsen's position is open to question, particularly her dating of the book in the pre-exilic period, her arguments underscore the importance of bloodline in defining insiders and outsiders in ancient societies.

Kinship is an important theme throughout the Hebrew Bible and forms the backdrop to the book of Ruth. The study of kinship systems is a well-established discursive field. In addition to the historical-critical method, biblical scholars have at their disposal many new tools from disciplines as diverse as anthropology, sociology, semiotics, structuralism, poststructuralism, and cultural studies. Whether the text is read as a means to provide historical data or as a literary product, the book of Ruth provides many interesting points for discussion, such as the characteristics and nature of levirate marriage in ancient Israel, the issues of endogamy versus exogamy and patrilocal versus virilocal marriages, and the form and style of genealogies.

The book is narrated in a way that assumes knowledge on the part of the implied reader of the practice of levirate marriage, which enables the continuation of the family line and the protection of property within the family (Deut 25:5-10). Out of distress and frustration, Naomi sends her two daughters-in-law away, lamenting that she has no more sons that can become their husbands (1:11). The encounter of Ruth with Boaz and the climax at the threshing floor are facilitated by the fact that Boaz is a kinsman of Naomi's husband (2:1). The anticlimax takes place by way of the public witness and decision regarding the legitimate next-of-kin to redeem family property and to marry Ruth (4:7-10).

In her intertextual study of the book of Ruth with the Tamar story in Genesis 38, Ellen Van Wolde points to the implied interest of establishing the male line, which frames the beginning and the end of the narrative (8-9). Both stories begin with a man leaving his home country: in the Tamar story, Judah leaves his home; in the book of Ruth, Elimelech from Bethlehem goes to sojourn in Moab because of famine. The stories of Tamar and Ruth are told from the Judahite perspective, and not from a Canaanite or Moabite point of view. Although the two women attract attention through their daring actions, they are both absent from the concluding scene of the story: the Tamar story ends with an account of childbirth, with no mention of Tamar's name; the Ruth story concludes with the birth of Obed and his place as the ancestor of David. Van Wolde writes: "The female protagonists, Ruth and Tamar, are in the end absent; they disappear in favour of their sons" (9). In both stories, the woman involved is a foreigner, who has to take radical action so that the man in question exercises the responsibility of the next-of-kin. The men, Judah and Boaz, are much older than the female protagonists. When Ruth gives birth to Obed, he is nursed by and identified as the son of the Judahite Naomi and not of Ruth the Moabite. Phyllis Trible points out that it is noteworthy that the child is named by the women and identified as the son of Naomi rather than of Elimelech (194-95).

The anxiety of the next-of-kin to establish his progeny through levirate marriage does not escape the notice of scholars. In Tamar's case, the closest kin, Onan, agrees to sleep with her, but safeguards his seeds and decides to "do it his way" (Van Wolde: 10, 15). In Ruth's case, the closest kin agrees to redeem the property for Naomi, but refuses to marry a foreign woman. He is willing to follow the law of redeemer but not the law of levirate (Bal: 80). This opens a possibility for Boaz to act against established customs and social roles: "He searches for ways to maximize his own advantage while maintaining his proper family honor; his solution bends the social rules about marriage while adhering to and exceeding the redemption law" (Berquist: 34). Since Boaz is an older man, his response to being sexually awakened by Ruth at the threshing floor and his concern about his virility are highlighted by some readers. Washed, perfumed, and dressed in her finest clothes, Ruth wakes Boaz, literally and figuratively, challenging Boaz to leave behind his pious public respectability. "The younger woman," states Francis Landy, "comes to sleep with the older man at a site marked symbolically by decision and fertility and temporally by the suspension of social norms" (292).

The story touches on endogamy and exogamy as well as on patrilocal versus virilocal marriages. The Jews were admonished not to marry foreign women and worship their gods. This was one of the reasons why the immediate next-of-kin refused to marry Ruth, because she was a Moabite. In fact, according to some rabbinical interpretations, Naomi's two sons, Mahlon and Chilion, were struck down by God because they had committed the sin of marrying foreign women (Darr: 62-63). But Boaz was able to cross the boundary and hence became the ancestor of David. Following Mieke Bal's study of the transition from patrilocal to virilocal marriage in Judges, David Jobling argues that the book of Ruth reads "like an apology for virilocal marriage" (133). Here Ruth disassociates herself from her father's family and joins her husband's family and participates in establishing the monarchy. Although Ruth gives birth to the baby and the women name the newborn, the child is reckoned according to Boaz's family line in the closing genealogy. The genealogy leaves out Judah and starts with his son Perez, so that Boaz will occupy the honorable seventh position and David the tenth. Katherine Doob Sakenfeld suggests that the formal and official genealogy serves several purposes in the book (85-86). The genealogy demonstrates that the blessing prayer for Boaz (4:12) is fulfilled and provides a literary link to I Samuel, in which the establishment of the monarchy and David's kingship is told. It also reminds Christian readers of another important genealogy in Matthew, namely, the genealogy of Jesus as a descendant of David. While the genealogy in the book of Ruth does not include any women, the Matthean genealogy includes four women (Tamar, Rahab, Ruth, and the wife of Uriah).

Finding a home for Ruth within the kinship system, either in terms of continuation of the male line in the family saga or in the political narrative of the rise of monarchy, has been criticized by feminist critics (Fuchs, 1989). Yet, as we have seen, both the narrative structure and the framing of the book lend themselves to such a reading. As a matter of fact, before the advent of feminist criticism, many women's stories in the Bible had been read as serving some grand purpose, such as the salvation of God or the political liberation of the people. Postcolonial feminist critics are quick to point out that women's issues have likewise been subsumed under the banner of national liberation in modern revolutionary narratives and that women's leadership roles have been overshadowed by men's. Furthermore, as Marcella María Althaus-Reid points out, women's sexuality has been appropriated figuratively both in the texts and in economic and political systems that treat their bodies as commodities or instruments. Here, Ruth's sexuality is not a private matter but is intimately related to finding security and means of survival for her and Naomi, as well as to the preservation of family land and property. Using the critical insights of Althaus-Reid, we can discern an omnipresent heterosexual system operating in the story through different economic and political arrangements and supported by theological discourse (40). Such critical observations lead us to the next clusters of issues when we consider home as patriarchal household.

Home as Patriarchal Household

The story presents problems for feminist scholars because the narrative does not challenge patriarchal and heterosexual familial structures: a widow can only find economic security through remarriage; marrying a man with some means (no matter the age difference) guarantees financial gains; giving birth to a son is the greatest responsibility of women; a male child is more valuable than a female child; and the authority of the mother-in-law is over the daughter-in-law (Sakenfeld: 11; Levine: 78-79). Armed with the hermeneutics of suspicion, feminist scholars want to retrieve liberating moments in the story, since it is rare to find women with such major roles in a book in the Bible.

Borrowing insights from feminist literary criticism, biblical scholars accentuate the roles, character, and subjectivities of female protagonists. Phyllis Trible, for example, stresses the courage and determination of Naomi and Ruth in "their struggle for survival in a patriarchal environment" (166). In the midst of poverty, famine, and dislocation, Naomi invokes the promise of Yahweh, and Ruth chooses life over death. In this way, they have changed from nonpersons toward personhood (168). In keeping with her narratological method, Mieke Bal looks at women's speech, focalization, and action as portrayed in the narrative (77-79). Susan Reimer Torn suggests that the book of Ruth preserves the ancient matriarchal tradition, in which powerful women forge their own identity and take initiative (345-46). It seems to me that many white feminist readings are interested in the recovery of the authoritative self associated with the modern female subject. Such overemphasis on individualist female subjectivity may sometimes overshadow other power dynamics at work in the story and suggest that the heroic acts of the protagonist can solve all problems.

Besides personal virtue and character, feminist commentators also elaborate on the interpersonal relationship between women. Some suggest that the book might stem from women's culture because the relationship of Naomi and Ruth is sharply different from the stereotypical biblical image of women as rivals (van Dijk-Hemmes: 136). It is rare in the Bible to find two women who commit their life and future to one another at such a deep level. For Ruth Anna Putnam, the story provides a model of female friendship, which sometimes requires stepping outside one's moral tradition (Ruth's "leaving home") and the courage to share the hardship in a friend's life (53-54). From the Taiwanese context, where mothers-in-law exercise great authority, Julie Chu cherishes the respect and devotion of these two women, who struggle together against patriarchal culture. However, such readings have the tendency to decontextualize the story, while trying to lift up moral ideals or universal truths for appropriation in other situations.

By far, the most interesting discussions center on Ruth's desire and sexuality, because in the process deep-seated assumptions about family, gender relations, and women's appropriate behavior are revealed. Scholars differ in interpreting the unconventional action of Ruth at the threshing floor. For Torn, there is no reason why women cannot take matters in their own hands, "even steering their male protagonists toward their chosen course of action" (344). She continues: "these biblical women, rather than bowing to some external, foreign authority embodied in the father, fully appropriate their prerogatives. They themselves seduce fathers and father figures. The importance of their directing—rather than submitting to—the father cannot be overlooked" (344). For Amy-Jill Levine, the issue at hand is not defining decent and indecent behavior of women in general, because the gender of Ruth must be read together with her ethnicity. Levine cautions that the story can be used to preach that Gentile women are bad models for Israelite women because they are sexually manipulative and dangerous. She states: "It is the reader's task to determine whether this book affirms Ruth or ultimately erases her, whether she serves as a moral exemplar or as a warning against sexually forward Gentile women" (79). The interpretation of this episode would lead readers to rethink their assumptions regarding the sexual behavior of women in a patriarchal household, gender relations in a cross-cultural context, and sexual myths about foreigners, especially foreign women.

A radical debunking of the ideology of patriarchal household is presented by lesbian readers, who focus on the love between Naomi and Ruth instead of the liaison between Ruth and Boaz. For Rebecca Alpert, the book of Ruth is an important source for the location of women who are lovers of women in Jewish history. The story provides important role models for female friendship for Jewish lesbians: committed relationship across the boundaries of age, nationality, and religion; commitment to maintaining familial connections and raising children together. But Alpert goes a step further to ask readers to "read between the lines of the text and imagine Ruth and Naomi to be lovers," because for her "without romantic love and sexuality, the story of Ruth and Naomi loses much of its power as a model for Jewish lesbian relationships" (95). To the critics who feel dis-ease with reading it as a lesbian love story, Alpert retorts that much sexual love between women is hidden from public view. Even though Ruth married Boaz in the end, she might have done so to protect herself and Naomi, for it was difficult for women to survive without male protection in biblical time (95). Alpert issues two challenges in proposing such a reading. The first one is epistemological: can the reader interpret the story without using a patriarchal heterosexual lens? The second one is ethical: can enough room be made for lesbian interpretations of the book of Ruth as a way of welcoming lesbians?

Home as Hospitality for Strangers

In the Jewish tradition, the book of Ruth is read during Shavuot, the Feast of Weeks in May, which is connected with the acceptance of Torah by the children of Israel. During the harvest of late-spring crops, the festival reminds the Jewish people of their covenantal relationship with God. Since they were brought out of the land of Egypt by God, they were exhorted to be merciful to the stranger, the orphan, and the widow among them. In the story, Naomi and Ruth embody all these marginalized qualities and challenge the Jewish world to live up to Torah ideals (Kates and Twersky Reimer: xix). For some commentators, the story exhibits a model of loyal living, in which the care and concern for others are reciprocated. The three major characters—Naomi, Ruth, and Boaz—act in ways that promote the well-being of others, and they are in turn praised in the book (Sakenfeld: 11). The attitude of Boaz is especially contrasted with that of the closest kin. Thus, Boaz protects and takes care of Ruth when she gleans in his field; exhibits moral rectitude and does not take advantage of the young woman at the threshing floor; and agrees to marry Ruth, even though she belongs to an enemy people.

But not all strangers are equally accepted by the people at home. Cynthia Ozick argues that the story offers two examples of strangers—Orpah and Ruth—whose destinies are quite different. Although Orpah might have been more daring than other women by marrying a Jew, she is no iconoclast and chooses to return to her mother's land and her gods (222). For ten years she has been with Naomi's family, but she has not fully absorbed the Hebrew vision (223). When given a chance to return to her homeland, no one would blame her for choosing the normal course, which most people would have taken anyway. On Orpah, Ozick comments: "She is no one's heroine. Her mark is erased from history; there is no Book of Orpah. And yet Orpah *is* history. Or, rather, she is history's great backdrop. She is the majority of humankind living out its usualness on home ground" (221). The real heroine is Ruth, whom Ozick characterizes as a visionary, for she thinks beyond exigency and is willing to commit herself to a monotheistic god. Contrasting Ruth with Orpah, Ozick says: "Ruth leaves Moab because she intends to leave *childish ideas* behind. She is drawn to Israel because Israel is the inheritor of the One Universal Creator" (227; emphasis mine).

Reading the story from a Jewish nationalist perspective, Ozick praises Ruth for her successful assimilation into the Jewish community and her conversion to the God of the Israelites. Her interpretation is criticized by Bonnie Honig, who argues that Ozick has neutralized the differences Ruth the Moabite represents, making her a model emigrée without threatening the identity of the Israelites. Honig notes:

> The contrast between Ruth and Orpah highlights the extraordinariness of Ruth's border crossing, as Ozick points out. But the contrast also has another effect: it suggests that Ruth's migration to Bethlehem does not mean that Israel is now a borderless community open to all foreigners, including even idolatrous Moabites. Israel is open only to the Moabite who is exceptionally virtuous, to Ruth but not Orpah. (55-56)

Honig has called attention to the imagined boundary created by interpreters between the home and strangers, the dangerous alien and the assimilated immigrant, a kinship-style (national) identity and a challenged and contested democracy (74). For her, Ruth's incorporation into the Israelite order is not without complications and ambivalence (60-61). She further argues that Israel, as the chosen people, needs to construct the foreignness of the Other, but that, at the same time, the foreign Ruth also threatens the very definition of the identity of Israel. In the next section, I will turn to some recent discussions that further interrogate the very definition of "home."

Home and Its Discontents

As new paradigms of interpretation emerge, the Bible is not only read for its religious and theological meanings in the context of the development of biblical scholarship but also for its broader cultural impact on shaping the values and norms of society. Mieke Bal, for example, explicitly states that she does not attribute moral, religious, or political authority to the biblical texts, but is interested in the "cultural function of one of the most influential mythical and literary documents" of Western culture (1). Literary critic Cheryl Exum foregrounds the textuality of biblical literature and examines the Ruth-Naomi-Boaz triangle through paintings, Hollywood films, and novels as metatexts. Similarly, Regina Schwartz and Laura Donaldson present two cultural readings that are particularly relevant to the American context: the former, through the lens of the reconfiguration of modern Jewish identity; the latter, from the perspective of the struggle for survival of Native Americans.

Home, Violence, and Identity Formation

Regina Schwartz begins her controversial book, *The Curse of Cain*, by sharing an encounter she had with a student while discussing the Exodus story. To the student's simple question, "What about the Canaanites?," Schwartz replies:

> Yes, what about the Canaanites? and the Amorites, Moabites, Hittites? While the biblical narratives charted the creation, cohesion, and calamities befalling a people at the behest of their God, what about all the other peoples and their gods? Having long seen the Bible put to uses that I could not excuse—hatred of Blacks, Jews, gays, women, "pagan," and the poor—I now began to see some complicity, for over and over the Bible tells the story of a people who inherit at someone else's expense . . . through the dissemination of the Bible in Western culture, its narratives have become the foundation of a prevailing understanding of ethnic, religious, and national identity as defined negatively, over against others. (ix-x)

Schwartz's attempt to reexamine how religious and national identities have been formed through the deployment of covenant, land, kinship, "nation," and memory in the Hebrew Bible has profound cultural and political implications for modern history. The themes of "covenant," "chosen people," and "promised land" have been used repeatedly by the Christian West to justify the colonization of non-Christians and the annihilation of Native peoples of the Americas. But the same belief system also undergirded the rise of modern Zionism and the displacement of Palestinians from their homeland. Schwartz's book emerged from the larger discourse of a critical scrutiny of modern Jewish collective identity. In his Jewish theology of liberation, Marc Ellis insists that Jews should never use the painful memory of Holocaust as a pretext to oppress other people. Along the same vein, Jonathan Boyarin raises the links between Zionism and European nationalism, questions the grounding of Jewish identity in a territory, and challenges the attempt to "escape history by a return to a mythic past" (116-29).

Schwartz makes several bold claims at the outset of her book. She argues that the acts of identity formation are themselves acts of violence, because for her "imagining identity as an act of distinguishing and separating from others, of boundary making and line drawing, is the most frequent and fundamental act of violence we commit" (5). At the center of her interest is how identity is related to monotheism, thus the subtitle of her book, *The Violent Legacy of Monotheism*. She explains: "Monotheism is a myth that grounds particular identity in universal transcendence. And monotheism is a myth that forges identity antithetically—against the Other" (16). But why would identity formation based on a monotheistic God spawn violence? The answer, she claims, is the principle of scarcity, which is also found in the Bible. This principle—encoded as one people, one nation, one land, and ultimately one God—demands exclusive allegiance and threatens with the violence of exclusion. Schwartz finds a paradigmatic account of the "original violence" in the story of Cain and Abel, wherein Cain kills Abel as a result of God's acceptance of the sacrifice of Abel but not his.

With these broad theoretical interests, Schwartz argues that the book of Ruth demonstrates that the principle of scarcity is at work and that kinship is attached to monotheism (90-91). The story associates the foreigner Ruth with the principle of scarcity. During a time of famine in her homeland, she travels with her mother-in-law into the land of Israel and is fed by a generous Israelite who takes care of her and later marries her. Throughout the story, the themes of fertility of the land and human fecundity are interwoven with the threat of famine and barrenness. On the surface, the fact that Ruth is generously treated would seem to suggest the inclusion of a foreigner within the kinship system and a broadening of the vision of monotheism. Upon closer scrutiny, however, one finds that the principle of plenitude and generosity is compromised because Boaz is providing not for a complete stranger but for his kin Naomi and for the continuation of his family line. While Ozick commends Ruth for her conversion to monotheism, Schwartz regards the adoption of the God of Israel as precondition for embracing the foreigner as highly problematic. Ruth's vow, "Your people shall be my people, and your God my God," binds kinship with monotheism by linking a people with one God and excluding other identities.

While Schwartz's reviewers have raised questions concerning the relation between identity formation and violence and the necessary link between monotheism and scarcity (e.g. Brueggemann: 536-37; Volf: 34; Smith, 1999:406-9), I am interested in the reading strategies she proposes to lessen the infliction of violence. First, she persistently demonstrates that in the Bible identity (people, nation, land) is a question and not an answer, provisional and not reified. As such, the Bible cannot be used unambiguously to justify nationalism, imperialism, and the persecution of the Other (142). Second, she does not see the Hebrew Bible as offering a coherent, unified, and developmental history to which Jewish people can unequivocally lay claim. She argues that the preoccupation with collective identity as God's chosen people and chosen nation was colored by German nationalism, which emerged at the same time with the historical-critical method (10-11, 122-23). Following Foucault, she regards history in the Hebrew Bible as a series of discontinuities, ruptures, and incoherences, in which identities need to be remade and reformed. Third, she pays attention to the triad of sex, power, and transcendence. There are many incidents in the Bible where sexual violation begets violence and war (e.g. the rapes of Dinah and the Levite's concubine). Sexual fidelity is related to divine fidelity in the attempt to construct kinship, nationhood, and monotheism (141). Fourth, she draws out contradictory biblical narratives on group identity so as to destabilize the definition of the stranger or the foreigner. She writes: "what I have been exploring here is not a single view of the Other that is somehow 'in the Bible,' but instead pursuing a strategy of reading the Bible that makes any single consistent ideological viewpoint difficult to defend" (103). Fifth, she suggests that, apart from the principle of scarcity, there is also the principle of plenitude and generosity in the Bible, though she does not concretely spell out how this will affect identity formation.

Home, Women's Sexuality, and the Pocahontas Perplex

In certain ways, Laura Donaldson's reading of the book of Ruth complements that of Schwartz. While Schwartz is interested in debunking the identities of kinship, chosen people, and monotheism, Donaldson lifts up the themes of projected sexual stereotypes of the Other and assimilating the Other into the same. Both Schwartz and Donaldson are trained not primarily in the Bible and biblical studies but in English literature and literary criticism and engage a wide range of reading strategies in their works. Donaldson also begins by making some bold claims. She maintains that the Bible has been introduced to Native cultures in the context of a colonizing Christianity and has facilitated culturecide of Native peoples. Yet, she argues that, through the long history of victimization, Native peoples have also read the Bible in their own terms (20-21).

Donaldson's intervention focuses on women's sexuality in the story and interprets it through the lens of the encounter between Native women and European colonizers. Her reading is significantly different from that of Schwartz on this point. Schwartz pays attention to sexual violation, rape, and adultery in the Hebrew Bible because she is interested in the relation between violence and identity formation. In Ruth's story, there is seemingly no sexual violence involved, and the sexual relationship between Ruth and Boaz does not matter much to Schwartz, except that they get married and a son is later born. Donaldson, on the other hand, sees the "voluntary" interethnic marriage as an assimilationist strategy, which has wrecked havoc on her people. Placing women's sexuality beyond the sex/gender framework, Donaldson differentiates herself from those feminist biblical critics who challenge the ideology of home as patriarchal household either by exposing its masculinist and heterosexist bias or by constructing a woman-identified love between Ruth and Naomi (23).

While traditional interpretations emphasize the genealogy of Boaz, David, and Jesus, Donaldson constructs another matrilineal genealogy from Lot's daughters to Rahab and Ruth. The Moabites allegedly are descendants of Lot and his daughters from incestuous encounters (Gen 19) and are excluded from the assembly of the Lord even to the tenth generation (Deut 23:3). Moabite women are portrayed not only as worshipping idols but also as hypersexualized and presenting enormous threats to Israelite men. Such stereotypical images of Moabite women, Donaldson argues, would have fitted the profiles of indigenous women held by European Christians (24). Ruth's other mother-in-law is Rahab, Boaz's Canaanite mother, whose family is spared by Joshua during the fall of Jericho because she has collaborated with the spies. Rahab's destiny foreshadows that of Ruth because "Rahab embodies a foreign woman, a Canaanite Other who crosses over from paganism to monotheism and is rewarded for this act by absorption into the genealogy of her husband and son" (30).

For Donaldson, the narrative figures of Rahab and Ruth are best understood as the Israelite versions of Pocahontas in Native history. In what Cherokee scholar Rayna Green has termed the "Pocahontas Perplex," the beloved daughter of Powhatan saves and falls in love with John Smith, the white colonist in Jamestown, Virginia, thus enabling the settlement of the English pilgrims. The mythology of Pocahontas prescribes that a "good Indian woman" is one who loves and aids white men, while turning her back against her own people and religion. In the biblical stories, Salmon and Boaz stand in for John Smith, and the loyalty of Ruth, the good Moabite, is praised by generations of biblical scholars, while Orpah is scorned as the bad Moabite.

Postcolonial critics have increasingly paid attention to the role sexuality plays in the representation of the Other in colonial discourse. By subjecting the story of Ruth to a sexualized reading, Donaldson helps us to discern more clearly how the representation of otherness is achieved through both sexual and cultural modes of differentiation. This does not simply mean paying attention to how Moabite woman or Moabite sexuality is represented. It also entails deciphering the ways in which representations of the other are interwoven by sexual imageries, unconscious fantasies, desires, as well as fears. As Meyda Yegenoglu has argued, to fully understand the double articulation of colonial discourse, we must explore the "articulation of the historical with fantasy, the cultural with the sexual, and desire with power"(26).

Homi Bhabha, a prominent postcolonial critic, argues that the difference between the colonizers and the colonized is never static or fixed, so that colonial discourse is never closed or unidirectional. In fact, colonial authority is always ambivalent, contested, and conflictual, characterized not only by the manifest power of domination but also by latent dreams, fantasies, myths, and obsessions (1994:71). Using psychoanalytic theory, Lacan's in particular, Bhabha articulates the colonizer's consistent and unconscious need or demand for psychic affirmation. The Pocahontas Perplex belongs to a genre of myths about an indigenous or native woman falling in love with a white man, longing for his return, and even willing to die for him. Other cultural specimens that represent the white male fantasy of sexy Asian woman falling for heroic white man include such figures as Madame Butterfly, Suzie Wong, and Miss Saigon.

Donaldson's reading of the book of Ruth illustrates several useful reading strategies. First, in this example as well as in her book

Decolonizing Feminisms, she insists that gender and sexuality must be examined in the wider contexts of race, class, culture, colonialism, conquest, and slavery. Second, she lifts up the voices that are marginalized in the text and in the history of interpretation. Orpah, who returns to her mother's house, becomes for Donaldson the story's central character, for Orpah does not abandon her mother's house and thus becomes a sign of hope for Native women. Third, she demonstrates that Native people must take response-ability for their own reading and interface the biblical text with their own history and struggles. In this particular case, reading against the grain means conferring positive value to a figure that has been censored in traditional interpretations (Darr: 62). Fourth, the meaning of the text can only be determined with reference to specific cultural and historical contexts. Much of the complexity of interethnic and interreligious encounters in the Bible can be fruitfully interpreted with the help of theories of the contact zone.

Reflection on Method

Several decades ago, when the historical-critical method was the reigning paradigm in the field, biblical scholars belonged to the same tribe, shared the same *habitus*, and read the same genealogy of scholars. Today, biblical scholars belong to many different tribes, and each tribe has its own sources of authority and its own genealogy of founding fathers and mothers. The fact that scholars can construct so many different "homes" for Ruth points to the radical expansion of the field and the diversity of reading interests. The "home" for biblical studies is fixed no more, but is constantly shifting and changing, being remade and recreated.

One important consequence of such a change is that the Bible is seen not only as a religious or historical product but also increasingly as a cultural product. Its interpreters are not limited to those within the faith community or teachers in divinity schools but are likely to include cultural critics coming from many disciplines in the secular university. Their research interests are not so much motivated by the search for religious truths as for cultural meanings promoted and endorsed by the Bible. Unlike the historical critic who traces the meaning of the texts diachronically to their original settings, the cultural critic is more interested in constructing meaning synchronically through reading the Bible with other cultural metatexts. While the former asks what the Bible said to its original audience, the latter asks what the Bible is saying to our contemporary situation. Since both the Bible and the contemporary contexts can be read in so many different ways, the issues of the ethics and accountability of interpretation are brought to the forefront. As Elisabeth Schüssler

Fiorenza stated in her 1987 presidential address to the Society of Biblical Literature:

> If the Bible has become a classic of western culture because of its normativity, then the responsibility of the biblical scholar cannot be restricted to giving "the readers of our time clear access to the original intentions" of biblical writers. It must also include the elucidation of the ethical consequences and political functions of biblical texts and their interpretations in their historical as well as in their contemporary context. (28)

Both Regina Schwartz and Laura Donaldson raise critical questions regarding the political functions of biblical texts and trace the problem not only to its history of interpretation but to the text itself.

As a Jew, Schwartz challenges the ways in which the Hebrew Bible has been read for millennia as a book defining the special identity of Jews as God's chosen people and Israel as the chosen nation. She notes that during the exile, when Jews lost their homeland and their temple, the memory of the Exodus and of Israel as the chosen people became paramount in defining their identity. After the Holocaust, many Jews linked their identity to a specific territory and evoked the memory of the past in justifying the establishment of the nation of Israel. Schwartz takes upon herself the responsibility of interpreting the Hebrew texts so that they will not perpetuate the violent ways that national, ethnic, and religious boundaries have been drawn. Thus, she argues for a diasporic understanding of Jewish identity that is fluid, destabilized, and open to negotiation in specific circumstances. Schwartz's iconoclastic reading puts her at odds with much rabbinic teaching and modern Jewish politics. She says: "Freud's courage to write his *Moses and Monotheism* in the midst of Nazi persecution gave me strength to criticize the biblical legacy despite a continuing tragic climate of antisemitism" (xiv).

In her postcolonial and Native reading, Laura Donaldson calls our attention to how the Christian West has appropriated the Jewish text and used it against the indigenous and colonized peoples. Instead of reading the text from a Jewish perspective, she is compelled to reexamine the relationship between Israel and her neighbors and to interpret the text from a Moabite perspective. She debunks the triumphant Christian claim that Christians have replaced the Jews as the chosen people of God and are entrusted with the "civilizing mission" of the world. She writes: "I can only hope that my indigenization of Ruth has located new meaning in the interaction between biblical text and American Indian context—a meaning that resists imperial exegesis and contributes to the empowerment of aboriginal peoples everywhere" (36).

In the postcolonial era, when many of the world's boundaries are being remade and redrawn, Schwartz and Donaldson challenge us to read the Bible not from the cozy "home" of traditional Jewish or Christian interpretations but from the experiences of those whose lives have been marginalized and oppressed by the Bible.

In conclusion, as we search for new ways of interpreting the Bible for the contemporary world, it is important to pay attention to critical and prophetic scholarship, often coming from marginalized communities in our society. As biblical scholars and theologians, entrusted with the task of interpreting and transmitting the tradition, it is imperative for us to recognize the violent legacy of biblical interpretation in the past and in the present. The Bible has fueled such beliefs as the "heavenly kingdom in America," the "manifest destiny" of the United States, and the "one country, under God" of the national motto. Since the United States has become the single superpower in the world, it is significant to look for ways to read the Bible that will help us to destabilize all hegemonic claims and that will make room for others to share the planet as their "home."

Works Consulted

Alpert, Rebecca
    1994   "Finding Our Past: A Lesbian Interpretation of the Book of Ruth."
           Pp. 91-96 in Kates and Twersky Reimer.
Althaus-Reid, Marcella María
    1999   "On Wearing Skirts without Underwear: 'Indecent Theology
           Challenging the Liberation Theology of the Pueblo': Poor Women
           Contesting Christ." *Feminist Theology* 20:39-51.
Bal, Mieke
    1987   *Lethal Love: Feminist Literary Readings of Biblical Love Stories.*
           Bloomington: Indiana University Press.
Berquist, Jon L.
    1993   "Role Dedifferentiation in the Book of Ruth." *JSOT* 57:23-37.
Bhabha, Homi
    1992   "The World and the Home." *Social Text* 31/32:141-53.
    1994   *The Location of Culture.* London: Routledge.
Boyarin, Jonathan
    1992   *Storm from Paradise: The Politics of Jewish Memory.* Minneapolis:
           University of Minnesota Press.

Brueggemann, Walter
   1998   "The Curse of Cain: The Violent Legacy of Monotheism."
          Theology Today 54:534-37.
Chu, Julie L. C.
   1997   "Returning Home: The Inspiration of the Role Dedifferentiation in
          the Book of Ruth for Taiwanese Women." *Semeia* 78:47-53.
Darr, Katheryn Pfisterer
   1991   *Far More Precious than Jewels: Perspectives on Biblical Women.*
          Louisville: Westminster/John Knox.
Donaldson, Laura E.
   1992   *Decolonizing Feminisms: Race, Gender, and Empire-Building.*
          Chapel Hill: University of North Carolina Press.
   1999   "The Sign of Orpah: Reading Ruth through Native Eyes." Pp. 20-
          36 in *Vernacular Hermeneutics*. Ed. R. S. Sugirtharajah. Sheffield:
          Sheffield Academic Press.
Ellis, Marc H.
   1989   *Toward a Jewish Theology of Liberation: The Uprising and the
          Future.* Maryknoll: Orbis Books.
Exum, J. Cheryl
   1996   *Plotted, Shot, and Painted: Cultural Representations of Biblical
          Women.* Sheffield: Sheffield Academic Press.
Fuchs, Esther
   1989   "The Literary Characterization of Mothers and Sexual Politics in
          the Hebrew Bible." *Semeia* 46:151-66.
George, Rosemary Marangoly
   1996   *The Politics of Home: Postcolonial Relocations and Twentieth-
          Century Fiction.* Cambridge: Cambridge University Press.
Honig, Bonnie
   1999   "Ruth, the Model Emigrée: Mourning and the Symbolic Politics of
          Immigration." Pp. 50-74 in *Ruth and Esther: A Feminist
          Companion to the Bible.* Second series. Ed. Athalya Brenner.
          Sheffield: Sheffield Academic Press.
Jobling, David
   1993   "Ruth Finds a Home: Canon, Politics, Method." Pp. 125-39 in *The
          New Literary Criticism and the Hebrew Bible*. Ed. J. Cheryl Exum
          and David J. A. Clines. Sheffield: JSOT Press.
Kates, Judith A. and Gail Twersky Reimer, eds.
   1994   *Reading Ruth: Contemporary Women Reclaim a Sacred Story.* New
          York: Ballantine Books.
Landy, Francis
   1994   "Ruth and the Romance of Realism, or Deconstructing History."
          JAAR 62:285-317.
Levine, Amy-Jill
   1992   "Ruth." Pp. 78-84 in *The Women's Bible Commentary*. Ed. Carol A.
          Newsom and Sharon H. Ringe. Louisville: Westminster/John Knox.

Nielsen, Kirsten
 1997 *Ruth: A Commentary*. Louisville: Westminster/John Knox.
Ozick, Cynthia
 1994 "Ruth." Pp. 211-32 in Kates and Twersky Reimer.
Putnam, Ruth Anna
 1994 "Friendship." Pp. 44-54 in Kates and Twersky Reimer.
Sagar, Aparajita
 1997 "Homes and Postcoloniality." *Diaspora* 6:237-51.
Sakenfeld, Katherine Doob
 1998 *Ruth*. Louisville: John Knox.
Schüssler Fiorenza, Elisabeth
 1999 *Rhetoric and Ethic: The Politics of Biblical Studies*. Minneapolis:
    Fortress Press.
Schwartz, Regina M.
 1997 *The Curse of Cain: The Violent Legacy of Monotheism*. Chicago:
    University of Chicago Press.
Segovia, Fernando F.
 1998 "Introduction: Pedagogical Discourse and Practices in
    Contemporary Biblical Criticism." Pp. 1-28 in *Teaching the Bible:
    The Discourses and Politics of Biblical Pedagogy*. Ed. Fernando F.
    Segovia and Mary Ann Tolbert. Maryknoll: Orbis Books.
Smith, Brian K.
 1999 "Monotheism and Its Discontents: Religious Violence and the
    Bible." *JAAR* 66:403-11.
Smith, Wilfred Cantwell
 1993 *What Is Scripture? A Comparative Approach*. Minneapolis:
    Fortress Press.
Torn, Susan Reimer
 1994 "Ruth Reconsidered." Pp. 336-46 in Kates and Twersky Reimer.
Trible, Phyllis
 1978 *God and the Rhetoric of Sexuality*. Philadelphia: Fortress Press.
Van Dijk-Hemmes, Fokkelien
 1993 "Ruth: A Product of Women's Culture?" Pp. 134-39 in *Ruth and
    Esther: A Feminist Companion to the Bible*. Second series. Ed.
    Athalya Brenner. Sheffield: Sheffield Academic Press.
Van Wolde, Ellen
 1997 "Texts in Dialogue with Texts: Intertextuality in the Ruth and
    Tamar Narratives." *Biblical Interpretation* 5:1-28.
Volf, Miroslav
 1998 "Jehovah on Trial." *Christianity Today* 27 (April): 32-35.
Yegenoglu, Meyda
 1998 *Colonial Fantasies: Towards a Feminist Reading of Orientalism*.
    Cambridge: Cambridge University Press.

8

Bible Translation and Ethnic Mobilization in Africa

Lamin Sanneh

Introduction: Race and Ethnicity in History

In an article entitled "The Diversity Myth: America's Leading Export," Benjamin Schwartz, a historian and foreign policy analyst, speaks of ethnicity as the "diversity myth" framing America's perception of and prescription for the world. Although a distortion and an oversimplification, this ethnic myth, he adds, constitutes "America's leading export." However, the immigrant populations that flocked into the United States, he points out, were subjected to a cultural process which did not so much cleanse America of its ethnic minorities as cleanse those minorities of their ethnicity. Thus, he argues, the American melting pot "celebrated not tolerance but conformity to a narrow conception of American nationality by depicting strangely attired foreigners stepping into a huge pot and emerging as immaculate, well-dressed, accent-free 'American-looking' Americans—that is, Anglo-Americans. Sinclair Lewis recognized the melting pot, in *Main Street*, as a means by which 'the sound American customs absorbed without one trace of pollution another alien invasion'" (62).

Schwartz cites a variety of testimonies to this effect. In 1786 John Jay, one of the Founding Fathers, wrote in his second *Federalist* paper that "Providence has been pleased to give this one connected country to one united people; a people descended from the same ancestors, speaking the same language, professing the same religion . . . similar in their manners and customs" (62). In 1916, the liberal writer Randolph Bourne reflected in a similar manner on what makes America unique: "English snobberies, English religion, English literary styles, English literary reverences and canons, English ethics, English superiorities" (62)—these are what held America together, a cultural tutelage that made mashed potatoes of non-Anglo ethnic groups. A popular guide for Jewish immigrants advised them to "forget your past, your customs, and your ideals" (62). In America, therefore, ethnicity was domesticated rather than celebrated.

155

When America as a new nation confronted the issue of ethnic and national difference—the issue, that is, of Native Americans and of national communities belonging to Britain, Spain, and France—it adopted a policy of forcible assimilation. Thus were created present-day Texas, California, New Mexico, Arizona, Nevada, Utah, and parts of Colorado and Wyoming. Schwartz contends that America was involved in a three-hundred-year-long ethnic conflict with Native Americans in which one of two solutions was acceptable: extinction of the native races or permanent quarantine in native reserves. Thus, for example, in 1830 Richard Wilde, a congressman from Georgia, declared concerning the destruction of Native Americans, "What is history but the obituary of nations?" (64).

All this historical evidence serves as indispensable background for understanding the force of ethnicity and what came to transpire in the radical transformation of Christianity in Africa. Africa was colonized on the basis of race theory—in particular, of white hegemony. Although Africans, in contrast to whites, as Hannah Arendt pointed out, "do have a genuine race origin, they have made no fetish of race, and the abolition of race society [in South Africa] means only the promise of their liberation" (205). When used of Africans, "race" and "tribe" carry the meaning of a people without history or a knowledge of history. These terms, however, are not self-applied designations: they have been imposed upon Africans in all of their dense meaning. They entail the cultural meaning of a people with no historical record—specimens of nature unrefined by discipline, struggle, and self-control, and thus incapable of logical thinking or polite behavior.

Such terms also refer to geographical regions where nature is particularly hostile, as reflected in the wild habits of the natives. Cribbed and confined by nature, the natives lost out in that struggle out of which, and only out of which, a specifically human character and a moral temper could develop. Instead, the natives perceived nature as their enchanted master and abandoned themselves to its mindless gyrations and mystifying impenetrability with awe and incomprehension. Such was the view of Hugh Trevor-Roper, at that time the Regius Professor of Modern History at Oxford University.[1] In a widely quoted remark, he insisted that there was no African history properly speaking, because, "there is only the history of Europeans in Africa. The rest is darkness . . . and darkness is not a subject of history." "Please do not misunderstand me," he pleaded, "I do not deny that men existed even in dark countries and dark centuries, nor

---

[1] As reported in *The Listener* (a BBC publication), 28 November 1963. The occasion was a series of BBC television lectures on the topic, "The Rise of Christian Europe," delivered at the University of Sussex. All the citations that follow are taken therefrom.

that they had political life and culture, interesting to sociologists and anthropologists; but history, I believe, is essentially a form of movement, and purposive movement too. It is not a mere phantasmagoria of changing shapes and costumes, of battles and conquests, dynasties and usurpations, social forms and social disintegration." Trevor-Roper cast his remarks in a global frame, contending that "The history of the world, for the last five centuries, in so far as it has significance, has been European history." As such, he concluded, Western scholars cannot afford to "amuse ourselves with the unrewarding gyrations of barbarous tribes in picturesque but irrelevant corners of the globe."

Consequently, lacking the intelligence and purpose denoted by a historical sense, Africans were classified under the categories of "race" and "tribe" and given an objective status in anthropology. Such classification acquired economic meaning: Africans were "drawers of water and hewers of wood." Subsequently, the political idea of domination and control merged all these meanings with the argument that the white race had attained through struggle the progress that separates human beings from nature, and so selected race inheritance established the hereditary genius of whites vis-à-vis non-white peoples. Thus, in the nineteenth century "race" was employed by writers such as J. A. Froude, in his *Short Studies on Great Subjects* (1867-1882), Charles Dilke, in his *Greater Britain* (1869), J. R. Seeley, in his best-selling *Expansion of England* (1883), and Cecil Rhodes, the arch-imperialist, as a political symbol of white power and black subordination. Symbols are anchored in what one holds to be true, in values, and as such are liable to change and shift, depending on circumstances and context. Thus, in the high imperial era—say, between 1890 and 1940—aspiring blacks would compete for the attributes of white power, knowing it was the only way to advancement and status, and in that competition they were sometimes among the staunchest defenders of a race society.

On this reading, Africa was afflicted with a double jeopardy. It served as an outpost of Europe's mastery, exploitation, and world domination, and, while thus repressed, it was held to standards of freedom and progress it had lost under European hegemony. The central question became whether, given the extent of Africa's absorption into the Western political scheme, concepts such as ethnicity, plural languages and dialects, and tribal fragmentation held in check under foreign overlordship, left any room for African initiative, for a distinctly African solution to emerge.

Ethnicity and the Modern Missionary Movement

Through the modern missionary movement, Africa was ironically offered a chance to answer the intellectual assault of the West, insofar as the same missionary movement that identified itself with colonialism and its agenda of modernization (schools, modern clinics and architecture, scientific agriculture, the emancipation of women, a bureaucratic state, town planning, and modern means of transportation and communication) also identified itself with indigenous societies by fostering the use of mother tongues in Bible translation and literacy. Many European and American writers followed a variation of Trevor-Roper's argument regarding the history of Africa as the history of Europeans in Africa by insisting that in instituting mother tongue development and literacy, missionaries were actually extending European hegemony over oral cultures, with the superior technology of writing and systematic documentation overrunning the backward values of oral tradition. Besides, it is argued, missionary motives were in any case suspect, both hostile to native cultures and bigoted in doctrine. Consequently, any work or interest in African languages represented unwarranted interference.

This is neither the place nor the time to pick through this line of reasoning, so provocatively stated by Trevor-Roper. Suffice it to say that such argumentation oversimplifies a complex theme and overlooks the point of the ability of so-called native victims to turn to their own benefit the things to which Europeans had introduced them, including mother tongue literacy, a development for which European motives could be discounted. Furthermore, African societies, insofar as they were living societies, were no more immune to change than other societies; to condemn them to lost authenticity as a result of their encounter with Europeans, therefore, seems particularly harsh, and without ground. Africans are not like children, fixed for life from the first white impressions. Thus, one does not have to deny the presence of Europeans in Africa to believe that African history abides by its own internal logic, that African agency is authentic, that African themes are original, and that an African outlook on life shapes people's historical and moral consciousness. I make those and similar assumptions in my work generally, and I do so here specifically.

Let me present the subject in this way. The missionary sponsorship of Bible translation became the catalyst for profound changes and developments in language, culture, and ethnicity—changes that invested ethnic identity with the materials for a reawakened sense of local identity. It is this claim that I should like to expand upon in what follows by way of historical and theological materials.

In approaching Africa through the fruits of European science and literature, the West was dealing with a version of its own identity, with what was recognizable and acceptable in terms of the West's ascendant values. African doctors, nurses, clerks, lawyers, mechanics, engineers, teachers, and factory workers were, as such, agents and mediators of Western medicine, law, engineering, education, and manufacture. Therefore, as long as Europeans were willing to accept Africans as equals, Africans would be allowed to compete on Western terms. Professor Diedrich Westermann of Berlin has observed in this regard, "It is fortunate that the Africans are patient and intelligent enough to meet these requirements: in the case of Togo and part of Kamerun (sic), the Natives had, within one generation, first to learn English, then German and now French" (1925:31). There would come a time, however, when such equality would be denied and those Africans who had gained their qualifications in those more favorable times would find that they had become the victims of affirmative action of the quota kind: senior level jobs would be taken and reserved for whites without regard to qualification. Africans were restricted to subordinate positions and kept in their place by virtue of their race, not because they were unqualified. The race policy of the colonial empire was one of the most wholehearted preferential quota programs ever undertaken in history, and it was blacks who paid the price for it.[2] Much of this policy was motivated by benign paternalism—the attitude that, as members of an inferior race, Africans needed to be placed under white oversight and grudgingly given promotion on the scale of civilization. Such was the white man's burden, to recall Rudyard Kipling's memorable phrase, the responsibility that destiny had placed on superior races everywhere.

The racism of apartheid is very different from this race policy, but only in degree, not in kind. Separate development is the answer to uppity black pretensions that spatial proximity with whites was apt to encourage. As long as Europe remained physically separate from Africa, there would be no need to introduce separate-but-equal policies. However, once Europe and Africa shared a common physical space, as happened with white-settler communities in North, East, Central, and Southern Africa, then race and ethnicity became tools of political and administrative policy. Thus, the categories of "race" and "ethnicity," "folk" and "tribe," were constructed to capture and distribute dislocated Africans, to entrap unsuspecting hinterland populations, and to punish the recalcitrant among mission-educated natives for being inclined to step outside their place in the scheme of things. There is little debate that Western

---

[2] Hannah Arendt states that the Boers in colonial South Africa discovered that British colonialism was not detrimental to their interests, and so "they demanded and were granted charity as the right of a white skin, having lost all consciousness that normally men do not earn a living by the color of their skin" (194). Within that framework, Africans passed from slavery to hired cheap labor, the dumping ground of mine and urban reservations.

missions in general aligned themselves accordingly on this political faultline, adding, for example, to the drama of race politics in Zimbabwe and South Africa the moral passion of a Manichean duel between good and evil, light and darkness, the messengers of God and the dupes of the devil, medical and development experts, and the incubus and succubus of witchcraft. Similarly, it was in this spirit that the French *mission civilisatrice* was launched in order to level the *native feudalities* and to abolish ethnic wisdom.

Bible Translation and the Ethnic Cause

The exception, at least in unintended consequences if not in deliberate design, to this wholesale Western assault on the Africa of ethnic classification was the launching of mother tongue projects of Bible translation. Such projects shifted the ground to a view of African languages as things of native origin, for which Africans had only God and the ancestors to thank, not the whites who had given such languages written form. In retrospect, it is hard for us to imagine what might have happened to Africans, and to the dark races in general, had Europeans gone through, as the master race, with the grim logic of domination and control to which they felt entitled by virtue of their technology and power. One should remember, for example, that the invention of the science of eugenics, of genetics as social policy, coincided with Europe's complete mastery of the non-white races. One should further remember that, through the writings of Madison Grant, America promoted race theory. However, two important forces intervened to avert universal ethnic genocide. One was the growth and influence in the eighteenth century of the evangelical and humanitarian movement in Europe (in Scandinavia, France, and Britain especially), a movement that spawned the antislavery movement; the other was the contemporary missionary movement, if not in rhetoric and ideology, certainly in its field policy of mother tongue development.

Accordingly, in the language projects of modern missions, Europe confronted the native character of non-Western races in its irreducible profundity, in its core self-understanding, rather than as space to be filled with European speech forms and habits only. In that confrontation only two responses were possible for Europeans. The first was to say that blacks were too different from Europeans to belong to the same category of *homo sapiens* and may accordingly be excluded from the privilege of membership in civilized company. The second was to say that, given this difference as a mark of human diversity, there was no basis for saying that one race was superior or inferior to another, but only that the human condition was deeply marked by variety and difference, as Herbert Spencer maintained, and that, given the uncontrived nature of the ethnic spirit, Africans might possess by that fact an advantage for the Gospel that Europe had chosen to abandon. Both attitudes were prevalent, although the second was much truer to the facts and more attuned to field experience than the first. Consequently, the tribes and ethnic groups of Africa came to be furnished with the necessary cultural and linguistic apparatus for mother tongue development, a development which gave them confidence not only in who they were but also in their reason for being.

I have argued in *Translating the Message* that the "central and enduring character of Christian history is the rendering of God's eternal counsels into terms of everyday speech. By that path believers have come to stand before their God" (1989:frontispiece). Bible translation has marked the history of Christianity from its very origins: the gospels are a translated version of the preaching and message of Jesus, and the epistles a further interpretation and application of that preaching and message. Christianity is unique in being promoted outside the language of the founder of the religion. Having abandoned the mother tongue of Jesus, Christians were freed to promote a Gentile religion, the religion of the uncircumcised and the non-Chosen People. Consequently, Christianity through Bible translation offered to the world a genuine share in the heritage of Jesus, however inferior in cultural attainment ethnic groups might be or might be deemed to be. Similarly, with regard to those languages and cultures that had attained the highest levels of civilization and thus transcended tribal life, Christianity by virtue of its open policy on Bible translation would not surrender to them as an exclusive right the heritage of Jesus.

In Bible translation hitherto taboo ethnic groups, along with their languages and cultures, were effectively destigmatized, while at the same time warlike cultures that preyed on their neighbors as a natural right were stripped of their right to constitute themselves into exclusive standards of access to God. In affirming weak and stigmatized languages and cultures, Bible translation bade farewell to Western cultural prerequisites for membership in the human family. Bible translation breathed new life into local languages and equipped local populations for participation in the emerging world order. This was a result of the fact that Bible translation was based on the idea that all languages were equal in terms of their value and right in mediating the truth of God but, by the same token, equally inadequate in relation to that truth. No one language could claim exclusive prerogative on the truth of God, just as conversely no one language was intrinsically unworthy to be a language of faith and devotion.[3] The message of God and the language of ordinary human communication shared the same moral universe, although no human language, however exalted or in any combination, was identical completely with that message. The quest for divine meaning was not exhausted by any one historical approximation, even though historical approximations were inseparable from the reception of God's message.

To reinforce this point, Bible translation looked to the common forms of local expression in all their rich diversity and paradox and, by a devoted study and use of the diverse languages of the world, enfranchised the ordinary people who utilized those forms rather than those with a vested interest in elitist culture. There were deepening repercussions for the affected societies and cultures. Where it happened, such indigenous social and cultural revival often set off mass social change.

Thus it was that indigenous religious and cultural categories received validation by their adoption in translation. In few fields was this principle more important than in the matter of adopting the names of what were essentially ethnic deities as the God of Scripture, for in those names were contained not only the religious worldview but also rules of property, social structure, and personal identity. Almost everywhere in the mission field, missionaries and local agents had to confront three fundamental questions: (1) How else can we transmit the faith except in the language and experience of the ethnic groups to whom the message is being brought? (2) How may such ethnic groups connect with the message unless there is in the message itself a point of contact? (3) Finally, how best can we ascertain that contact point except through systematic attention to ethnic specificity as revealed in language usage and culture? Even for those missionaries who confined themselves deliberately to the development and technical side of mission, it was impossible to escape entirely the repercussions of theological engagement with the local communities in which they lived. Indeed, the striking mark of Christianity in its mission was its confidence that, since God had spoken to us all, all human speech in its concrete ethnic diversity was hallowed for our ordinary and consecrated use. As a result, missionaries plunged into hitherto neglected lan-

---

[3] Such a favorable view of indigenous languages was not universally shared. Saul Bellow's famous attack on African languages as unworthy of great literary merit is a case in point. Some ethnographers expressed similar sentiments; see, for example, E. F. Sayers, who wrote of one Sierra Leonean language as follows: "Limba is a very fourth-rate language in which, so far as my experience goes, it is almost impossible to get any fine shades of meaning expressed" (113). In contrast, speaking of vernacular Bible translation, Westermann remarks: "No African languages have hitherto been found into which the Bible could not be translated" (1925:28).

guages and cultures to engage their immense potential for the message and
to bring that potential into public harmony with the values of choice and
ethnic fulfillment. Through mother tongue translation, Christianity would
crystallize not into a cultural confectionery as such but rather into a power
that would make God sound as sweet music to ethnic ears.[4] As such, mother tongue translation conformed to the insight of the incarnation: divinity
is not a human loan word; rather, humanity is the chosen language of
divine self-expression. God—who for the tribes was imageless, ineffable,
and speechless breath—became for Christians the one whose utterance in
the word-made-flesh gave humble tongues native dignity.

Diedrich Westermann, a former missionary to Africa himself, has
well expressed the general principle of Christianity's success as ethnic
fulfillment rather than ethnic self-rejection. In each people, he argues,
mental life has evolved to produce an individual shape and a proper mode
of expression. In so doing, Westermann provides a striking illustration of
what today we would call "inculturation":

> In this sense we speak of the soul of a people, and the most immedi-
> ate, the most adequate exponent of the soul of a people is its lan-
> guage. By taking away a people's language we cripple or destroy its
> soul and kill its mental individuality . . .We do not want Christianity
> to appear in the eyes of the Natives as the religion of the white man,
> and the opinion to prevail that the African must become a pseudo-
> European in order to become a Christian, but we want to implant the
> Gospel deep into the soil of the African mind, so that it may grow
> there in its own African form, not as a gift of the white man but as
> the gift of God. . . . If this is to be effected, the Gospel and the whole
> Christian education must take root in the mother soil of the vernacu-
> lar. Only in this way will it enter into the African mind and become
> the medium of a new life—not of new forms of life—and of a regen-
> eration of the people's soul. . . . If the Christian Church in Africa is
> to be really African and really Christian, it must be built upon the
> basis of the indigenous peculiarities and gifts of the people, it must
> become part of the African genius, and these will for ever be embed-
> ded in the mother language. A people without a language and a tra-
> dition of its own is individually dead, it has become part of a mass
> instead of being a living personality. . . . If the African is to keep and
> develop his own soul and is to become a separate personality, his
> education must not begin by inoculating him with a foreign civiliza-
> tion, but it must implant respect for the indigenous racial life, it must
> teach him to love his country and tribe as gifts given by God which

---

[4] In the preface to his Zulu dictionary, R. C. A. Samuelson, the interpreter to King
Cetywayo, affirms, "it is the mother-tongue which is sweet" (xxxviii).

are to be purified and brought to full growth by the new divine life. One of these gifts is the vernacular, it is the vessel in which the whole national life is contained and through which it finds expression (1925:26-28)

The Theological Dimension: Domesticating the Transcendent

The field dimension of Bible translation came to grips with this language issue and, in so doing, activated a profound religious process in African societies. James Green, the Church Missionary Society agent in South Africa, wrote that the issue concerning the word to be used by the church to instruct the Zulu about God the Creator belonged directly to the task of theology (Green). He did not wish to minimize questions of philology and other technical features of language work, but he was convinced that, at the heart of the enterprise, lay the theological question: Has God been known to the Zulu in former times, and, if so, how can we ascertain that? To answer that question, the only reasonable course of action was to embrace the terms that the Zulu, in God's own providence, had been accustomed to employ. This Zulu frame would shape what missionaries brought, or thought they were bringing, for, in the Zulu way of receiving the message, missionaries would awaken to the God who had preceded them among the Zulu. That was the first order of business. It was a necessary step. It had to be taken, and it was taken willingly and without delay.

In taking that step, however, missionaries committed themselves to a further step as well: the natural developments in the Zulu worldview that Christian translation would have stimulated belonged with Zulu self-understanding and lay, therefore, well beyond the power of the missionaries to control. This additional step many missionaries were unwilling to take, or allow to be taken, although there was little they could do to stop it. Green saw the problem clearly and moved courageously to confront it. He spoke of the phases of God's instruction of the human race:

> God revealed Himself to men by degrees; adding to that knowledge, from time to time, as they were able to receive the increase. We find, in addition, that God, in His ineffable love, when He began to raise fallen man to dwell in His Presence, humbled Himself to the level of man's ignorance, as witness the wording of the First Commandment. Those words, *'Thou shalt have none other gods but Me,'* would be received by those on whose ears they first fell, as admitting that there were other gods besides the Lord, God of Abraham, and of Isaac, and of Jacob. (4-5)

By seeking to penetrate ethnic cultures and societies with the message of the Bible, translators faced the paradox of needing to reconcile opposites. Green, facing the issue, insisted, "we must look into the heart and mind of the Zulu, ascertain the principal features in his character, and denote God in the Zulu tongue by a word related to that distinguishing characteristic" (24). For Green, the task was not to have the Africans embrace the principles of scientific rationality, since, as colonial administrators insisted, that was beyond the power of the "natives." Bible translation proceeded, therefore, without commentaries, dictionaries, and lexicons—the fruits of the Western intellectual tradition. In the process, ironically, African societies were shielded spiritually from the West. The exception was theological training, which affected the relatively few Africans educated in the Western tradition of commentaries, exegesis, and systematic thought. Yet, even such Africans had to deal with the mass of Christian Africans weaned on mother tongue Scripture.

Scriptural translation thus enabled ethnic empowerment, such as the discovery of Zulu ways of thought and patterns of life as the functioning frame for Christianity. Mother tongue fluency became a justification for communicating the message, for "the law which holds the earth in its orbit and regulates the fall of a pin, is the same law which has directed the Greek to call God *theos* [and] has guided the Zulu to speak of Him as *Unkulunkulu*. And that law we must accept with its consequences" (41). As a result, Bible translation advanced the empowerment of mother tongue agents.

A corresponding double effect attended the work of missionaries themselves. By translating the Bible into the mother tongue, missionaries, with the assistance and leadership of local language experts, learnt the vernacular and so made the strategic shift from the familiar Western idiom to a totally new system. Thus, Bible translation in its consequences affected ethnic sensibility, giving it material expression, moral affirmation, and a historical vocation,[5] even if it mediated at the same time the spread of European cultural ideas. In so many places in Africa—from the Ashanti of Ghana, the Kaka of Cameroon, and the Gikuyu of Kenya, to

---

[5] In this regard, see Westermann (1949:124):

The missions have realized from the beginning that if they wanted to reach the heart of the Africans and to influence their inner life, they could do so only through the medium of their own language, and they have kept to this principle; even where a considerable section of the people know a European language, Church work is with rare exceptions done in the vernacular, and it is characteristic that most African books and periodicals deal with religious subjects. Only in this way was it possible and will it be possible in the future to build up an indigenous African Church.

the Ndebele and Shona of Zimbabwe and the Zulu of South Africa—we find in Bible translation work this ethnic theme taken up, not as a cruel design to foment inter-tribal bigotry but as a critical historical effort to reclaim and refocus the race instinct. Thus, David Barrett, in his *Schism and Renewal in Africa*, described the many examples of Bible translation work and fellowship helping to break down inter-ethnic barriers and overcome the cumulative residue of tribal grudge. This is a theme to which John Taylor gave theological voice in his suggestive book, *The Primal Vision*. Yet, it is curious to see how historians continue to be dominated by the rubrics of ethnicity and tribe from European race theory. In fact, such concepts are colonial and missionary constructions, examples of negative agency: primitive tribes as afflicted by endemic malice toward one another and thus in need of the intervening hands of Europeans to tame and civilize them. In their status as subjects of primitive and backward customs, the tribes represent an invention of the European imagination, set up to meet the demands of colonial control and domination. The history and scholarship of Africa became thereby a question of superimposition and capture. Typical of such imaginative construction is the use of dialogue passages in European writings to represent the natives as speaking in defective "dialects" because of their inability to understand language. Such representation proved so powerful that even today people continue to refer to African languages as tribal "dialects." Edward Said expounds on this issue in his *Orientalism*.

The projects of vernacular Bible translation departed radically from this tribal and ethnic redefinition of Africans. The notions of ethnicity and language received a completely different understanding. On the face of it, missions did impose a written form on oral cultures and thereby interfered with internal morphological processes; at the same time, mother tongue literacy freed up mother tongue reserves for creative adaptation, as Albert Gérard has shown. Similarly, ethnic identity was reclaimed by the meaningful step of recognizing that the "genealogies in the Gospel linking Christ himself with the unnumbered myriad of the [ancestors] are a symbol of the unbroken cord with which God will finally draw Adam back to Paradise" (Taylor: 171). Students of culture may profit from understanding the theological nature of the missionary engagement with non-Western cultures, because, in their systematic and successful cultivation of the mother tongue for translating the Scriptures, missionaries embraced living cultures for their human and religious potential.

In this respect, James Green was convinced that, in looking for the right Zulu concept to adopt for God, missionaries should resist their own scholastic bias, reject abstract terms and imported ideas, and settle instead on those terms that have within them the idea of personality. (Let me, in parenthesis, refer to Steve Bevans's exceptionally well done study of John Oman, the Cambridge theologian, who wrote on this theme of the personal God.) Our conception of God as infinite, unconditioned, and absolute, though justified, Green demanded, should not be allowed to obfuscate the idea of personality in Scripture. Biblical theology, Green insisted, warranted our having the paradox of these two contrasting conceptions of God—the paradox of God as both unconditioned infinity and personal deity. True knowledge of God demanded the concurrent validity of these two apparently contradictory ideas, so that what in strict logic could not be predicated of God as Spirit and Architect became, in the reality of religious life, a necessity. The scholastic tenor of the question, "Did human beings first believe in an infinite deity and then, by faith, ascribe to such a deity personality, or did human beings first know God as the personal God and then go on to acknowledge His infinity?," was resolved by the historical nature of Biblical faith. In other words, the whole debate in evolutionary anthropology about whether monotheism or polytheism was the first or final stage of religious development is not as illuminating as the discovery of the concrete terms by which the first dim awareness of God was signaled to people, whether in Africa or among the ancient Hebrews. And we have, Green continued, the warrant of the Bible for this view, because in it the divine is revealed as a person, not just as an idea.

The question whether, in using personal attributes for God, we have not incurred too great a risk for any reasonable and proper notion of God's infinity is really, at heart, a religious question. In other words, it was the awe of the religious mind that prompted it to veer towards a sense of human inadequacy before divine transcendence—the human inability, for example, of uniting infinity with personhood, of reconciling an incomprehensible transcendence with the human celebration of a personal God. Modern philosophy, Green objected, took infinity as a principle of speculative thought and in so doing sundered it from its religious roots in order to claim it as the perfection and crown of the system of human cognition. Thus, the philosophy of religion ended, as it began, in rootless speculation, speaking to the elite few of an abstraction rather than to flesh-and-blood humanity of a progressive relationship founded on divine instruction. Consequently, if we started from the religious roots of knowledge, we should see that the impulse to understanding is grounded in the encounter with a personal God, a God who has spoken and acted and a God who, as the source of living and meaning, is graciously available to us in the habits and languages of human community, in ethnic particularity if you will. In philosophy it is the accepted custom to speak of God as the Supreme Being; in religion, as the living God. As long as we keep close to the soil, we would not split God between an abstract form and a personal deity. Such was the spirit in which Green and his missionary colleagues approached their work.

In the mission field this split, which has been such a fateful mark of modern Western thought, was not made, or, at least, not made with the same effect.[6] Green (10) cited a remark on this point, to the effect that,

> All ancient religion, as distinguished from the primitive, laboured under the total inability of even conceiving the idea of the *worship of God.* It split and went to pieces upon that rock; acknowledging, in a speculative sense, one God, but not applying worship to Him. The local, the limited, the finite, was, as such, an object of worship; the Infinite, as such, was not. The one was personal; the other impersonal. Man stood in relation to the one; he could not place himself in relation to the other.

In that formulation, the particular and the concrete merely functioned as an idolatrous diversion, while the general and universal were emasculated of any specific content or power. That procedure sat poorly with experience and tradition, and so the question for religion at this point was how the conception of a universal God could be reconciled with worship of God in all the particularity and concreteness necessarily involved in worship as such—notably the particularity and concreteness of language, symbol, ritual, aesthetics, music, dance, and art. It turns out, however, that these were not opposite conceptions but different levels of apprehending the real. The truth, of which ethnic particularity was a concrete historical channel and instrument, was still possible at a different level of thought, of more general, conceptual expression.

Like other people, Africans inhabit a field of concentric circles connected by mother tongue recognition: family, clan, tribe, village company, initiated associations, and so on, to the farther regions where spirit dwells. Words and gestures directed, say, to the innermost circle of spir-

---

[6] Westermann (1949:128) stressed this as one of the most important effects of education in the mother tongue. He writes:

> The teaching of the vernacular is by many considered as a waste of time; this may be true for the pure rationalist and for those who regard knowledge of a European language and education as two almost identical things. But if education in Africa means the full development of personality and of the organic growth of a new society, it cannot lose sight of the soil out of which the existing society has grown and the human values it has produced. The medium for studying and appreciating these things and for assigning them their due place in the new order of things is the Native language, and from this point of view it is one of the important means of education.

its and divinities to be placated would carry the burden of joy and sadness; grudges and grievances, as well as feats of giving and forgiving; the fear, distrust, remorse, and desolation, as well as the courage, support, and assurance of everyday wear and tear. Farther away, at the remote circumference, deference and due acknowledgment of spirit would assume the more stylized, indirect, poetic pleading of general humanity. In religious life something of God clings to all levels of spiritual encounter and apprehension enough to mitigate opposition and separation between matter and spirit or between perception and concept, so that subjective self-interest is not reserved for those closer at hand and altruistic generosity for a remote, hypothetical humanity. God who is far away may, in supplication, be spoken of in telescopic terms as parent, friend, and ancestor, suggesting a narrowing and tightening of the distant circle until the one God arrives to the praise of a thousand tongues of tribal exuberance. This is the paradox of the "One and the Many," of the *one* God breaking through the *many* representations in anticipated fulfillment.

This theme is taken up in the perceptive defense of a converted traditional African diviner against missionary criticism. The diviner argued that the Christological exclusiveness of the missionaries was not consistent with the missionaries' own adoption of the pre-existing African name for God, to whom traditional Ifa divination has typically accorded many complementary attributes (such as the "great Almighty one," the "Child of God," "the One who came whom we have put to death with cudgels causelessly," "the One who is mightiest among the gods and prevailed to do on a certain occasion what they could not") (cited in Ajayi: 235, footnote). There are echoes here of Isaiah, if only the old diviner knew. What once hung on the clouds of myth now condenses into a real historical figure, the one crucified under Pontius Pilate. Separation between myth and history is thereby overcome, and the diviner may be forgiven for being unwilling to let slip the old moorings, to forego the company of the old spirits. For Africans, too, it is not good for "man," or divinity for that matter, to be alone (Gen 2:18). Many rude surprises awaited missionaries who threw themselves without much forethought into Bible translation, setting off thereby a process that helped in naturalizing the Bible in African culture.

Thus, Johannes Christaller, the great missionary-linguist, urged Africans, especially Christian Africans, "not to despise the sparks of truth entrusted to and preserved by their own people, and let them not forget that by entering into their way of thinking and by acknowledging what is good and expounding what is wrong they will gain the more access to the hearts and minds of their less favoured countrymen" (cited in Danquah:

186). Thus, too, did Edwin Smith inveigh against foisting an artificial culture on Africans, for the African "cannot be treated as if he were a European who happened to be born black. He ought not to be regarded as if he were a building so badly constructed that it must be torn down, its foundations torn up and a new structure erected on its site, on a totally new plan and with entirely new materials" (295).

On the issue of the imposition of European languages such as English by colonial authorities, Smith was cogent: "to insist upon an African abandoning his own tongue and to speak and think in a language so different as English, is like demanding that the various Italian peoples should learn Chinese in order to overcome their linguistic problem" (303). Westermann, as the passage cited above on "inculturation" reveals (1925:26-28), agrees with Smith about the theological value of mother tongue literacy. The mother tongue, he argues, is a divine gift to be used for moral instruction and development of national life. Both Westermann and Smith knew of the contrary policy adopted for India by Alexander Duff, and they were determined not to repeat it in Africa.

As an intellectual matter, we are familiar with the dilemma which theology has rightly construed as the incompatibility of idolatry and worship of God, of self-moralization and trust in God. Yet, we have not noticed, or not noticed to the same extent, how the operative theology of Bible translation acts as a solvent on the race or ethnic problem, as it responds to the latter's enduring yearning for messianic consolation, and gives it the central figure of the New Testament, the figure of Nazareth, a tribal Jewish figure. In the historical record of the missionary encounter with African societies, this Jesus—born of Mary in Bethlehem, who grew up in Hebrew society and culture and was marked with all the Jewish characteristics of time, space, and blood—became the Africans' brother, example, and savior. By contrast, the cosmic Christ—stripped of the inconveniences of his tribal Jewish heritage, equipped with standardized toneless gestures, and refined in the astringent essence of rational formalism—never took root among the tribes. As Edward Wilmot Blyden noted, "Voltaire, who denounced the god brought to his country, was condemned as an infidel. But he could not recognize in the Christ brought from Rome the Jesus of Nazareth, of Bethlehem, of Bethany, of the Mount of Beatitudes or the Sea of Galilee, and in the rush of patriotic impulse exclaimed, 'Dieu n'est pas Français'" (31). Blyden further cites a report from Alexander Fraser in *The Church Missionary Review* of February, 1908, regarding the objection of an Indian, Keshub Chunder Sen, to the effect "that the Christ that we to-day preach in India is an English Christ, an Englishman, with the customs and manners of an

Englishman about him, and the acceptance of whose message means denationalisation, and who, therefore, must raise hostility in every true son of India" (31). Thus, for example, my adopted Creole grandmother, Cecilia Moore, could say of the Jesus of Nazareth, the Jewish Jesus, "Na we yone," "He is our own," but not of the cosmic Christ we study in the philosophy of religion.

As Blyden insisted, Christ's cosmic transformation tribalized him for Europeans, whose intellectual elites harmonized him with the Western philosophical ideal, thereby evading the inconvenient facts of their own history. The Western quest for the historical Jesus ended as a quest for the primacy of critical method, for what will conform to the West's rational scruples and cultural tastes. Accordingly, Jesus was constructed as an iconic symbol with a thick patina of prevailing tastes and agendas.[7] (Indeed, Edward Said may have underestimated the extent to which Europeans "constructed" their own culture before doing the same to the cultures of others.) New discoveries outside the idiom of cultural invention were ruled out, and hence the possibility that an African Christianity, founded on mother tongue affirmation and expressed in ethnic accent, could rise to take its place in the universal human quest for transcendence.

The courageous if forlorn career of Albert Schweitzer of Franco-German Alsace, who later served as a missionary in Lamberene, Gabon, serves as a good example in this regard. The author of the celebrated *The Quest of the Historical Jesus*, Schweitzer's New Age creed of "reverence for life" left little room for African ideas of God or for Africans themselves, whom he kept at arm's length though he lived among them. Schweitzer has become an icon of the West—an Enlightenment hero who forsook a lucrative, secure career in Europe for a life of danger and deprivation in the jungles of Africa. Yet, such Western adulation of Schweitzer contrasts with African attitudes to him. Schweitzer thus embodies a strange controversy: while Europeans honor him for not preaching to Africans, Africans resent him for his aloofness and condescension. Schweitzer did not believe in evangelizing Africans, only in doing good for them and being entitled to their gratitude. In his view, Africans lacked the cultural qualifications presupposed in Christianity, and it was the duty of Europeans to remedy such cultural deficiency without requiring Christianity. Schweitzer's formula of religion as reverence for life, freed of creed and sacrament, appealed to the modern mind for its elegance and inclusive simplicity but left him with no obligation to learn from Africans. Schweitzer was an irony: he came to Africa by a process of self-abdication, but he remained in Africa by a

---

[7] For a summary of such treatment, see Charlotte Allen, who, for example, describes Renan's *Life of Jesus* as a wishful self-portrait.

process of self-insulation. He knew Africans only on his terms, and so Africans could not otherwise know him. The divide remained, both as a race and as a cultural issue. The race matter was transmuted into a cultural matter, but, even in that cultural guise, it was still a matter of race. Who would have suspected that the ideology of the cosmic Christ and the Enlightenment dalliance with the historical Jesus would create cultural barriers with African Christians? Or that Africans who flocked almost by herd instinct to the Jewish Jesus in preference to the enlightenment Christ would end up paying their ethnic homage in mother tongue hymns, songs, and prayers to the ruler of the Universe?

Example of Samuel Ajayi Crowther of Sierra Leone and Nigeria

There are too many examples of such convergence between mother tongue affirmation and the appeal of the figure of Jesus of Nazareth to fit into the restricted space of an essay. Its foundation was laid with the pioneering work of African agents, among whom Samuel Ajayi Crowther (1806?-1891), Bishop of Sierra Leone and Nigeria, ranks among the most outstanding (Sanneh, 1999). Crowther was the chief architect of the plan to open up West Africa to the antislavery movement. Born around 1806, the year before the abolition of the Slave Trade, Crowther (a name adopted from his missionary benefactor) came from the Yoruba town of Oshogun, where he was captured by invading Yoruba Muslim forces and then sold to a Portuguese slave ship in Lagos. By a series of remarkable coincidences, he was eventually rescued (April, 1822) by the British Naval Squadron and brought to Freetown, where he came under instruction.

Crowther was all too conscious of the danger of Britain imposing its cultural habits on rescued Africans as the price for their emancipation, offering thereby the hapless refugees the choice of civilization at the expense of indigenous self-respect. Accordingly, under the terms of British suzerainty, Crowther looked for room to promote what he saw as the necessary African transformation of Christianity. I reproduce below his testimony regarding his own mother tongue, set against the background of the newly created recaptive settlements in Sierra Leone. Here he describes an event that occurred in Freetown in 1844, where Yoruba was used for the very first time as the language of liturgy. (The first celebration of the Christian ritual among the Yoruba took place in Abeokuta in 1842 under Thomas Birch Freeman, who was normally based in Cape Coast, but that celebration was not in the Yoruba language.)

A large number of Africans crowded thither to hear the words of prayer and praise for the first time in their own tongue in an English church. "Although it was my own native language," says the Rev. S. Crowther, "with which I am well acquainted, yet on this occasion it appeared as if I were a babe, just learning to utter my mother-tongue. The work in which I was engaged, the place where I stood, and the congregation before me, were altogether so new and strange, that the whole proceeding seemed to myself like a dream. . . . At the conclusion of the blessing, the whole church rang with *ke oh sheh*—so be it, so let it be!" (Oduyoye, 251-52).

With his linguistic and ethnographic inquiries, Crowther formulated terms for Christianity as an African religion, using African languages in Scripture, prayer, worship, and study to provide the new anthropology required for inculturation. This became a central plank of his vocation. Thus, when he came under pressure to submit to missionary directives from London, Crowther responded by pleading African priority. He argued that the time was drawing near for him to retire from the Niger Mission altogether and turn his attention to his linguistic work and the translation projects that had suffered neglect on account of the heavy demands of travel and administering stations on the River Niger. When the time was right, Crowther pleaded, "I should like to spend the remainder of my days among my own people, pursuing my translations as my bequest to the nation" (cited in Ajayi: 184).[8]

Yet, if Crowther was wary of harmful Western assimilation, he was no less mindful of the mischief of romanticizing traditional Africa, and so he launched a public campaign to scrutinize political structures and native institutions in the light of the new ethic of antislavery. Crowther's moral commitment to antislavery, sharpened by the events of his own personal history, sprang nevertheless from much wider principles. Africans, he argued, were no exception to the rule of righteousness, a rule opposed to any compromise with slavery and its supporting chiefly and priestly structures. Crowther would not denounce or applaud indigenous institutions and native authorities merely for being African. Rather, he demanded of them an unyielding, stringent compliance with the credo that slavery is "a great abomination in the sight of God." Pledging his total commitment to the cause, he wrote, "For Zion's sake will I not hold my peace, and for Jerusalem's sake will I not rest, until the righteousness thereof go forth as brightness, and the salvation thereof as a lamp that burneth."[9] He

---

[8] Crowther's journal entries show him in impressive form when engaging matters of language and translation; see Page (1888a:108; 1888b:91).

[9] Samuel Crowther, September 30, 1851, citing Isaiah 62:1, in a personal inscription written on the inside cover of *The Church Missionary Intelligencer*, 1850. Isaiah 62:2 goes on to speak about God's righteousness being extended to the Gentiles and rulers, a thought that would have been very much in Crowther's own mind.

would not spare tainted institutions and customs or exempt them from the purifying pains of critical historical scrutiny. The African transformation of Christianity demanded no less of Africa itself. Crowther's approach to Christianity carried this historical view of the religion, not as a neat doctrinal package draped in approved Western forms and imposed on Africans in the interest of preserving religious dogma, but as a mediated teaching that must run its African course.

Crowther had encountered more militant alternatives to his policy of accommodation. On the one hand, there was the view of those we may call cultural prescriptivists, who believed that a ready-made, one-size-fits-all imported template should be imposed on Africans, if need be at the tried and trusted hands of civilized West Indians, but in any case under imperial tutelage. On the other hand, there was the view of evangelical pietism, which, with its gnostic tendencies, eschewed having any truck with worldly arrangements, including primitive cultures, and trusted instead in the preaching of the word to effect the wholesome moral and social emasculation necessary for salvation.

Sir Richard Burton, a founding officer of the Royal Anthropological Institute, who trumpeted his ideas of race supremacy throughout the length and breadth of Africa, was a cultural prescriptivist very much in the tradition of Madison Grant and Randolph Bourne, from which position he attacked Crowther's work as pretentious, as a delusory view of Africa's civilized capacity. He derided the recaptives as "half-reclaimed barbarians clad in dishclouts (sic) and palm oil" and cankered with ethnic malice. For Burton, Africans, whether native or Creole, were a setback for "the ruling race" and for progress (1:217; Burton returned to the subject of recaptives in reference to Cape Coast, Ghana, 2:72-73). Such recaptives and their evangelical allies, Burton charged, were an obstacle to the real interests of Africa, whose people would be better off under firm colonial control. Instead, Burton lamented, the evangelicals and the humanitarians had succeeded only in combining with free enterprise advocates to transfuse imperial doctrine with "homoeopathic doses of scientific political economy" (2:48). Aiming a barb at Crowther and his campaign to expand the cause to Nigeria, Burton declared, "No one is more hopeless about the civilization of Africa than the semi-civilised African returning to the 'home of his fathers'" (1:210).

As for the evangelicals of the period, they were at one with the cultural prescriptivists in rejecting any agency role for Africans or African culture, convinced that only Europeans could achieve the objectives of true conversion in Africa. From this position, Crowther's work was deemed inadequate in the light of a reawakened sense of colonial and evangelical paternalism. Andrew Walls describes the general historical background and context as follows:

> European thought about Africa had changed . . . the Western powers were now in Africa to govern. Missionary thought about Africa had changed since the days of Henry Venn; there were plenty of keen, young Englishmen to extend the mission and order the church; a self-governing church had now seemed to matter much less. And evangelical religion had changed since Crowther's conversion; it had become more individualistic and more otherworldly. A young English missionary was distressed that the old bishop who preached so splendidly on the blood of Christ could urge on a chief the advantages of having a school and make no reference to the future life. (19-20)

The answer Crowther gave to cultural prescriptivism was similar to the answer he gave to evangelical pietism: the need for receptivity to African culture. Christianity, he argued, did not come into the world to undertake to alienate or destroy national cultures. Even where it sought to correct false and oppressive ideas and structures, Christianity would still have to do so, he declared, "with due caution and with all meekness of wisdom" (cited in Ajayi: 224). The system of mutual aid that might be found in African society should not be condemned or despised but appreciated for the example it offered Christians entering the culture for the first time. Even those aspects of traditional culture that might strike the foreigner as puerile amusements that excluded the ideas of the spiritual and the eternal (such as stories, fables, proverbs, and songs), Crowther claimed, were actually a storehouse of knowledge and original thinking, as Christaller's investigations in Ghana proved. Africa did not have to become Black Europe to be Christian, for salvation was neither a matter of producing a breed of sanitized, blow-dried citizens, nor of putting to rout local systems of ideas and practice. Consequently, Africa's encounter with the West required separating Christianity from the West's political project and uniting it with Africa's own cultural priorities.

In looking to Africa's own cultural priorities, Crowther was drawn to African languages—it is scarcely possible to think of living cultures without a language—and their indispensable role in the historical development of traditional societies. Yet, Crowther was also drawn in particular to African religious and moral ideas as the index of cultural priorities. For this reason, combining the techniques of field ethnography and the methods of moral reasoning, Crowther made extensive observations during his explorations of the Niger on people's ideas of God. Thus, although he noted somber aspects of their customs and traditional practices, Crowther was nevertheless enthusiastic about what he learnt of religion among, for example, the Igbo people. He found that they had very concise and clear ideas about God, ethics, and moral conduct. He states that he had heard references to such things among the Sierra Leoneans of Igbo background but had refrained from presenting them as facts "before I had satisfied myself by inquiring of such as had never had any intercourse with Christians . . . Truly God has not left Himself without witness!" (cited in Page, 1888a:57). The idea that pre-modern Africa had anticipated in all relevant respects Christian teaching was stated by Crowther with such natural conviction that it marked him as a native mouthpiece, not just a foreign agent. His views had none of the collateral safeguards of planned economic development as a Christian prerequisite.

Crowther credited the Igbo with crucial theological advantage. On this point his journal is worth citing at some length:

> The Igbos are in their way a religious people, the word "Tshuku" [Chukwu], God, is continually heard. Tshuku is supposed to do everything. When a few bananas fell out of the hands of one into the water, he comforted himself by saying, "God has done it." Their notions of some of the attributes of the Supreme Being are in many respects correct and their manner of expressing them striking. "God made everything. He made both white and black," is continually on their lips. Some of their parables are descriptive of the perfections of God, when they say, for instance, that God has two eyes and two ears, that the one is in heaven and the other on earth. I suppose the conception that they have of God's omniscience and omnipresence cannot be disputed.
>
> It is their common belief that there is a certain place or town where Tshuku dwells, and where he delivers his oracles and answers inquiries. Any matter of importance is left to his decision, and people travel to the place from every part of the country.
>
> I was informed today that last year Tshuku had given sentence against the slave trade. The person of him is placed on a piece of ground which is immediately and miraculously surrounded by water. Tshuku cannot be seen by any human eye, his voice is heard from the ground. He knows every language on earth, apprehends thieves, and if there is fraud in the heart of the inquiring he is sure to find it out, and woe to such a person, for he will never return. He hears every word that is said against him, but can only revenge himself when persons come near him...They sincerely believe all these things, and many others respecting Tshuku, and obey his orders implicitly; and if it should be correct that he has said that they should give up the slave trade, I have no doubt that they will do it at once." (Schön and Crowther: 50-53)

In Onitsha Crowther took notes on what he and his party observed of the cult of Tshi, a deity with power to preserve people from witchcraft. A goat was sacrificed to the deity, the blood allowed to run into a bowl, and an invocation made over the victim: "I beseech thee, my guide, make me good; thou hast life. I beseech thee to intercede with God the Spirit, tell Him my heart is clean. I beseech thee to deliver me from all bad thoughts in my heart; drive out all witchcrafts; let riches come to me. See your sacrificed goat; see your kola-nuts; see your rum and palm wine" (Page, 1888a:127, 1888b:107). (It is an intriguing to see how the invocation equates witchcraft with "bad thoughts in the heart," showing, as Evans-Pritchard observed in his classic study of witchcraft and magic among the Azande, that it is witchcraft that establishes the existence of the witch, and not the other way round.)

Crowther virtually invented the methods of field anthropology long before the latter would become an academic discipline and social evolutionary theory would arise to dominate the field completely. In that early period, in agreement with much contemporary mission theology, Crowther deemed African culture a fitting anticipation of the Gospel, to be strengthened by European moral influence. In the later era of social evolutionist thought that followed the publication of Charles Darwin's *The Origin of Species* (1859), such indigenous anticipation of Christianity was discounted as too precocious and European influence deemed as corrupting of primitive society. James Green, for example, was struggling against that intellectual Darwinist tradition when he felt moved to propound his views about the welcome implications of Christianity adopting the African name for God. Crowther's field methods demonstrate the stimulating effects of the missionary movement on academic disciplines like anthropology and linguistics, not to mention religious studies in general. Within this framework, Christianity was an outward-looking, form-fitting religion, best adapted to respond to the needs of those most at risk from the collision with the European commercial machinery—an exception to the law of the survival of the fittest.

Conclusion

Both race theory and colonial tutelage offered little scope or indication for the kinds of adaptations that characterized Christianity's theological transformation in Africa. Crowther's anthropological method, functional but not relativist, placed Christianity on solid indigenous foundations. He spoke with such confidence about Olorun and Chukwu and the numerous other deities as none other than the God of Scripture that one would suspect he had received training in the central ideas of cultural anthropology. Yet, this was a discipline that would not come into being for another half-century. Only the unsuspecting gravity of the translatability of Christianity pulled Crowther in directions that felt natural to the acute indigenization of the gospel and, with it, the cultivation of an inculturated leadership.

In spite of serious political and cultural obstacles, African leadership remained crucial for the course and final outcome of Africa's encounter with the West in its colonial and missionary phase. Ultimately, mother tongue affirmation would complicate the logic of continued foreign overlordship—an affirmation that Bible translation and literacy did a lot to advance. In Africa and elsewhere the boundaries of Christianity's cultural frontiers were expanded and deepened rather than merely repeated, resulting in a shift of key and scale to local initiative, local enterprise, and local paradigm. Western forms of the religion, in themselves transformations of an earlier commensurate vernacular process, were scrambled within the African setting by the process of reappropriation and adaptation.

A further issue concerns the liberating and empowering effects of Bible translation on the native idiom. We need not insist here on an original affinity between a translated and translatable Christianity and the infinite series of complex indigenous adaptations and idioms arising therefrom. What remains a fact was the novel and empowering response on the ground—a response that the native idiom inscribed into the thoughts and habits of millions of people. The spectacle of a translated Bible, at the same time novel and patriotic, empowered victim and marginal populations to take charge of their lives. For example, both Nelson Mandela and Z. K. Matthews, his nationalist contemporary, spoke of Christianity's empowering effects on their struggle for racial equality in South Africa.

Let me return for a final time to the question of race and empire. It is a paradox of the West's missionary expansion in Africa that early nineteenth-century mission should have made the close link that it did with the antislavery movement in the strategy for developing native leadership. The antislavery movement established free settlements along the African coastline, and those free settlements opened the way for the intrusive impulse of colonial rule, but also for colonialism's nemesis with the rising aspirations of a resurgent class of recaptives. The fact that the movement should produce the new African mobile classes whose demonstrated ability would question the hegemonic claims of colonialism shows something of the deeper significance of the antislavery campaign. Mother tongue development had a double duty in this sense: bolstering the cause of cultural renewal and attaching it to the matter of ethnic identity. From

Africa's complex engagement with Europe's presuppositions about non-Western cultures, then, a distinctly African Christianity eventually emerged, admittedly bearing all the marks of the West's exploits, the West's machinery of literacy and the authority of the text, but still sufficiently endowed with mother tongue assurance to connect with the African love of storytelling. African Christianity became distinguished by the idiom of the mother tongue in translation and by its indigenous transformation as a mass movement of people fluent in the native Scriptures, unhindered by Western borrowings, and able to respond to local life and values with inborn confidence.

Works Consulted

Ajayi, J. F. Ade
    1969   *Christian Missions in Nigeria, 1841-1891: The Making of a New Élite*. Evanston: Northwestern University Press.

Allen, Charlotte
    1998   *The Human Christ: The Search for the Historical Jesus*. New York: Free Press.

Arendt, Hanna
    1964   *The Origins of Totalitarianism*. Cleveland and New York: Meridian Books of the World Publishing Company.

Barrett, David
    1968   *Schism and Renewal in Africa: An Analysis of Six Thousand Contemporary Religious Movements*. Nairobi: Oxford University Press.

Bevans, S.
    1992   *John Oman and His Doctrine of God*. Cambridge, UK and New York: Cambridge University Press.

Burton, R. F.
    1991   *Wanderings in West Africa*. 2 vols. New York: Dover Publications. Original ed.: London: Tinsley Brothers, 1863.

Blyden, Edward Wilmot
    1908   *The Three Needs of Liberia: A Lecture Delivered at Lower Buchanan, Grand Bassa Country, Liberia, January 26, 1908*. London: C.M. Phillips.

Danquah, J. B.
    1944   *The Akan Doctrine of God*. London: Lutterworth Press.

Evans-Pritchard, Edward E.
    1936   *Magic, Witchcraft and Oracles among the Azande*. Oxford: Clarendon Press.

Gérard, Albert S.
    1971   *Four African Literatures: Xhosa, Sotho, Zulu, Amharic*. Berkeley and Los Angeles: University of California Press.

Grant, Madison
   1916   *The Passing of the Great Race, Or the Racial Basis of European History*. New York: Charles Scribner's Sons.
Green, James
   N.D.   *An Inquiry into the Principles which Should Regulate the Selection of a Word to Denote "God" in the Language of a Heathen Race; With Special Application to the Case of the Zulus*. N.P.
Oduyoye, Modupe
   1978   "The Planting of Christianity in Yorubaland: 1842-1888." Pp. 239-302 in *Christianity in West Africa: The Nigerian Story*. Ed. Ogbu Kalu. Ibadan: Daystar Press.
Page, Jesse
   1888a   *Samuel Crowther: The Slave Boy of the Niger*. London: S. W. Partridge & Co. Reprinted, 1909. (London edition)
   1888b   *Samuel Crowther: The Slave Boy Who Became Bishop of the Niger*. New York: Fleming H. Revell. Reprinted, 1909. (New York edition)
Said, Edward
   1978   *Orientalism*. London and Henley: Routledge and Kegan Paul.
Samuelson, R. C. A.
   1923   *The King Cetywayo Zulu-Dictionary*. Durban: The Commercial Printing.
Sanneh, Lamin
   1989   *Translating the Message: The Missionary Impact on Culture*. Maryknoll: Orbis Books.
   1999   *Abolitionists Abroad: American Blacks and the Making of Modern West Africa*. Cambridge, MA: Harvard University Press.
Sayers, E. F.
   1927   "Notes on the Native Language Affinities in Sierra Leone." *Sierra Leone Studies* (old series) 10:112-114.
Schön, James Frederick and Samuel Crowther.
   1970   *Journals*. 2nd edition. London: Frank Cass.
Schwartz, Benjamin
   1995   "The Diversity Myth: America's Leading Export." *The Atlantic Monthly* (May): 57-67.
Schweitzer, Albert
   1906   *Von Reimarus zu Wrede: Eine Geschichte der Leben-Jesu-Forschung*. Tübingen: J. C. B. Mohr (Paul Siebeck). English trans.: *The Quest of the Historical Jesus: A Critical Study of Its Progress from Reimarus to Wrede*. With a Preface by F. C. Burkitt. New York: Macmillan Co., 1959.
Smith, Edwin W.
   1926   *The Golden Stool: Some Aspects of the Conflict of Cultures in Modern Africa*. London: Holborn Publishing House.
Taylor, John B.
   1963   *The Primal Vision*. London: SCM.

Walls, Andrew F.
  1992   "The Legacy of Samuel Ajayi Crowther." *International Bulletin of Missionary Research* (January): 15-21.
Westermann, Diedrich
  1925   "The Place and Function of the Vernacular in African Education." *The International Review of Missions* 14:25-36.
  1949   *The African To-day and To-morrow*. 3rd edition. London: Oxford University Press for the International African Institute.

9

Evangelicals and the Bible Yesterday, Today, and Tomorrow

John G. Stackhouse, Jr.

The B-I-B-L-E
Yes, that's the book for me!
I stand alone on the Word of God
The B-I-B-L-E!

All Christians love and venerate the Bible. But no tradition of Christianity loves and venerates it more than evangelical Protestantism. The renowned English pastor and writer John R. W. Stott, one of the current generation's leading evangelical statesmen, pronounces evangelicals to be, above all, "Bible people" (65). Lutheran sociologist Peter Berger famously writes of Protestants purging Roman Catholicism of most of its myth and mystery, leaving the Bible at the core of humanity's revelational connection with God (110-13). Evangelicals "stand alone on the Word of God" as faithfully as any Protestant—even to what many Protestants, including most Lutherans, would deem an extreme.

Precisely because of this setting aside of other religious resources in favor of the Bible, the identity, activity, and vitality of evangelicals has depended crucially upon the Bible in their midst. In this essay, I would like to trace three moments in the role of the Bible among evangelicals, and especially evangelicals in Canada and the United States. The first is the historical sketch: how the Bible has figured in evangelical life over the last couple of centuries and especially in recent generations. The second is the sociological and journalistic: how the role of the Bible is under stress amid sweeping changes in contemporary evangelicalism today. And the third is the prophetic—or, more modestly, the merely "punditic": how individuals and organizations that care about the Bible, such as the American Bible Society, can encourage evangelicals to continue to love and venerate it in the new century before us.

My thesis, then, is simple and three-fold. The Bible has played an enormous and complex role in evangelical life. Almost every feature of

183

that role, however, is under challenge today. Those challenges are not likely to disappear, and so evangelicals and others who share their regard for the Bible will need to meet those challenges with pious hope and prudent discernment.

Who Are the Evangelicals?

An academic cottage industry has sprung up among historians, sociologists, and theologians, debating answers to this question. For the purposes of this essay, however, let us agree on a widely accepted general definition (cf. Bebbington: 1-19; Marsden: viii-xvi; and Stackhouse, 1993:6-12).

Historically, evangelicalism emerged in the eighteenth-century revivals associated with the work of John and Charles Wesley, George Whitefield, and Jonathan Edwards. Individuals and movements who descend from these origins and who have not departed from the concerns that marked them can be called "evangelicals," along with those groups that latterly identified with these concerns and the network of groups that espouse them. Evangelicals thus would be found among Methodists, Presbyterians, and Baptists in the former set, and among Mennonite Brethren and the Christian Reformed in the latter.

Evangelical concerns are perhaps best seen as a cluster of five. First, "evangelical" comes from *evangel*, or "gospel." Evangelicals prize the classic good news of God being in Christ, reconciling the world to himself. Doctrinally, then, evangelicals are creedally orthodox (whether or not they happen to recognize the authority of the Apostles', Nicene, and Chalcedonian symbols, which many do not) and concentrate particularly on the career of Jesus Christ—his incarnation, life, death, resurrection, and ascension. Evangelicals believe that only in the work of Christ is salvation secured, and only through faith in Christ is salvation received.

Second, evangelicals hold to these beliefs, as well as all of their other religious tenets, because they believe that the Bible teaches them, and the Bible is the Word of God in written form. "Jesus loves me—this I know, for the Bible tells me so." The Bible is fully inspired by God such that it is God's own book. Most evangelicals specify that the Holy Spirit inspired the very words of Hebrew, Aramaic, and Greek in the Bible's canonical form, while others believe that God allowed the limitations of the human authors to show up in relatively minor matters. All agree, however, that the Bible is the fundamental and supremely authoritative reference for religious life, once given by God in inspiration and subsequently taught by God's Spirit in illumination of all who read it in faith.

Third, evangelicals believe in conversion. And they believe in it in two respects. Because of each person's inherited sinfulness and many individual acts of willful sin, he or she must be converted away from sin and toward God, raised from spiritual death to eternal life—in a phrase, "born again." Furthermore, evangelicals believe in "full conversion"—a life of increasing holiness, of disciplined and fervent piety that conforms increasingly to Christ's example of obedience and goodness. This aspect of conversion is not completely fulfilled until the believer reaches complete maturity, or "glory," in heaven.

Fourth, evangelicals believe in mission. They particularly support the work of evangelism, the act of proclaiming the gospel and calling for decision regarding it. But they also have been busy cooperating on other fronts to accomplish what they see to be the divine mission in the world, especially in ameliorating evils. Thus, they have sponsored hospitals, schools, farms, and other institutions that care for the body and mind as well as the spirit.

So far, of course, these four emphases are generically Protestant and, with the exception of the emphasis placed on the supremacy of scriptural authority, basically Christian. What makes evangelicalism distinctive is its fifth emphasis, namely, a transdenominationalism that holds the other four concerns as so primary that evangelicals recognize anyone as kin who both holds them and is willing to work together on that basis. Thus, evangelical Pentecostals, Methodists, Anglicans, and Mennonites, for example, all share the first four concerns and go on to cooperate in the World Evangelical Fellowship, World Vision, Inter-Varsity Christian Fellowship, and a multitude of other institutions. Those Christians who happen to hold the first four concerns with evangelicals but who do not privilege them and see them as a sufficient basis for fellowship and service together (for example, some Mennonite, Baptist, and Lutheran groups) would thus properly not be called "evangelicals" in this context, however truly "gospel-oriented" and thus "evangelical" they are in a more basic sense (Dayton and Johnston).

Evangelicals and the Bible: The Past

Christ and Salvation

The "original evangelicals" were, of course, the sixteenth-century Protestant Reformers who saw themselves as champions of the true gospel against Roman Catholic distortions and accretions. The famous Reformation slogans—*sola fide, sola gratia,* and *sola scriptura*—epitomized the Protestant agenda of stripping away the husk of medieval superstition that had obscured the gospel kernel for centuries.

Modern evangelicals have continued to understand Christ and salvation in terms that self-consciously reject Roman Catholicism's putative excesses: all those intermediary saints and clergy; all those rituals, pilgrimages, and relics; all those extra duties entailed by confession and penance; all those elaborations of the cosmos such as limbo, purgatory, and various angelic realms; and all those dubious additional doctrines, whether the Immaculate Conception of Mary or the infallibility of the Pope.

Indeed, it is this last doctrine that highlights the role that the Bible plays in the evangelical articulation of the gospel. Evangelicals understand themselves to teach what the Bible teaches—nothing more and nothing less. Roman Catholics, however, teach much more, drawing as they do on what they understand to be divinely-inspired tradition mediated to the Church through the centuries and clarified particularly in the *magisterium*, or "teaching office," of the Church, personified by the Pope. Evangelicals are radically Protestant in this respect: the Bible is a sword that evangelicals use to cut through all of Roman Catholic teaching and practice that is not conformed—to evangelical satisfaction, at least—to the teaching of the Scriptures alone.

Evangelicals see a symmetry here. Roman Catholics teach "too much," adding unhelpfully to the gospel message because they draw on "too much" in the way of revelational resources. Disqualifying tradition as inspired revelation and ignoring Catholic claims of papal authority reduces evangelicals to sorting out what the Bible says and thus reduces the version of the gospel they preach to a simpler, even starker, message.

The other group, however, over against whom evangelicals have defined themselves since the origin of "evangelicalism" in the eighteenth century is the tradition of liberal theology. To be sure, most textbooks trace the origins of liberal theology to the career of F. D. E. Schleiermacher, whose first book was not published until 1799. Yet some of the polemics of Jonathan Edwards—perhaps most famously his treatise *On The Freedom of the Will* (1754)—are addressed to theological positions that clearly anticipate nineteenth-century liberalism. And whereas evangelicals have seen Roman Catholics to add improperly to the "store" of God-given revelation and thus end up with a theology and piety that is too elaborate, evangelicals have seen liberals as subtracting from the Bible's authority and thus commending a theology that is attenuated in every major respect.

In the evangelical view of liberal theology, the Incarnate Son of God shrinks down into a "very, very, very, very good man," in the incisive phrase of H. Richard Niebuhr. Salvation becomes merely our imitation of Jesus' example of godliness—without need of atonement. In many versions of liberalism, the Christian religion itself becomes just one of many salvific paths to God. Given the acids of what evangelicals have called "irreverent" and "destructive" historical criticism of the Bible and the preference for the deliverances of contemporary reason and experience over the orthodox doctrine harvested faithfully from the pages of Scripture over the centuries, liberalism is left with a thin theology and a merely moralistic (and perhaps mystical) piety wrought out of a thoroughly corroded Bible.

Positively, then, evangelical summaries of doctrine typically provide "proof-texts" for each proposition, not only as glosses but as authorities: we believe X because the Bible teaches it *right here*. Orthodoxy is *not* merely the position of the strongest party in church disputes. Evangelicals maintain instead that orthodoxy is simply a digest of the Bible in correct delineation and emphasis.

The Bible

The evangelical commitment to *sola scriptura* has played out in a number of respects, some of them paradoxical, some of them even contradictory. Evangelical theology was formed in the crucible of the Enlightenment, and much of it continues to show traits of that movement. Evangelical sermons and Bible study materials, for example, typically emphasize "word studies," the tracing of etymologies and semantics through the Bible. Evangelical laypersons often possess reference volumes of this sort (*Vine's Expository Dictionary* being perhaps the most popular) in their home libraries. Such word studies often depend on Enlightenment-style univocity, that "one word means one thing." Thus, many evangelicals confidently discuss a term such as "glory" or "righteousness," flipping lightly over vast tracts of scriptural material with the aid of their concordances. Here, ironically, is a built-in disregard for hermeneutical context, a disregard that punishes the blithe exegete all the more when symbols are in play: thus, "fire" *always* connotes "judgment," and "leaven" *always* connotes "sin."

The most obvious sign of evangelical regard for the text of Scripture is the habit of proof-texting. Evangelicals assume that truth is found in the very words of Scripture, and every truth (at least, every truth of faith and religious practice) therefore can be demonstrated as emerging from particular texts of the Bible, cited by chapter and verse. Such an inclination is not confined to the more radical "biblicistic" evangelical traditions, whether Plymouth Brethren, Mennonites, or Baptists. Evangelical theologians, scholarly or popular, such as Luther and Calvin, Edwards and Wesley, Hodge and Finney, or Moody and Graham, habitually cite verses of Scripture as the authority for whatever point they wish to make.

Many evangelicals, however, have been slow to take stock of just what role should be played, and in fact is played, by reason, experience, and tradition in their theologies. Wesley formulated his famous "quadrilateral" to coordinate these four resources, but few evangelicals outside the academy have explicated just what goes on in their theology besides mere Bible study. Thus, the dispensationalist believes that such a system is merely the end result of careful exegesis, not a paradigm that, once adopted, bends recalcitrant texts to its pattern. The Calvinist does the same, ingenuously claiming that his system is merely the distillation of biblical truth.

The most obvious giveaway of such a lack of theological self-consciousness is the widely recommended evangelical practice of so-called inductive Bible study. Taught in dispensational Bible schools, denominational seminaries, and transdenominational Bible study guides alike, the practice of inductive Bible study seeks to expose the Bible reader to the text without the interference of "theology" or "tradition." Readers instead are given a particular passage to read (but who selects the beginning and end of a passage and according to what criteria, when the earliest texts have neither paragraph nor even sentence divisions?) and customarily are provided also with a few "guiding questions" meant to help the reader come to his or her own conclusions (albeit within the terms of the questions interposed between the reader and the text!). The Reformation doctrine of the "perspicuity of Scripture" therefore plays out in evangelical regard for and reading of the Bible in ways that are sometimes perplexing and even self-defeating.

The authority of the Bible as evangelicalism's primary theological resource is reinforced in evangelical use of the scriptural text as symbol. Scripture texts are calligraphed or cross-stitched for decorating rooms both domestic and ecclesiastical. And Bible texts in some evangelical traditions replace even the cross as the symbol emblazoned upon the front wall of the sanctuary—an aesthetic that resembles Islam's resistance to pictorial representation and embrace of the Quranic text for both ornamentation and devotional focus.

What is true of the biblical text is true also of the Bible itself as a holy object. A massive Bible typically adorns a prominent lectern at the front of the church—in some traditions, occupying the place of honor reserved in other churches for the elements of communion. In traditional evangelical homes, one can count on each family member owning a leather-bound, gilt-edged Bible. One also can count on these Bibles being shelved in places of honor, with many evangelicals practicing the folkway that no other book shall be placed on top of it. Each family member possesses that personal Bible, furthermore, because evangelicals typically have marked important rites of passage with the presentation of new Bibles: birth and (perhaps) infant baptism, beginning a new phase of education, believer's baptism or confirmation, graduation from school, and marriage. Such Bibles often include pages for the recording of milestones in one's life, just as the family Bible serves as the register for the life of the clan. In these and other ways, then, evangelicals affirm the preeminence of the Bible both practically and symbolically (McDannell: 67-102)

Conversion

Conversion in the sense of evangelism will be discussed under "Mission" below. Conversion in the sense of the progressive transformation of the sinner into the image of Christ is an equally important theme in evangelicalism.

When evangelicals assemble to worship, the Bible always figures prominently. Evangelicals have long championed preaching as the focus of the worship service. Good preachers are valued everywhere, but in no tradition more than evangelicalism—so much so, that the pastor is sometimes referred to simply as "the preacher." The sermon normally comes at the climax of the liturgy, and evangelical sermons are almost always longer than they are in non-evangelical churches.

Evangelical sermons tend to feature the actual words of Scripture. Many preachers simply exposit the Bible book by book, chapter by chapter, verse by verse. Others follow a lectionary or set of themes, but the evangelical impulse is always to refer frequently to the text of the day. "Let's look now at verse x" is a familiar phrase in evangelical churches, with the expectation that people will have their Bibles open throughout the sermon to follow along with the preacher to see that the Bible does, in fact, say what the preacher says it does. Evangelical churches typically have pew Bibles, but regular attendees bring their own Bibles and commonly take notes on the sermon either in the margins of those Bibles or in pads brought along expressly for that purpose. People in evangelical churches typically expect to learn more about the Bible each time they hear a sermon.

Scriptural knowledge is to be gained in other ways as well. Children in evangelical Sunday Schools hear Bible stories, not just cute fictions meant to illustrate Christian truths. They learn the order of the books of the Bible, engage in contests (known colloquially as "sword drills") to find a particular passage first, and are encouraged to memorize Scripture, whether key verses or whole passages such as the Ten Commandments or the Beatitudes.

Adults also typically engage in Bible study in a small group, whether in a Sunday morning class or in a midweek home fellowship. Laypersons commonly own at least one single-volume commentary on the Bible and often invest considerable sums in a reference library of Biblical commentaries, concordances, and other study aids. Such aids assist them in their personal study and devotional reading that, again, normally focuses upon Scripture (as opposed to, for example, devotional readings from the Church Fathers or contemporary spiritual writers).

Scripture is also embedded into music. Adults—from sixteenth-century Psalters to Vineyard Church's songs today—sing Scripture in church, while Sunday Schools feature Scripture songs for the kids. Indeed, many evangelical children learn most of the "memory verses" they know by singing them rather than merely reading them.

The role of Scripture in forming Christians, whether individually or in community, also emerges in verbal clues offered by the by. Ethical issues are discussed in church board rooms, at annual meetings, and in Christian homes with reference to snatches of Scripture: perhaps a proverb here or a beatitude there. Allusions and catchphrases show up as a matter of course in informal speech at church dinners and in correspondence with other believers. And jokes are made, whether from the pulpit or over Sunday lunch, that presume a general knowledge of the Bible that is sometimes very specific and might include in particular a knowledge of the King James Version (e.g., "Who was the first smoker in the Bible? Rebekah, because she lighted off a camel [Camel]"; "What man had no parents in the Bible? Joshua, the son of Nun [none]").

Mission

The Bible is woven throughout the evangelical subculture. It naturally plays a large role, then, in the witness of this tradition to the larger world. Evangelicals have a long record of providing for the needs of others at home and around the world. But when evangelicals offer help—such as medicine, education, or food—they typically tie it to evangelism. Furthermore, evangelicals do not merely commend the gospel to others. They argue for its validity and virtue, and they do so typically with open Bibles. So the apologetic as well as the evangelistic modes of evangelical mission deserve a look, and both show once again just how important the Bible is to evangelicalism.

In apologetics, evangelicals typically concentrate attention on the Bible because it is the supreme guide to their faith. Thus, evangelicals argue for the historical reliability of the Bible's accounts, the prophetic accuracy of its predictions, the beauty of its poetry and prose, the glory of its moral teachings, and the fundamental reality of its divine inspiration and authority. On the basis of this peerless volume, others are invited to look at the Bible's central subject, Jesus Christ, and come to faith in him.

In the act of articulating the gospel message, evangelicals do not only rely on the Bible's authority for the truth of that message. They use the Bible in that proclamation quite directly. Heeding promises such as "my word shall not return unto me void" (Isaiah 55:11), evangelicals freely salt their presentations with phrases, verses, and even whole chapters of Scripture. Billy Graham has epitomized the evangelical who confidently proclaims, "The Bible says… ," even to audiences who are not yet convinced of the Bible's authority. Graham *is* convinced, and so he speaks and reads from it with assurance that the very words of the Bible are charged with divine blessing and will be used for the divine mission by the Holy Spirit in the evangelistic encounter. Evangelicals at Bible schools and evangelism training workshops offered in their local churches or by groups such as the Billy Graham Evangelistic Association are taught to memorize key Scripture texts at the heart of the gospel and urged to deploy them in evangelistic conversations. The Bible is not quite seen as magical here, as a book of charms merely to be recited to effect the desired outcome, but it is trusted as the vehicle through which God promises to work as a matter of course.

Thus, evangelicals learn the Bible themselves to aid them in witnessing to the gospel, and they encourage their neighbors to read it in the course of their investigation of the Christian faith. Such reading means that evangelicals have worked hard to make Scripture available to their neighbors—which brings us to our last heading.

Transdenominationalism

In order to venerate and use the Bible and in order to learn, memorize, teach, and evangelize from the Bible, the Bible has to be intelligible and available. Thus, evangelicals have enthusiastically supported means of translating and disseminating the Bible. Whether as individuals struggling to produce translations on missionary frontiers (with the pioneer missionary William Carey's Bengali translation as an epitome of such efforts), or as major international organizations (with the Wycliffe Bible Translators/Summer Institute of Linguistics perhaps the best known), evangelicals have worked hard and even sacrificially to render the Bible into the languages of the world.

Evangelicals have worked no less diligently at the tasks of producing and transporting Bibles. Colporteurs in the last century brought Bibles to the borderlands of rural and urban America alike, to remote farmers and forgotten slum dwellers. In our time, Brother Andrew, "God's Smuggler," has inspired a generation of evangelicals with his swashbuckling escapades on behalf of Scripture distribution behind the Iron Curtain.

In these tasks, then, evangelicals typically have worked cooperatively with other evangelicals. For nothing is more basic, more uniting, and less contentious among evangelicals than the value of the Bible. So the great Bible societies arose as mainstays of evangelical ecumenism. Translation projects became one of the few enterprises in which evangelical scholars of various traditions worked together—in our day producing the New American Standard Bible (1960), the New International Version (1973), and the Living Bible (notably its revised edition, 1997), among numerous versions issued among Anglophone North Americans.

The culture of North American evangelicalism, then, features the Bible in every important respect. But in those same respects, the place of the Bible is under challenge in North American evangelicalism today.

Evangelicals and the Bible: The Present

While the traditions of evangelical regard for and use of the Bible continue to the present, in each area of concern new challenges have arisen. In academic theology among evangelicals, three areas of debate have opened up in this generation, each of which has the Bible at its heart. The first two regard the gospel message. The third deals with the nature and function of the Bible itself.

Christ and Salvation

The first question deals with world religions and the fate of the unevangelized. All evangelicals reject the option of "pluralism," the position associated with scholars such as Wilfred Cantwell Smith and John Hick, and with varieties of Hindu and New Age religion. Pluralism affirms all spiritual paths as salvific—or, at least, affirms all *good* spiritual paths as salvific. (No one wants to endorse, say, infant sacrifice to Moloch in the ancient world or National Socialism in our own era.) But evangelicals divide into two broad camps of "exclusivists" and "inclusivists" on the question of the salvation of those who do not hear and understand the propositions of the Christian gospel (Sanders, 1992; 1995).

Exclusivists maintain that hearing and responding to the gospel is normally required for salvation (hardliners would remove the qualifier "normally") and that the best one can hope for others is that God might do some mysteriously gracious thing about which we have no clue. Exclusivists, of course, have their proof texts, such as Romans 10:14 ("How shall they hear without a preacher?") and Acts 4:12 ("for there is no other name under heaven given among mortals by which we may be saved").

Inclusivists respond that the Bible is full of examples of people who have saving faith without knowledge of Jesus Christ: most obviously, every believer in the Old Testament qualifies as such. Furthermore, inclusivists press, what about infants, or the mentally incompetent, or the schizophrenic, or others who are incapacitated and cannot understand the propositions of the gospel? Surely God will not abandon them all?

Both sides, to be sure, deploy both proof texts and examples. Exclusivists point to Cornelius as an example of a God-fearer who nonetheless had Peter sent to him by God to bring him the gospel (Acts 10); inclusivists wield verses such as John 10:16—"I have sheep not of this fold."

This debate has yet to mature into a full-blown theology of religions, although there are some new ventures in that direction (Pinnock, 1992; McDermott). Neither side, however, is challenging fundamental orthodoxies regarding Christ or salvation. And both clearly see the Bible as the fundamental resource for exploring and resolving this conflict.

The same terms apply to a controversy much more far-reaching than the inclusivism-exclusivism debate. Led by theologians Clark Pinnock (1994) and Gregory Boyd, some evangelicals have reacted strongly against what they see to be a view of God distorted by Platonism via the Augustinian tradition. This view of God, they believe, portrays him as static in his timelessness, loveless in his impassibility, and utterly domineering in his sovereignty. Instead, this new group recommends that evangelicals prize the "openness" of God: God goes through time as we do, feels in some way as we do (whether love or hate, dismay or celebration) as events come and go and as his purposes are frustrated or fulfilled, and cooperates with his creation toward an ultimately beneficent end.

The majority of evangelical theologians currently look askance at this movement. Some share its unhappiness with the classical categories of timelessness, impassibility, and so on, but believe that many streams of evangelical orthodoxy provide the resources to differ with those categories without adopting what seems dangerously close to the categories of process thought, albeit without all of the Whiteheadian vocabulary and detail. Others denounce the whole enterprise as simply heretical, compromising the glory of God both metaphysically and morally: God is no longer omniscient and omnipotent and is himself subject to doubt, confusion, and fits of rage from which he needs sometimes to be talked down (e.g., Exodus 32:7-14).

It is stories like these in the Bible, of course, that provide grist for the "openness" mill. And they have developed their theology considerably beyond these perennial Bible puzzles. The "openness" advocates fundamentally assert that they are simply reading the Bible better than their opponents and that they are more faithful to the text of the Bible and less dominated by non-Christian philosophical presuppositions.

No one in this debate doubts the creedal affirmations regarding Christ and salvation as far as they go. Clearly, however, the nature of God's work in Christ, the nature of God's program of salvation, the nature of the church's relationship with God, and the eschatological hope of the church all are affected by the change in viewpoint advocated in the "openness" model.

The Bible

The third leading edge of evangelical theological development is at the level of methodology. Whether the championing of Karl Barth's theology by an earlier generation of evangelical theologians, most notably Bernard Ramm and Donald Bloesch, or the exploration of postliberal views in the current one, evangelical theologians have been wondering aloud about just what biblical inspiration and authority mean (Dorrien). Some have come to the conclusion that the Barthian/postliberal acceptance of higher criticism, followed by a kind of "second naïveté" that affirms the Bible's truth and authority within the discourse of the Christian community, points the way out of two hundred years of controversy between evangelicals and liberals. Many evangelicals, however, wonder whether the Barthian/postliberal program really does anything other than sidestep the question both traditional evangelicals and liberals want to keep asking: However "true" the Bible seems to be for those within the Christian fold, what claims can be made, if any, for the truth of the Bible in the world at large? Is the Bible just "our book," or is it really God's book to the world (Phillips and Okholm)?

Such methodological debates have yet to seep very far into evangelical popular culture. What is striking in some cutting-edge evangelical churches is a sort of embarrassment toward or at least a downplaying of the Bible as symbol. "Seeker-sensitive" churches typically avoid any traditional religious symbolism, including the Bible. No great Bible sits splendidly at the front of these auditoriums. Rarely are there Bibles available for those in the pew to read. Instead, if viewing any Biblical text is deemed necessary, it is projected onto a screen or wall for a few moments and then, surely with unintentional irony, extinguished. Or perhaps a few verses are printed in the program for that service, only to be discarded as trash once the service is finished. Opponents who neither understand nor sympathize with the agenda of seeker-sensitive churches easily score cheap shots against such churches. But it remains a matter of fact that the Bible is purposely much less evident in these meetings than in traditional evangelical sanctuaries.

As for the Bible in the private lives of evangelicals, some still have Scripture texts on the walls of their homes, but this practice is fading fast. As for other kinds of adornment, evangelicals do not typically go to the Hasidic extreme of binding actual texts to their bodies, of course—except that some now do: in T-shirts emblazoned with snatches of Scripture, ballpoint pens and pencils imprinted with more, and even candy and gum that "bear witness" via Bible verses on their wrappers. The "Jesus junk" of contemporary evangelical paraphernalia thus contrasts sharply with former evangelical traditions of the Bible as holy object.

Conversion

Evangelical preaching in many places is as traditionally expositional as ever. But two other traditions of preaching vie increasingly with it. Evangelicals influenced by the "narrative" school of homiletics (American Fred Craddock is perhaps the best known of these) are encouraged to reach the postmodern mind by jettisoning the old, linear, argumentative form of preaching and adopting an impressionistic, quick-cutting style that emphasizes story-telling over declamation.

In the Pentecostal and charismatic wings of evangelicalism, preachers still unabashedly wave open Bibles about as they speak and still quote Scripture aplenty. The Bible, that is, continues to occupy the sermon both symbolically and materially. But many of these preachers perpetuate a "ranting" tradition of homiletics that ironically also fits some people's understanding of the postmodern mind: its preference for the episodic, allusive, and affective. In this style of preaching, the speaker selects a theme and then proceeds to make his points in turn while studding each one with portions of Scripture—sometimes an extended quotation and often merely a quick phrase. The effect is not unlike the more refined homiletics of the "narrative" school in the combination of storytelling (or "testimonies"), Scriptural allusions, and punchy exhortations.

What is difficult to judge in either form of such quickly-changing, kaleidoscopic presentations is whether what the preacher is saying really emerges from the authoritative Word of God or whether the preacher might just be grabbing convenient bits from here and there to justify a point he was going to make anyway. In sermons that increasingly resemble MTV videos as nonsequential, rapid-fire "experiences," it is also unclear here whether anyone is learning much about the Bible.

Evangelicals apparently are still learning about the Bible in small group studies. Yet many of these groups read other sorts of books together, whether guides to healthier marriage or family life, handbooks on evangelism or apologetics, or even popular Christian novels. To be sure, any and all of these pursuits can be part of a good program of adult Christian education. But an observer might still wonder where, if not in these groups, evangelicals are engaged in an ongoing study of the Bible.

Preachers report, and pollsters on both sides of the border confirm, that both churchgoers and nonchurchgoers alike show a declining grasp of even basic Bible content (Bibby; Gallup and Jones). The experiential-cum-therapeutic cultural wave of the late twentieth-century has tended to turn even genuine Bible studies into encounter groups in which people offer their impressions of "what this Bible passage means to me" or perhaps, in good evangelical pragmatist fashion, "what this Scripture encourages me to do," without lingering upon the prior question of "what the Bible actually says." "Sword drills" are quaint relics of a rapidly disappearing subculture, along with the discipline of Scripture memorization. Indeed (to take the phenomenon of humor seriously as an anthropological marker), one could not tell a joke to a typical church audience today that assumed any particular item of Scriptural knowledge with confidence that everyone would get it. The Bible, in short, is disappearing on several fronts within evangelical precincts, as well as in the culture at large.

Mission

In terms of apologetics and evangelism, traditional methods and resources still prevail. Evidentialist and rationalist apologetics dominate the market, and most evangelistic programs still emphasize proof texts as part of an appropriate gospel presentation.

The rise of "friendship evangelism," however, is not without its ambiguities. At its best, such an emphasis encourages evangelicals to eschew the bad old days of seeing neighbors as souls to be saved, as targets for proselytization. The gospel is lived out, and in time is articulated within the context of genuine love for one's neighbor. At its worst, however, such an approach allows for the benign and inoffensive vagueness of mere goodwill, without the specificity and challenge of a scripturally informed conversation.

At the other end of the scale lies the popular "Alpha" program originating from Holy Trinity-Brompton (HTB) Anglican Church in London, England, and readily imported to North America in recent years. Drawing on previous evangelistic programs, most notably the supper meetings of the Oxford Group Movement of two generations ago, the Alpha program has been employed enthusiastically by groups that share neither HTB's Anglicanism nor its charismatic emphasis.

And therein lies the rub. For this presentation of "basic Christianity" is actually devoted very largely to a clearly charismatic presentation of the work of the Holy Spirit in the individual and the church, from the controversial teaching of the "baptism of the Holy Spirit" in classical Pentecostal terms to extended discussion of spiritual gifts. Such teachings, however true they might be to the charismatic tradition in its distinctive cultivation of believers, seem oddly prominent in a program designed to evangelize those who do not attend church and are not confessing Christians of any sort. Indeed, they seem oddly out of keeping with the evangelistic emphases of the New Testament itself, which concentrates instead on the saving work of Jesus Christ particularly in its accounts of apostolic proclamation. One wonders in both cases, then, how deeply informed by the Bible evangelical thinking has become nowadays even regarding the fundamental enterprise of Christian mission.

Transdenominationalism

When it comes to the projects of translating and disseminating the Bible as key zones of evangelical transdenominational cooperation, one might conclude that the evangelical story is an entirely happy one. Domestic translations have proliferated with huge sales across denominational lines. Publishers have devised more and more ingenious "niche" Bibles to serve what they perceive to be the needs of homemakers, fathers, mothers, professionals, youth of various ages, college students, divorced persons, pastors, evangelists, apologists, and other groups. (For more on this, see Chapter 4. —Ed.) And international translation continues apace, with Wycliffe Bible Translators weathering various storms, from accusations of complicity with the CIA overseas to the kidnapping and even murder of some of their staff.

Yet not all has been well in the field of Bible translation. Controversy over English translations—not a new phenomenon, of course—most recently rocked American evangelicalism over the proposed revision to the New International Version (NIV). The NIV, evangelicalism's most popular modern translation, was revised as it had been previously for a new edition. This time, however, inclusive language for human beings in various places in Scripture was systematically included. (The New Revised Standard Version [1989] had anticipated this change by a decade.) Some prominent evangelical scholars and activists took umbrage at what they saw to be the not-so-thin edge of a feminist wedge that would perhaps lead to outright goddess worship, as inclusive language spread like a virus throughout the Bible. Many evangelicals saw these fears as hysterical, but the American publisher backed off and refused to print the new edition. (The British publisher had already begun distribution.) Actual matters of Bible translation are indeed at stake: there might well be something important lost, for example, in rendering Psalm 1 as "Blessed are those" (that is, a group) rather than the more literal "Blessed is the man…" (that is, a faithful individual). But more than a few observers have seen the conservative reaction as beholden at least as much to anti-feminist ideology as to scriptural fidelity. In that respect, this was the first translation controversy *not* clearly about orthodox doctrine of God, Christ, and salvation, but perhaps about secondary or even tertiary matters of differing evangelical opinion (Stackhouse, 1999).

Other critics have found the very proliferation of translations to have affected evangelical piety and community. No longer are the cadences of a single translation (the King James Version or KJV) familiar to everyone, and therefore useful for reference and allusion. Evangelical congregations now are filled with people having to do their own quick translating between the version they had brought to church and the version from which the preacher is reading. Furthermore, because the new translations have aimed to produce idiomatic and accessible English, and usually have succeeded, many bemoan the loss of nuance and poetic expression that had made the KJV a classic of English literature. "Who wants to memorize this banality?" some ask.

Finally, the phenomenon of the "niche" Bible, usually published with a variety of Bible "helps," prompts some to wonder whether evangelicals are now unwittingly reintroducing a whole new set of intermediaries between the reader and the text. Moreover, these intermediaries are not nearly as distinguished as, say, Thomas Aquinas, Augustine, or other saints, but are merely contemporary Bible scholars, popular pastors, or simply hack writers hired to find material somehow germane to the target group. Furthermore, the very attempt to package these Bibles in various covers and designs in order to appeal to a particular taste has had the unfortunate symbolic effect of conforming the Bible to an individual's own chosen "lifestyle," rather than marking it out as a holy object to which one ought to conform one's lifestyle.

In all of these respects the current changes in evangelicalism have involved important changes in the way evangelicals regard and use the Bible. What, then, lies before those concerned to assist evangelicals in these respects on the road ahead?

Evangelicals and the Bible: The Future

That evangelicalism has changed is a truism. Every movement changes over time, and evangelicalism has taken on the contours of a succession of cultural impulses from its eighteenth-century origins to its current position at the beginning of a new century and millennium. So, too, has evangelicalism's relationship to and use of the Bible varied over time, in several subcultural versions. The mere fact, then, that the present does not look like the past should not necessarily provoke either dismay or joy (Bebbington; Hatch and Noll; Noll).

Change, indeed, often brings both loss and gain, and sometimes both unavoidably together. The case of the Bible is a splendid case in point. This last section traces out some of these combinations and concludes with some suggestions for how foreseeable changes can be negotiated most helpfully by those who promote the Bible among evangelicals.

Christ and Salvation

Doctrinal controversy may be allowed to distract the church from its worship, fellowship, and mission when only trivial matters are at stake. But discussions of the fate of the unevangelized or of the nature of God in the "openness" controversy are hardly trivial matters.

As the religious pluralization of North America proceeds apace, the task of understanding other religions in theological terms becomes more and more urgent—not merely the establishment of grounds for apologetic polemics, but also the clarifying of just how these religions figure in the providential plan of God. The authority of the Bible is a touchstone for such discussions, both in its inspired portrayal of God's revelation to Israel and the church in the context of other religions, and also in the very question of the authority of the Bible vis-à-vis other sacred scriptures. Thus, the popular controversy nowadays regarding the canon of the New Testament that excludes the Gnostic gospels ultimately leads to the question of the *world's* "canon" and the place of the Bible among the Quran, Bhagavad Gita, Dao De Jing, and so on. Suddenly, it seems, theologians and pastors need to dust off their class notes regarding the emergence of the biblical canon and consider afresh just why this set of ancient books was judged to constitute God's holy Word in a way that no other books were. Those who seek to promote regard for the Bible can aid the church by reminding us of those principles of canonization in the midst of a plethora of alternatives.

As for the question of the "openness" of God, this is hardly a matter of mere metaphysical speculation, as all sides agree. Pastors are always struggling to explain God's providence to those who are earnestly trying to make life decisions, improve their prayers, or deal with suffering. The "openness" dispute touches on all of these matters and more. One pastor involved in this discussion reported to me that this was the first time in his twenty-year career that his church members were fascinated by a theological subject. And in their fascination, he continued, they were reading and discussing the Bible as never before on matters that, he concluded with satisfaction, really matter.

The Bible

The methodological conversation between evangelicals and postliberals remains mostly within the academic cloister. But it has immediate ramifications for every evangelical's use of the Bible: How does one profit best from higher critical commentary? How do we apply the Bible to one's life or to the church's life today? And what role can the Bible play, if any, in conversation with neighbors who do not grant its divine authority?

As for the role of the Bible in public worship, missiological as well as liturgical sensitivity will continue to be the key to striking the right balance for any Christian group seeking to honor God in its particular setting among its particular neighbors. Keeping Christian symbols to a minimum in a "seeker-sensitive" meeting can be easily defended on the grounds of hospitality, the way one might be careful not to overwhelm guests in one's home with Christian symbolism upon their first visit. But hospitality also requires "truth in packaging" and requires that we present ourselves honestly at first and always. Critics of the "seeker-sensitive" model have yet to be convinced that such wholesale evacuation of Christian symbols from the meeting place does not in fact amount to a fundamental misrepresentation of the Christian ethos at the heart of the meeting. The best of these churches, however, make clear that such meetings are not aimed at Christians, but at seekers. Thus, when the church gathers for its own worship and fellowship (so this logic proceeds), Scripture is given its proper symbolic prominence, congregants are expected to bring their own Bibles, and the teaching is as expositionally substantial as in any other church.

The use of biblical texts to adorn or decorate is also not a new issue. Scriptural texts and motifs bloomed throughout many nineteenth-century American and Canadian homes, whether on walls or on teapots. Critics must therefore be careful to ensure that their criticism is not just a matter of aesthetic taste dressed up in theological garb. What to one person may be a sacrilegiously tacky bathroom mirror Scripture text or T-shirt slogan might be another person's daily reminder to piety or heartfelt testimony to salvation. Some uses of the Bible might well be the result of misplaced zeal or crass commercialism and deserve denunciation as such. These phenomena, however, challenge everyone concerned for the dignity of the Bible to recall just what the Bible is given us to do and to beware of an excessive reverence that would prevent the Bible from functioning as fully as it might in people's lives.

Conversion

There are few who would suggest that North America enjoys a golden age of preaching at the turn of the new millennium. Preaching that blithely strays from the solid path of the biblical text leads no one to a good end over time. Blame, however, cannot be laid solely at the door of a particular homiletical style. Most pastors are so busy with the multitude of tasks with which most churches encumber them that *any* sort of sermon in *any* style that shows *any* serious preparation can be commended. If churches want pastors to preach the Bible well, they must equip pastors with the time, space, and books to do it.

Adult Christian education, with a strong component of Bible teaching and with the continual theme of relating all of learning to the Bible, should constitute an essential part of evangelical church life. It does, indeed, in many congregations, but hardly in most. A sermon or two per week, expositing a few verses or perhaps a chapter or two, is hardly a sufficient diet of scriptural teaching. Furthermore, preaching rarely lends itself to the discussion of matters that should show up in a class, whether historical questions of provenance and purpose of a particular Bible book, geographical situation, or context in the canon. In small churches, pastors might be assisted by only a very few laity, if any, with the expertise necessary to teach these subjects well. Such churches must again decide whether they will assist the pastor in other works of ministry in order to free him or her to prepare and deliver this teaching.

What is true for adult Christian education goes for youth programs as well. Entertainment and socialization into quiet behavior too often seem to be the priorities of Sunday school teaching, with a little moralizing to take home. Evangelicals have done better than most other religious believers in North America in retaining the allegiance of their youth into adulthood. But the sad state of most churchgoers' knowledge of the Bible testifies to the poor quality of Sunday School teaching such "cradle Christians" have received. Evangelicals of previous generations took such teaching seriously, holding regular seminars and rallies for Sunday School teachers and encouraging young people to go off to Bible school in order to equip themselves for lifelong ministry as lay volunteers in such programs. Such concern for the quality of Christian education is encountered rarely today, outside of larger churches that can afford to hire Christian education specialists.

One bright note must be acknowledged, however, regarding the knowledge of Scripture among children. Cassette tapes and CDs with Scripture songs have lulled many a child to sleep at night, and an increasing number of Bible stories have come to life on video. Evangelicals have been quick to use these new media to bring the Bible to children, and it is through them that many children are learning what they do know of its text and narrative.

Evangelicals used to be accused of being "biblicistic" and even "bibliolatrous" as they reflexively referred any problem of life to a Bible text. That accusation can rarely be leveled anymore, and it is not necessarily because evangelicals have become more theologically sophisticated. Many instead have become just as ignorant of the Bible as anyone else.

Mission

Some evangelical apologists and evangelists have left behind the inherited models of mission and have adopted a different posture and voice in their public addresses. Such defenders and commenders of the faith now offer the Christian tradition without claims to its universally demonstrable superiority. Instead, they acknowledge respectfully the outlooks of others and offer the Christian tradition to such others with the acknowledgement that Christians do not have a corner on truth and goodness, but we do believe we have been introduced to the God who is Truth and Goodness. Such apologetics and evangelism does not give up traditional confidence in the Christian tradition. But it does take seriously the postmodernist *and Christian* teaching that humans are both finite and fallen and therefore that each must humbly offer what he or she has found to his or her neighbor without pretensions to infallibility (e.g., Morris; Stackhouse, 1998).

Thus, the Bible is offered without embarrassment to one's neighbor as "our book" in the same way that the neighbor might loan an evangelical a copy of the Adi Granth or Book of Mormon. Those who seek to equip evangelicals for such exchanges, therefore, might well consider the publishing of Bibles with front matter than introduces it to those who do not have a Christian background.

As for trends in evangelistic technique, they will come and go, and time will sift them. But while they are among us, evangelicals who know the Bible will be responsible to serve the church by doing some sifting as well. In the best cases, such people will re-shape these evangelistic approaches to resemble more closely both the examples and teachings of the Bible. In the worst cases, such people must point out the incompatibility of such approaches with biblical norms.

Transdenominationalism

The controversy over the inclusive-language NIV raises two important questions for evangelicals: the issue of gender in both society and in the Bible (over which evangelicals continue to argue), and the perennial translation tension between striving for intelligibility to a particular culture, on the one hand, and remaining faithful to the foreign cultures of the Bible's own literature, on the other. While some critics in this controversy appear to be straining out linguistic gnats or chasing paranoid fantasies, others have raised valid points that cut to the heart of how the church tries to understand God's Word and make that Word understood to its neighbors. Those who promote the Bible therefore have the opportunity here to equip the church for truly edifying argument by teaching the church the principles of good Bible translation and warning about the inevitable differences of opinion that result even among people of good will and sound skills. Such a teaching opportunity not only can promote regard for the Bible but even more importantly can remind Christians of the command to love each other even in, and especially in, the midst of passionate dispute.

The production of Bibles with various "helps" interposed between the reader and the text is hardly a new phenomenon for evangelicals. Many today continue to accept C. I. Scofield's famous "notes" as simply a digest of scriptural truth, bound in as they have been for almost a century with the King James Version. Those who promote Bible reading today need not retreat into a "Bible alone" purism, since everyone who reads necessarily brings along some sort of interpretative framework. But the fair-minded critic might yet wonder about the propriety of giving just one celebrity pastor's view of things in a version bearing his name, when evangelical transdenominationalism could bring a number of orthodox viewpoints to bear on scriptural commentary and reduce the risk that mere idiosyncrasy is substituting for community wisdom.

One also might pause before agreeing with the criticism of modern translations as so banal as to be unfit for memorization, particularly when compared with the putative majesty of the King James Version. As revisers of the KJV itself have agreed through the centuries, there is little to be spiritually gained by memorizing words that in fact have changed their meanings over time, let alone become simply opaque. Furthermore, the Bible itself is not uniformly written in fine style. So there is a fundamental translation question here not to be overlooked: if Peter or John wrote like fishermen, should not their epistles sound that way, rather than like the prose of a highborn wordsmith? Also, should they all sound more or less the same as Paul, Matthew, Isaiah, and Solomon?

An old question of Bible use also resurfaces in the age of the Internet, CD-ROMs, and hypertext. Electronic Bibles have been a great boon to preachers, scholars, and students of the Bible, yet the specter of Thomas Jefferson methodically cutting and pasting (!) the Bible into a form that met his own ideological preferences looms over hypertext versions of the Bible. Does the convenience of these electronic editions militate against the sense of fixed authority that printed Bibles convey? Will Scripture readings be presented to churches nicely pruned of objectionable phrases or stories?

One must be careful not to overreact in this regard. Lectionaries already routinely tell readers what parts of which Psalms are appropriate for public reading and which parts (even to the division of a verse) should be left out. New technology does not necessarily entail either blessing or bane: as Neil Postman tirelessly reminds us, new media bring new ways of doing things, with gain and loss necessarily combined.

Therefore, at the dawn of a new century, it would be well not to attempt too much prediction. Historians can assure a public eager for prophecy of the future that whatever we predict will, in many respects, be either wrong or incomplete. What those who love the Bible do not doubt, however, is that "the Word of our God stands forever" (Isaiah 40:8) and will accomplish God's purposes in the new century—whether via paper, phosphors, or media not yet invented—just as it has in the previous twenty.

Works Consulted

Andrew, Brother, et al.
    1987   *God's Smuggler*. New York: New American Library.
Bebbington, David W.
    1989   *Evangelicalism in Modern Britain: A History from the 1730s to the 1980s*. London: Unwin Hyman.

Berger, Peter L.
   1967   *The Sacred Canopy: Elements of a Sociological Theory of Religion.*
          Garden City, NY: Doubleday.
Bibby, Reginald W.
   1987   *Fragmented Gods: The Poverty and Potential of Religion in
          Canada.* Toronto: Irwin.
Boyd, Gregory A.
   2000   *God of the Possible: A Biblical Introduction to the Open View of
          God.* Grand Rapids, MI: Baker.
Dayton, Donald W. and Robert K. Johnston, eds.
   1991   *The Variety of American Evangelicalism.* Downers Grove, IL:
          InterVarsity.
Dorrien, Gary
   1998.   *The Remaking of Evangelical Theology.* Louisville: Westminster/
           John Knox.
Edwards, Jonathan
   1957   *Freedom of the Will.* Ed. Paul Ramsey. New Haven: Yale University
          Press.
Gallup, George, Jr. and Sarah Jones
   1989   *100 Questions and Answers: Religion in America.* Princeton:
          Princeton Religion Research Center.
Hatch, Nathan O. and Mark A Noll, eds.
   1982   *The Bible in America: Essays in Cultural History.* New York:
          Oxford University Press.
McDannell, Colleen
   1995.   *Material Christianity: Religion and Popular Culture in America.*
           New Haven: Yale University Press.
McDermott, Gerald R.
   2000   *Can Evangelicals Learn from World Religions?* Downers Grove,
          IL: InterVarsity.
Marsden, George M.
   1984   "Introduction." Pp. vii-xix in *Evangelicalism and Modern America.*
          Ed. George M. Marsden. Grand Rapids, MI: Eerdmans.
Morris, Thomas V.
   1992   *Making Sense of it All: Pascal and the Meaning of Life.* Grand
          Rapids, MI: Eerdmans.
Noll, Mark A.
   1986   *Between Faith and Criticism: Evangelicals, Scholarship, and the
          Bible in America.* San Francisco: Harper & Row.
Phillips, Timothy R., and Dennis L. Okholm, eds.
   1996   *The Nature of Confession: Evangelicals and Postliberals in
          Conversation.* Downers Grove, IL: InterVarsity.
Pinnock, Clark H.
   1992   *A Wideness in God's Mercy: The Finality of Jesus Christ in a World
          of Religions.* Grand Rapids, MI: Zondervan.

Pinnock, Clark H., ed.
  1994   *The Openness of God: A Biblical Challenge to the Traditional Understanding of God*. Downers Grove, IL: InterVarsity.
Postman, Neil
  1985   *Amusing Ourselves to Death: Public Discourse in the Age of Show Business*. New York: Penguin.
Sanders, John
  1992   *No Other Name: An Investigation into the Destiny of the Unevangelized*. Grand Rapids, MI: Eerdmans.
Sanders, John, ed.
  1995   *What About Those Who Have Never Heard? Three Views on the Destiny of the Unevangelized*. Downers Grove, IL: InterVarsity Press.
Schleiermacher, Friedrich
  1958   *On Religion: Speeches to its Cultured Despisers*. Trans. John Oman. New York: Harper Torchbooks.
Stackhouse, John G., Jr.
  1993   *Canadian Evangelicalism in the Twentieth Century: An Introduction to Its Character*. Toronto: University of Toronto Press.
  1998   *Can God Be Trusted? Faith and the Challenge of Evil*. New York and Oxford: Oxford University Press.
  1999   "The Battle for the Inclusive Bible." *Christianity Today* 43:83-84.
Stott, John R. W.
  1999   *Evangelical Truth: A Personal Plea for Unity, Integrity, and Faithfulness*. Downers Grove, IL: InterVarsity.
Vine, William E.
  1997   *Vine's Expository Dictionary of Old and New Testament Words*. Nashville: Nelson.
Wolterstorff, Nicholas
  1995.   *Divine Discourse: Philosophical Reflections on the Claim that God Speaks*. Cambridge, UK: Cambridge University Press.

10

The Bible and Popular Culture
Engaging Sacred Text in a World of Others

Mary E. Hess

This essay was sparked by the conversations begun at a conference sponsored by the American Bible Society entitled *Futuring the Scriptures: The Bible for Tomorrow's Publics*. I am interested in the issues raised by that conference because I am a religious educator who works primarily with adults (I teach in a seminary and support adult Christian education in parish settings). My concern for new paradigms for Bible study very much grows out of my attempts to find ways to help persons of faith remain embedded in communities of faith and also be true to their vocations in other cultural spaces as well. For many years I lived in an inner city neighborhood in Boston, Massachusetts, one in which questions of crime and violence were not particularly foreign, and pop music and soap operas formed the basis of many conversations. At the same time I was teaching in a graduate program in pastoral ministry and religious education at a Jesuit college situated on a hill in the suburbs. Now I live in a large upper Midwestern city, St. Paul, Minnesota, and teach at a Lutheran seminary. Most of my teaching takes place in middle class, white contexts and with people who find themselves drawn to ministry as a vocation. Pop culture has not disappeared from the mix, however, with films, television, music, and the Web still interwoven in the lives of my students and neighbors.

I will make two arguments in this essay. First, I believe that engaging Scripture at the time and place in which I am located (see above) requires engaging mass-mediated popular culture. Second, that process of engagement is often difficult and strange, and thinking about it as a process of encountering an "other" is particularly fruitful for those of us who are intent on finding ways to think through Scripture into the twenty-first century and beyond.

Thinking through Scripture by Way of Thinking through Others

What does it mean to "think through Scripture"? I have in mind a process that is lively and embodied, that has cognitive or rational components, but that also has affective and physical elements. As a religious educator, I try to help people come to a sense of themselves and their communities that is bound up with, intertwined with, perhaps even constituted by, the sacred texts at the heart of Christian life. So thinking through Scripture is living with and through it. It is a process that requires active Christian practice, not merely adequate Christian belief. But how do we facilitate this kind of scriptural practice in the midst of cultures, at least in the contemporary United States, where what is considered "sacred" is under contention and, even within graduate theological education, what is considered "Scripture" is at times in question?

My first response, as always, is that we go back to the stories that are at the heart of the Christian community. In that central place, at least when read in terms of Jesus' life and engagements, we encounter a praxis of shared involvement with "others," those persons found at the margins or those outcast from community altogether. Jesus frequently shared table fellowship with those defined as "other," and the gospel writers often recall teachings related to embracing "others." How can we live those stories now? What does it mean to embrace "others" in our contemporary contexts?

These questions only raise more, because one immediate response is that we Christians have not learned how to do this. We have instead learned the opposite: how to name and create "others" as a means of strengthening our own identities. In many ways the warfare between various elements of the Christian community has rarely been so brutal. The civil war in Rwanda would be one particularly compelling example, but clearly the troubles in Northern Ireland, in the former Yugoslavia, as well as in the United States (here I am thinking of the violence involved in hate crimes and in attacks on abortion clinics) are all illustrative as well. Far from embracing "others," we are rarely capable of sharing our own differences in peaceful and just ways.

I have struggled with this dilemma for many years. My work has focused on understanding the ways in which mass-mediated popular culture contributes to the shaping of religious identity. At first I began that study convinced that pop culture contributes to that process only in destructive ways. I thought that there were clear and obvious connections between representations of "otherness" and the construction and maintenance of that otherness, often through violent means. Now I am not so sure. Indeed, in recent years I have come to engage questions of difference, of "otherness," that emerge *within* specific religious communities—differences identified by gender, by race, by class, and so on—at least as much as differences that are apparent *between* faith communities.

So how might popular culture function in shaping identity, and why would such a question be relevant in the context of a book that seeks to engage new paradigms for Bible study? To answer that question, I need to make an assertion and then process the implications of that assertion in a variety of ways. Let me begin by borrowing an assertion from Herbert Anderson and Edward Foley. They argue that storytelling is at the heart of human being. "Part of the power of narrative," they write, "is that it enables us to make deep human connections that transcend unfamiliarity in locale and experience. . . . It is as if stories have mystical power to invite us, willingly or unwillingly, to enter unknown worlds" (4). Anyone who has ever been caught up in a film or television show knows that the power of narrative is even more deeply underlined by the addition of moving images and music.

My primary assertion, growing out of theirs, is that human storytelling, at least in this time and place, is thoroughly embedded in and permeated by mass-mediated popular culture. Pop culture shapes our narratives in multiple ways, including our explicitly religious narratives. While many creative people are exploring various aspects of this assertion, the implications I would like to explore in the rest of this essay grow out Anderson and Foley's idea that stories invite us into unknown worlds. They invite us to encounter things and people, places and practices, that are in some ways "other" to us. Both Scripture and mass-mediated popular culture invite us into the unfamiliar, invite us to encounter the "other." But how do we do that constructively? How do we do that in ways that lead us into deeper relationship rather than into deeper division? And what, if anything, might encountering the unfamiliar in popular culture have to do with encountering the unfamiliar in Scripture? I will devote the rest of this essay to exploring these questions.

"Thinking by means of the Other"

Richard Shweder is a cultural anthropologist who has spent decades studying very diverse religious cultures. He describes four ways in which anthropologists go about thinking through others: "thinking by means of the other," "getting the other straight," "deconstructing and going beyond the other," and "witnessing in the context of engagement with the other." Each of these proves evocative in relation both to popular culture and Scripture, and I would like to consider each in turn. None of these four modes should be considered more valuable than the others; rather, each provides resources and processes by which we can ensure that our encounter with "otherness," particularly in the contexts of both pop culture and Scripture, can be constructive and honest.

Shweder's first category, "thinking by means of the other," has to do with engaging some aspect of the "other" as a means to learn more about ourselves: "Thinking through others in the first sense is to recognize the other as a specialist or expert on some aspect of human experience, whose reflective consciousness and systems of representations and discourse can be used to reveal hidden dimensions of our selves" (108). There are many ways in which mass-mediated popular culture attempts to function as an "expert" of sorts. One example would be the way in which pop culture has become a ritual in which we participate and which provides the "data" that we share in our attempts to communicate with each other. "Did you see that game?" someone asks, or, "What do you think about that candidate?" or, "Did you hear about that flood?" Most of the time the questions as well as the answers come from our listening and viewing in pop culture contexts. Mass-mediated popular culture also presents itself as an expert on what engages a "mass" of people. In both of these cases the expertise comes from defining the language (by which I mean more than simply the verbal issues) that we use in our attempts to communicate with each other.

But how does it reveal "hidden dimensions"? One obvious answer is that it gives us access to situations, feelings, settings, and actions that used to be entirely private. Indeed, the ability to enter a person's bedroom, even live between his or her sheets, is one of the most problematic ways in which communities of faith encounter the "otherness" of television, film, and other mass media. Representing and portraying a multiplicity of sexualities is just one of the ways in which popular culture invites us to reveal (sometimes to our detriment) the hidden dimensions of ourselves. However, television news and other pop culture genres have also brought to public attention various sexual abuses that communities of faith have perpetuated.

How is Scripture an expert? In particular, how might Scripture be an "other" who is an expert on something for which we yearn? More and more we find that the language of popular culture, while revealing some emotions and some contexts, hides others. There are in our sacred texts multiple expressions of emotions and ideas, modes of being and practice that are very alien to our contemporary context and that are consequently more valuable by virtue of that alienness. Finding ways to understand that joy and sorrow are intimately co-mingled, for example, is not easy within popular culture. Scripture, however, provides a route into that recognition.

But there is another way, one directly tied up with both Scripture and popular culture, in which it is important to "think by means of the other." Many people today find living with and through Scripture very alien simply because they are unfamiliar with the experience of living with a sacred text that has been communally defined. Many young people in the U.S. inhabit this space, particularly those whose families have no involvement with communities of faith and who, in attending public schools, have had little or no exposure to the sacred texts of any community of faith. At the same time, many of these people have in recent years had multiple opportunities to engage stories from Scripture in the context of mass-mediated popular culture. Increasingly, television and film have drawn on scriptural stories (Moses and the various Jesus stories being just a few). Popular music is replete with songs that use scriptural references, and the Web is rapidly being permeated by sites that use scriptural references in a multitude of ways. Indeed, the shallow and often careless manner in which these media have used biblical stories has on occasion angered communities of faith, even touching off public protests in some cases.

From the point of view of these young people and others who have not had the opportunity to live with and through Scripture (as opposed to simply being familiar with the plot lines and characters of scriptural stories), engaging sacred text is very much "other." At the same time, from the point of view of communities of faith, the modes and manner in which scriptural stories are wrested from their living contexts and employed in mass-mediated popular contexts is very "other." Whichever side of the dividing line you live on, you are likely to see the opposite side as "other" to your own identity.

I believe we need to take seriously Shweder's notion of "thinking by means of the other" and engage both sides of this line as possibly disclosive, even revelatory. Speaking as a religious educator, I am obviously located within a community of faith, so from that "side of the line," I urge communities of faith not to boycott or ignore popular culture, but to ask deeper questions of it. Why do particular scriptural stories have resonance for people living wholly outside of the communal confines of a specific community of faith? How might the disturbing ways in which young people and others are claiming the insights and images of Scripture be new and possibly disclosive?

When I have the opportunity to do so, I ask people living on the "other side of the line," to consider the ways in which living in a community of faith might have something compelling to offer. I join them in exploring a pop culture "text," a film like *The Matrix*, for instance, and invite them to think about how communities of faith have lived into the question of what is real and how we know to what end we are committed in our lives (both of which are questions central to that film). This process does not end here, however, for as Shweder notes, there are many ways to think through others.

"Getting the Other Straight"

Shweder's second process is something he terms "getting the other straight," by which he means "providing a systematic account of the internal logic of the intentional world constructed by the other. The aim is a rational reconstruction of indigenous belief, desire, and practice" (109). Much biblical exegetical work, particularly from the historical-critical frame, would be familiar in this mode. There are many anecdotes told by people beginning graduate theological education about the consequence of engaging historical-critical tools—"I've lost my Bible!" is a common refrain. The underlying anxiety or humor (depending on the perspective) has to do with coming to grips with a text they thought they knew, but in exploring its internal logic discovered that it was something "other."

The goal in this mode goes beyond simply learning the outlines of a narrative or becoming familiar with the major characters in the Bible. It requires digging deeply into the contexts of scriptural texts, learning how to "read" them in their multiple genres. Some of the resources emerging from new technologies are very helpful here. For example, scattered across the Web are numerous, credible sites that introduce people to the geography of the Bible. These sites help people to explore the etymology of various words used in the Bible, provide vast, easily searchable concordances, and provide images and music that reflect our best guess as to what we might have seen and heard in antiquity.

But what about "getting the other straight" in terms of mass-mediated popular culture? By what means can we read the underlying logics and discern the "beliefs, desires, and practices" that form the foundation of pop culture? Media educators have worked on these questions for some time and have begun to develop a range of tools that are, in some ways, very similar to biblical exegetical tools. These educators help students discover the different genres of popular culture; they explore the various grammars (visual and otherwise) that permeate pop culture. In particular, as a central aspect of their pedagogy, they introduce students to the unique production characteristics of particular genres of media. They do so not because they expect their students to master the technical aspects of film making, for instance, or to become adept at recording and editing musical scores, but because in performing these practices their students gain a more vivid, deep, and critical appreciation for film and for music. As with Scripture, there are numerous Web sites available to provide ready access to these tools and methodologies.

"Thinking by means of the other" and "getting the other straight" are very useful modes, then, for beginning to engage Scripture and for becoming more aware of mass-mediated popular culture, but both can remain simply an interesting side trip, a way to be a "tourist" in a different culture without allowing that culture to be integrated into one's own identity. It is possible to engage "others" in this frame and yet remain in a position of differentiation without ever moving to "reintegration." That is, it is possible to engage sacred texts as an interesting and compelling example of meaning-making without having them bound up in one's core way of making meaning in the world. It is equally possible to venture into popular culture without coming to a deep appreciation of its ubiquitous presence in the process of shaping identity. How might religious educators facilitate moving beyond this kind of differentiation?

"Deconstructing and Going Beyond the Other"

Shweder believes that the next step, at least from the point of view of anthropology, involves "going beyond the other." Many educators would identify their next step as "critical reflection," which shares much with Shweder's assertion that "'thinking through others' . . . comes later, after we have already appreciated what the intentional world of the other powerfully reveals and illuminates, from its special point of view. 'Thinking through others' is, in its totality, an act of criticism and liberation, as well as discovery" (109-110). "Going beyond the other" is perhaps the mode of learning and knowing most feared by our contemporary religious institutional authorities (speaking from within my Catholic tradition), and is often painfully practiced by religious outsiders. Far too often this mode has *not* been the "third sense," as suggested by Shweder, coming after "we have already appreciated what the intentional world of the other reveals," but instead is often the first mode practiced, before sufficient respect—or even simple attention—has been given to understanding each other's worlds. I often find Catholic persons in positions of religious authority condemning mass-mediated popular culture as a vast wasteland of violence and illicit sexuality, while religious outsiders (younger generations, in particular) condemn such religious authorities as closed-minded and repressive arbiters of meaning. Neither seeks to understand the other from within the other's perspective.

We have not recognized the extent to which our complicated relationship with Scripture and culture has led to a drawing of sharp boundaries around Scripture that, in granting it normativity, have paradoxically narrowed and limited its reach. We as persons of faith have sought to be "in the world, but not of it," and in doing so we have become increasingly irrelevant, as we have refused to recognize how permeable cultural boundaries are and how much our worlds are interpenetrating each other.

There are some Christian communities, for instance, that have actually forbidden encounters with media that offer radically new and challenging interpretations of Scripture. Yet without the opportunity to "think beyond" the ways in which we have previously engaged Scripture we cut ourselves off from an essential part of the process of adult learning and growth. "Going beyond," especially when it is a mode by which one can encounter the paradoxical and conflicting claims of tradition and faith, is a crucial mode of encounter and meaning-making. Robert Kegan, a noted adult educator, recognizes how central this process is when he identifies the process of "contradiction" at the heart of adult learning. Deconstructing and going beyond the other begins to open us up, not just by way of critically engaging the "other," but primarily by practicing a critical perspective that inevitably transforms our own self-perception. As Kegan notes, this process is often painful and is one for which little educational support is provided.

Kegan's description of the learning process is noteworthy in this context, because he believes that human development in general, and meaning-making transformation in particular, proceeds by way of "confirmation, contradiction and continuity." Teachers can support authentic growth and development by attending to this tripartite process. "Confirmation" has to do with the extent to which the way a person "makes up" the world is confirmed by others. Religious educators attempt this kind of confirmation when we meet people where they are and assess their current knowledge and mode of understanding before we challenge it.

"Contradiction" is a process of moving through and beyond such meanings to new and different ways of understanding the world. Contradiction occurs both inadvertently and naturally, as well as through deliberate intervention. Entering graduate theological education often has this impact on students in relation to Scripture study, but crises of health or relationship can also have this impact. Teachers often call the skills involved in processing contradictions those of "critical thinking."

Confirming reality for students and then proceeding to contradict that reality only creates confusion, at best, and rigidity of belief, at worst; therefore, we must simultaneously provide what Kegan terms "continuity." Continuity is the crucial process of finding ways to connect one's current construction of the world with those that one has made in the past. Religious educators can bring historical-critical biblical tools to bear on the tale of Noah's Ark, for example, but unless we help our students come to grips with the ways in which Bible stories "are all true, and some of them really happened," we risk our students falling either into biblical literalism or biblical irrelevance.

In describing this cycle of "confirmation, contradiction, continuity," Kegan explores the ways in which we carry along and construct our definitions of "self" and "other." He also explores the ways in which tremendous amounts of pain can be experienced amidst the learning process. "How I am" becomes "how I was" *before* shifting to "how I am now." The very process of that transition involves a fundamental revisioning of one's self and a distinct "dis-embedding" of oneself from a particular culture as part of the process of reintegrating into the next understanding. Far too often that pain can be externalized onto some "other" that is readily at hand.

It is this kind of "externalizing" onto an "other" that is at the heart of much our contemporary brokenness, particularly the violence and humiliation that characterizes some of the more painful conflicts within and between communities of faith. I believe that in providing new paradigms for biblical study, we must at least break open this process and find ways to support people through the painful encounter with the contradictions and discontinuities of our lives as lived in communities of faith. One such source of contradiction and discontinuity is our struggle over the relevance of Scripture to popular culture, and vice versa. Engaging the "otherness" of both Scripture and popular culture as similar, rather than specifying that one is "sacred" and the other "secular," offers an integrated approach that can succeed where the continuation of a polarized dualism cannot.

In dealing with these contradictions, we need to approach the process carefully. Religious educators need to think about how we faithfully demonstrate critique of religious insider stances, for instance, if we are to erase gradually the line between "insider" and "outsider" within our faith communities. How, for instance, can I as a Catholic educator take up questions of supporting persons who are gay, while I am trying to be faithful to the ways in which I represent institutional Catholic interpretations of Scripture on homosexuality? How might I, as a Catholic woman, embody educational leadership in community in such a way as to break open the scriptural issues around women's leadership in worship? These issues are alive in popular culture and are also lively within communities of faith.

These are difficult questions raised by Scripture and popular culture from within my own location, but there are equally difficult ones in others. If we can begin to engage them we might at the same time be able to change our stance towards those "others" beyond our self-defined boundaries. We might be able to educate toward a religious identity that can truly and thoroughly embrace difference. To do so, however, we have to find a way beyond differentiation and into reintegration. It is Shweder's fourth mode of "thinking through others" that brings us to the kind of continuity Kegan suggests is necessary for this kind of transformative learning.

"Witnessing in the Context of Engagement with the Other"

Shweder's fourth step recognizes that the "process of representing the other goes hand in hand with a process of portraying one's own self as part of the process of representing the other, thereby encouraging an open-ended, self-reflexive, dialogic turn of mind" (110). What does it mean to recognize that in thinking through others we are intimately engaged in portraying ourselves as part of that process? I began this section of this essay quoting Anderson and Foley's assertion that human beings are story-making people. Later in that same book, the authors suggest that the goal of story-telling "is not just to discover a world or provide an interpretation of a world that allows us to live in it but rather to discover and interpret a world that allows us to live with ourselves. We retell incidents, relate occurrences, and spin tales in order to learn what occurred, especially to *me*" (5). Indeed, in some manner, we make ourselves up in the process of making up the world. I will have more to say in the second section of this essay about the relational and communal consequences of this story-telling, but right now, I will explore the implications of this statement for Bible study.

"Making each other up" is often a legitimate concern many communities of faith have about popular cultural representations. Indeed, anyone who pays sustained attention to television in particular will sense that the reality constructed through it implicitly supports systems of oppression far more often than it explicitly deconstructs them. Many people of faith would affirm the normativity of Scripture, "Truth with a capital T," because it provides a way in which to confront the negative representations and destruction through omission that they can clearly identify in popular culture. This understanding of normativity, however, tends to equate truth with a particular set of statements or convictions that hold over time and across cultures and that create identity over and against "others."

Is there a way to address questions of normativity that allows us to affirm that we do, indeed, make each other up, but that does so without losing transcendence or without losing our ability to speak of universals? The concern over universality arises in large part because knowledge frameworks that specify that knowledge is socially constructed eschew any notion of an abstract neutral universal. Yet the inability to speak of a universal in abstract, disembodied terms does not require us to give up the possibility of finding an embodied, specific way to speak in universal terms. Catholic theologian Roberto Goizueta, for example, writes that "we discover the whole, or the universal, not by adding up the particulars, but by entering fully into their very particularity, *within which* we will encounter their universal significance: 'To know is to recognize the specific phenomenal activity that, in each case, reveals to us the Universe.' In the words of the poet William Blake, we can 'see a world in a grain of sand and a heaven in a wild flower'" (97). This description, an organic theological anthropology arising from within the U.S. Hispanic/Latino community, pushes us to recognize the ways in which we are inextricably bound to each other and yet still remain individual persons loved by God. Relationality is the very fabric of our existence; it is, in Goizueta's terms, "constitutive" and "preexistent." As Goizueta notes: "Only if I affirm your own concrete particularity and uniqueness will I be able to understand how your own life and history reveal a universal truth that is also true for me" (157).

This description provides further impetus for engaging in a complex and holistic process of "thinking through others," for how else might we come to "understand," as Goizueta puts it, "how your own life and history reveal a universal truth that is also true for me" (157)? I cannot believe that it is possible to be respectfully present to others without also recognizing the ways in which mass-mediated popular culture swirls around us in the process. So we are back to the implication of the assertions I made at the beginning of this essay: human beings are story-tellers whose stories are permeated by popular culture; in engaging them through both Scripture and popular culture, we engage ourselves and each other.

This kind of "witnessing in the context of engagement with others," however, is not often an easy or comfortable process to pursue. We need powerful and passionate metaphors and role models to help us embrace this struggle, particularly as we confront our own brokenness and the divisions that threaten to tear us apart. Daloz et al. speak of a "responsible imagination" that is capable of paying attention to images of dissonance and contradiction, "particularly as revealing injustice and unrealized potential." This is precisely the kind of imagination religious educators need to call upon (151-152).

There are multiple examples of ways in which educators have tried to support this kind of imagination, and in the process provide access to the continuities of Christian community. Here are two multimedia productions, by way of short example. The first is the animated videotape series for children from BigIdea Productions, entitled *Veggie Tales*. These videos translate scriptural texts into a world of animated vegetables that act out stories on a kitchen counter top. Each episode begins with the veggies out of costume, discussing some pressing question. They then perform a story "in costume" that attempts either to portray a specific biblical text (as in the story of Daniel in the lions' den) or to cull it out of a specific dilemma (as in the story of Madame Blueberry, whose tree house collapses under the weight of the "stuff" she has purchased from "Stuffmart," thus giving new meaning to the phrase, "troubling one's house"). At the end of the show, the veggies return to their "natural" state and pose a question to "QWERTY," the computerized Bible, who responds with a specific Scripture verse.

These shows captivate young children and college students alike not simply because they contain sophisticated digital animation, good music, and silly humor, but because they weave provocative references to mass-mediated popular culture throughout their references to biblical culture. Parents of young children in this digitally mediated world are challenged to find ways of integrating biblical imagination into the media children like. Television and particularly videotapes are a familiar feature of pre-school and elementary school age lives, and *Veggie Tales* provides a way to make Bible stories present within that context. They also model one mode of engaging Scripture: searching it for answers to troubling questions. The downside of these productions is that like any image-driven medium, video meaning is not easily constrained to one message. The meaning one person draws from a production might be quite different from the meaning intended by the author of the production. Nor are the questions posed as easily answered as these productions suggest. They are appropriate for young children and are amusing for adults, but are by no means the only way in which to present scriptural texts. Still, they provide access to one way to live with Scripture in the midst of a digitally-mediated culture.

Given our current cultural illiteracy of history, providing access to the ways in which faith communities have engaged Scripture over time and across multiple contexts is of equal or greater importance. For this challenge, the American Bible Society CD-ROMs are a vital resource. These digital media provide a hypertext approach to Scripture, giving the user the primary responsibility for providing the path through the materials, for evincing the necessary questions in search of multiple answers. They are rich in various instantiations of the text in question: music versions of the text, images based on the text, music videos of various versions of the text. The CD-ROMs also provide exegetical resources that allow the user to trace the meaning of various words in a passage and link that passage to a specific geographic context. Finally, they offer an introduction to story-boarding, enabling people to develop their own video interpretation of a text. By providing multiple translations of a text—translations that include not simply various print versions but also musical and image choices—the CD-ROMs open up the process of biblical translation and interpretation by making it accessible to people.

Theological Entry Points into Responsible Imagination

We need more than multimedia productions of biblical texts to provide continuity, however. We need new metaphors for bringing biblical themes to bear in contemporary contexts. Earlier in this essay, new voices in theological anthropology provided insight into questions of normativity and universality. Here they can provide new routes by which educators can support a responsible imagination. One entry point that is profoundly helpful from the educational standpoint of "providing confirmation, contradiction and continuity" grows out of the work of Miroslav Volf:

> The struggle for survival, recognition, and domination, in which people are inescapably involved, helps forge self-enclosed identities, and such self-enclosed identities perpetuate and heighten that same struggle. This holds true for relations between genders no less than for relations between cultures. To find peace, people with self-enclosed identities need to open themselves for one another and give themselves to one other, yet without loss of the self or domination of the other. (176)

Part of this opening up comes with the recognition that we are inextricably, constitutively bound to one another. But that recognition alone does not erase hatred, domination, systemic oppression, or any of the other sins with which we live. Instead, as Volf suggests, we must ask

> the right kind of question, which is not how to achieve the final reconciliation, but *what resources we need to live in peace in the absence of the final reconciliation. . . .* Both the modern project of emancipation and its postmodern critique suggest that a *nonfinal reconciliation in the midst of the struggle against oppression* is what a responsible theology must be designed to facilitate. (109-110)

Searching for such a nonfinal reconciliation can lead us to self-descriptions that are more complex and ambiguous, more embracing of "others," and more capable of sustaining the critical continuity that Kegan suggests that our contemporary situation demands of us. Asking what these resources could be is a question that grows organically out of Shweder's notion of "thinking beyond the other" and Kegan's descriptions of dealing with contradictions in meaning frame. I am convinced that new paradigms for Bible study must ask this kind of question.

Such a question does not search Scripture for definitive answers to final questions, but looks to stories and places in which we can find ways to struggle. Indeed, the struggle itself is the goal; a phrase very similar to the feminist chant that "the process is the goal." I am reminded of the word image that Buckminster Fuller, the man who created the geodesic dome, coined within architecture for describing the essential stability of structures created by holding opposing forces together with respect for their integrity: "tension" + "integrity" = "tensegrity."

As I wrote at the beginning of this paper, I have been looking at cross-cultural work as a way of thinking about communicating across various "sub-cultures" within the Christian church. In no way do I believe that these groups of "religious insiders" or "religious outsiders" actually inhabit separate spaces. Rather, I have been looking at ways in which we might find some larger common ground and engage our real differences rather than recognize our differences, hide them, and deny their reality within the church. While Volf speaks about the realities of Christians and other religious communities engaging each other across large geographically-induced cultural divides, I think he is equally relevant when we consider the generational divides that exist within Christian churches.

Volf writes that "one of the most basic tenets of the Christian faith is that *we* are the perpetrators who crucified Christ, *we* are the godless whose godlessness God exposed. For us, sinful and limited human beings, following in the footsteps of the Crucified means not only creating space in ourselves for others, but in creating space for them making also space for their perspective on us and on them" (215). What is required to make this kind of space in ourselves and in our paradigms for Bible study? As I noted earlier, Shweder and Kegan suggest that at a minimum we must cultivate ways of thinking through others that allow us to see not only our differences or the authentic utility of each other's ways of being in the world, but also the limitations and constraints of our own and others' modes. Beyond that, we must grow to understand the ways in which our explorations lead to a more full understanding of ourselves and of how we, quite literally, make each other up.

There is perhaps no source for our identity that is more central than Scripture, and so it is Scripture that *must* help us both engage these limitations and support us in engaging *its* limitations. Volf vividly describes the ground necessary for this kind of pedagogy, although I should point out that I read his image through my own Catholic lenses, which like Goizueta, show me a reality where "community is the *source* of individuality" (152). Volf suggests that by considering how we engage in a *literal* embrace, such as a physical hug, we can understand more deeply how we can and must embrace our differences without losing either our self-identity or our constitutive community in the process. He identifies four steps in an embrace: "opening arms, waiting, closing arms, and then opening arms again" (141ff):

> Open arms are a gesture of the body reaching for the other. They are a sign of discontent with my own self-enclosed identity, a code of *desire* for the other. . . . More than just a code for desire, open arms are a sign that I have *created space* in myself for the other to come in and that I have made a movement out of myself so as to enter the space created by the other. . . . Finally, open arms are a gesture of *invitation.* (141-142)

Religious educators need to ask ourselves, how open are our arms? Have we reached out to all those within our community who might be alienated from the institutional church? Alternatively, if we speak from within an alienated community, have we opened ourselves up to relationship within the institutional church? Have we been willing to desire such an invitation? Have we opened ourselves up to the kinds of meaning-making that await us with others? Have we tried to "think by means of others" and tried to "get the other straight"? Have we, within institutional contexts, immersed ourselves in mass-mediated popular culture by listening to music, going to films, surfing the internet, hanging out at the mall, or going down to the local teen hangout? Have we, within alienated contexts, believed it worth doing to "think by means of" or to "get the other straight"? Have we, as young people, tried to figure out why sitting in silent prayerful meditation with Scripture might bring new insight?

Volf identifies waiting as the next step within physical embrace. "Waiting . . . [is] the halted movement of the arms outstretched toward the other" (142).

> The waiting self *can* move the other to make a movement toward the self, but its power to do so is the power of signaled desire, of created space, and opened boundary of the self, not the power that breaks boundaries of the other and forces the fulfillment of desire. The other

cannot be coerced or manipulated into an embrace; violence is so much the opposite of embrace that it undoes the embrace. If embrace takes place, it will always be because the other has desired the self just as the self has desired the other. This is what distinguishes embrace from grasping after the other, and holding the other in one's power. Waiting is a sign that, although embrace may have a one-sidedness in its origin (the self makes the initial movement toward the other), it can never reach its goal without reciprocity (the other makes a movement toward the self). (142-143)

It is here that the pain of the dilemmas that emerge can be felt. Do we truly desire this embrace? How long must we wait? How do we hold ourselves open without submitting ourselves to coercion? What do we do if the embrace is rejected? Can we remain open to try again? The educational questions are myriad and deep. How can we teach in such a way as to remain open to that which might emerge? Can we sit in silence and allow silence to create a space for an invitation? Any classroom teacher knows how agonizing fifteen seconds of silence can be after a question is asked. Can we teach in such a way that our students and our faith communities grow more able and willing to wait for embrace? Can we provide the adequate support to enable the tension and pain of this transition, of this "not-knowing," of this waiting for final reconciliation, rather than the certainty of it? Can we inhabit our questions even more fully than we have asserted answers?

Volf does not leave us here, however, for he points out that open arms can draw the other in, at which point we close our arms again:

Closing the arms . . . is the goal of embrace. . . . It takes *two* pairs of arms for *one* embrace; with one pair, we will either have merely an invitation to embrace (if the self respects the other) or a taking in one's clutches (if there is no such respect). In an embrace a host is a guest and a guest is a host. Though one self may receive or give more than the other, each must enter the space of the other, feel the presence of the other in the self, and make its own presence felt. . . . For such free and mutual giving and receiving to take place, in addition to reciprocity, a *soft touch* is necessary. I may not close my arms around the other too tightly, [but] . . . I must keep the boundaries of my own self firm. . . . At no point in the process may the self deny either the other or itself. (143-144)

What is this reciprocity like in a teaching setting? How do we communicate the treasures of a tradition without shutting down the creative, improvisational abilities of new generations of faithful? Religious educators are often trained to bring answers to questions, not to allow questions to emerge. What does it mean to create a space within Scripture study where those who are alienated from various parts of a faith community or of a tradition are invited into the learning event and embraced as essential and integral partners in the learning process? How do we practice this kind of "soft touch" within an institutional culture that far too often appears to be relying on hard repressive pressures? We can do so by practicing the kind of "thinking through others" that Shweder advocates, keeping in mind Kegan's cautions about the pain and benefits of such a process.Volf's description of the final element of embrace is that of "opening the arms again":

> What holds the bodies together in an embrace is not their welded boundary, but the arms placed around the other. And if the embrace is not to cancel itself, the arms must be open again (Gurevitch 1990, 194). . . . As the final act of embrace, the opening of the arms underlines that, though the other may be inscribed into the self, the alterity of the other may not be neutralized by merging both into an undifferentiated "we." (144-145)

The best teachers I have encountered, those who inspire in me the vision of teaching to which I aspire, teach with precisely this kind of embrace— one that gathers me into a reciprocal and energizing study of a particular topic, sharing the resources that the teacher brings to the task and helping me to identify those that I bring, and then opening up the embrace again to let each of us continue to grow in our own ways. Scripture at its best can be this kind of teacher, and we must bring this kind of teaching to the tasks of Bible study, of enlivening our faith communities, and of supporting their embrace of all the vivid difference they now hold within them. If we cannot do that with each other, I hesitate to imagine how we might do it across larger boundaries. Finding a way to do it within our own boundaries, embracing the rich and painful differences that endure within us, only supports our efforts to live, work, and embrace our larger, overlapping cultures.

Works Consulted

Anderson, Herbert, and Foley, Edward
    1998   *Mighty Stories, Dangerous Rituals: Weaving Together the Human and the Divine*. San Francisco: Jossey-Bass Publishers.
Beaudoin, Tom
    1998   *Virtual Faith: The Irreverent Spiritual Quest of Generation X*. San Francisco: Jossey-Bass Publishers.

Daloz, Laurent, Cheryl Keen, James Keen, and Sharon Daloz Parks
 1996 *Common Fire: Lives of Commitment in a Complex World*. Boston:
    Beacon Press.
Goizueta, Roberto
 1995 *Caminemos con Jesús: Toward a Hispanic/Latino Theology of
    Accompaniment*. Maryknoll: Orbis Books.
Kegan, Robert
 1982 *The Evolving Self: Problem and Process in Human Development*.
    Cambridge, MA: Harvard University Press.
 1994 *In Over Our Heads: The Mental Demands of Modern Life*.
    Cambridge, MA: Harvard University Press.
Shweder, Richard
 1991 *Thinking through Cultures: Expeditions in Cultural Psychology*.
    Cambridge, MA: Harvard University Press.
Vella, Jane
 1994 *Learning to Listen: Learning to Teach*. San Francisco: Jossey-Bass
    Publishers.
Volf, Miroslav
 1996 *Exclusion and Embrace: A Theological Exploration of Identity,
    Otherness and Reconciliation*. Nashville: Abingdon Press.

11

Rethinking Local Bible Study in a Postmodern Era

Randy G. Litchfield

At the beginning of the twenty-first century, religious education professionals in North America are working to engage the challenges and opportunities of a culture in transition. This is nothing new. As part of the process of helping people make religious meaning, religious educators have always dealt with the intersections of a faith community's tradition and contemporary culture. The current times are particularly challenging, though, because of the magnitude of the cultural changes. These changes have been so deep that labels such as "*post*modern" are used to indicate that changes are occurring at the level of our core assumptions about the world. Some of the marks of postmodern culture include skepticism about universal truths, recognition of pervasive diversity, engagement with the politics of knowledge, widespread use of electronic media, reconsideration of the relationship between individuals and communities, and movements for human liberation. Because faith is formed and transformed in a variety of ways, religious education involves an ecology of forms composed of congregational worship, interpersonal relationships, prayer, and shared times of service to others, as well as church school. Many religious educators are considering the intersection of postmodern culture with these various forms through which education takes place.

My concern in this essay is to consider the intersection of postmodernism and religious education in the form of local Bible study. When religious educators address postmodern paradigms, we are tempted simply to teach *about* postmodernism and to overlook the impact that the postmodern situation has on the overall educational project. A paradigm change means that core assumptions are changing. Therefore, my approach to rethinking local Bible study in a postmodern era will be to consider postmodern responses to key educational questions, such as: What are the *purposes* of studying/teaching the Bible? What is the *content* of local Bible study? What *processes* are desirable in studying the Bible? How are the *people* involved in local Bible study understood?

The responses to these questions depend a great deal on one's context. Academic responses differ from parish responses. In this essay I use "local" in reference to congregational, para-church programs and small group contexts. The responses I offer are general—ultimately these questions must be answered from within specific locations. Also my responses emerge from my personal identity mix: European American, male, straight, Midwestern, college professor, lay leader, married parent, mixed denominational heritage, ex-engineer, etc.

My reflections in this essay are in five parts. The first part briefly introduces postmodern issues about the Bible as these are being discussed in conferences sponsored by the American Bible Society. Many of the insights emerging from ABS conversations reflect some form of postmodern assumptions. The second part relates these issues to local Bible study through the educational questions about purposes, content, processes and people. The final three parts will deal with implications for institutions seeking to support local Bible study, one possibility for a local Bible study approach, and summary conclusions.

1. Some Contemporary Issues about the Bible

The American Bible Society's report on its February 6, 1999 consultation, entitled *Futuring the Scriptures: The Bible for Tomorrow's Publics*, summarizes six themes reflecting postmodern issues for biblical study. I wish to highlight certain aspects of these that are relevant to my project. The first theme raises questions about ongoing revelation, ways that communities and individuals form their own canons, and the role of the Bible as a centering force. The second theme deals with issues of pluralism, diversity and uniqueness in relation to reading the Bible. Of note here is the observation that "no longer is the academic tradition of scriptural interpretation the only valid one; nor is it the privileged one. Instead, it is but one reading tradition among a rapidly increasing number of other traditions" (5). Reading is contextual, but how does one identify or understand that context? The third theme involves issues of continuity and discontinuity in the biblical message. Again there are observations about the privileged nature of some readings and the need to read the text in light of global, gender and ethnic realities. It is also observed that the survival of the biblical message depends on people engaging the Bible in ways that are mutually transforming. The fourth theme addresses the relation between the medium and the message of the Bible. The fifth theme engages the concern of approaches to the authority of Bible. Issues include how a source of authority can provide identity and norms that are either liberating or tyrannical, how the Bible is but one source of theological reflection, and that the authority of the text is a claim made for the text by a believing community. In summary, "a particular text may be primary within a given community but it's not self-sufficient. Each community will have multiple centers of authority" (14). The final theme addresses issues of racism, feminism, and antisemitism—is the Bible being used to enfranchise or disenfranchise people? The key point seems to be the recognition that the reading of the text is a part of the social formation of particular groups, traditions and communities. Two quotes from the report are worth sharing:

> Interpretation is a political act. Who says, 'the Bible says'? Individuals and groups selectively appropriate the biblical narratives, which then lead to social formation and group identity. When a group forms the boundaries of its social identity, who becomes 'the other' over against which the group defines itself? (15)

And later in the same section:

> [Struggles over the text take] place within the decision that the story is worth interacting with in ways that form real communities. Communities are formed in the struggle to preserve the text, and the future is created in the process of active decision making, not passive reception. (16)

These themes express postmodern assumptions that cannot help but impact our educational understanding of local Bible study. Biblical interpretations are increasingly understood as fluid and contingent upon the interpreter's perspective. One important source of perspective is the local culture of particular communities. The truthfulness of an interpretation is in relation to the community doing the interpretation. At the same time, the very acts of interpreting the Bible contribute to the development of community. Another aspect of understanding perspective is the interplay of the ways difference is embodied in gender, ethnicity, and class. These formative aspects of our lives underscore diversity as a pervasive characteristic of the world. Various media are also powerful forces in the construction of meaning. The interplay of differing perspectival interpretations is political, i.e., involves power and impacts the way people are able to live.

2. Educational Questions Related to Local Bible Study

With the preceding synopsis of postmodern themes in relation to Biblical study in mind, it is time to consider local Bible study in the future. I will do so in relation to four educational questions.

2.1 "What are the purposes *of studying and teaching the Bible?"*

Traditionally, several reasons are given for engaging in local Bible study. Some significant reasons include maturing in one's Christian discipleship, experiencing God as mediated by scripture, developing Biblical literacy, and seeking guidance for life decisions. In light of various purposes for Bible study, multiple ways of engaging the text exist and may be given new twists in the postmodern context.

In light of the interplay of the perspectival and political themes described above, the purposes of local Bible study might also include formation and transformation of community, formation and transformation of self-identity, stewardship of the texts of traditions, and sponsoring ethical responsibility. Including these aspects as part of the reasons for Bible study is an attempt to make implicit dynamics explicit, thus making Bible study intentional, constructive, and ethical.

The purpose of *forming and transforming of community* acknowledges the fluid, communal aspect of perspective. This goal is important to highlight because so many postmodern attitudes reflect the recognition that reality is a social construction. Indeed, the Bible is one of the most crucial centering forces of a Christian community. This is not so much a theological claim about its authority as it is a sociological observation about group process. In the act of engaging the Bible, individuals in a community dialogue, debate, argue and negotiate interpretations and their implications. In so doing, they are negotiating the relationships between themselves, their predecessors and their heirs. This Bible-mediated conversation weaves individuals together into a tradition and community.

The purpose of *forming and transforming self-identity* involves the postmodern concern for the interplay of gender, ethnicity and class. The postmodern self is understood as fluid and socially constructed. The self emerges as an intersection of many strands, such as gender, ethnicity and class. The configuration of the self depends greatly on the narratives used to weave these strands together. Various narratives are used at different times, and these highlight certain strands in one's identity. Reflection on the identities and norms presented by the Bible and other recognized authorities shape social and individual ways of being in the world.

The purpose of *stewardship of the texts of the tradition* acknowledges the community's role in defining the ongoing shape of the canon. The first two purposes might seem to imply that the dynamics of Bible study are unidirectional—flowing from the Bible to community and self. However, canons emerge in relation to communities. The communal and intrapersonal negotiations occasioned by the interpretation of the Bible also continually renew and reinvent the canon. In the midst of all the communal and intrapersonal strands, points of relevance can seemingly always be constructed out of elements of the Bible. As Elaine Pagels said, "We know it [the text] will only survive as people care about it and engage it in some way so the various stories transform it and live through it" (American Bible Society: 7). Engagement with the Bible entails a stewardship of the Bible.

The purpose of *sponsoring ethical responsibility* requires, in a post-modern setting, engagement with the politics of interpretation and identi-ty. *How* one reads is an ethical category because of the formative role read-ing has on the nature of community and self. Put another way, the act of reading a community's sacred texts opens one to a reinterpretation and renegotiation of relationships, which is in turn an ethical endeavor. If read-ing is related to context and each context entails norms and visions for right relationships, i.e., ethical standards, then how one reads is a political and ethical act. Since power and privilege are a part of the fabric of read-ing and studying the Bible, a sense of responsibility must be fostered for the way one reads and the actions that flow into and from study.

To deepen our understanding of the purposes of local Bible study, let us remember that engaging the Bible in a local community of faith is a religious practice. In such locations, biblical study is part of a quest for the sacred. Craig Dykstra and Dorothy Bass define a Christian practice as "things Christian people do together over time in response to and in the light of God's active presence for the life of the world" (5). They describe such practices as addressing human needs and conditions, providing help for "human flourishing," possessing standards of excellence, and creating awareness of "how our daily lives are all tangled up with the things God is doing in the world" (6-8). According to their definition, Bible study as a practice of faith is historical, communal, spiritually enriching, both hon-ored and abused, and contributes to human flourishing.

A major question for this description of the purposes for local Bible study is its acceptability within evangelical contexts, since the assump-tions about the social construction of reality is in tension with evangeli-cal convictions about universal truths revealed in scripture. This tension is one of several issues receiving attention within a "postconservative" movement, led by evangelical theologians such as Clark Pinnock, Henry H. Knight III, and Stanley Grenz. Postconservative evangelicals are in the process of reinterpreting evangelicalism in light of the postmodern con-text. Of particular relevance is the postconservative sensitivity to diversi-ty and the recognition of the significant role of community in interpreting the Bible.

2.2 *"What is the* content *of local Bible study?"*

The question of what is to be studied in local Bible study draws an obvious initial response: it's the Bible! But how do postmodern perspectives about the Bible potentially change our understanding of the content of study? If we look at the Bible in the postmodern world, we find that important assumptions about biblical content seem to have changed. One assumption involves the internal uniformity of scripture. Greater effort is being given to honoring the Bible's internal diversity that resulted from the various communities and experiences involved in the creation of the canon. This change in assumption means that differences within the Bible no longer need to be forcibly harmonized. The internal dialogue of scripture is much like the dialogue of contemporary communities who labor to find a faithful path by which to work out their salvation and vocation. Another assumption involves the source of meaning regarding a biblical text. Fernando Segovia notes in his analysis of the pedagogies of contemporary biblical criticism that the adoption of historical-critical methods did not change the assumption that the text holds a specific meaning and the scholar-teacher has the key to unlocking it (6). Postmodern perspectives about the location of meaning have moved from the modern view of meaning being somehow embedded in the text to meaning emerging from an interplay of text-reader-context. So the content of Bible study is always more than the text itself.

To understand the content of study we should also ask, What must be "known," in various ways, in order to accomplish the previously suggested purposes of Bible study? In order to accomplish the traditional and suggested purposes of local Bible study, there are several elements to include as content in addition to the text itself. To *form and transform community* calls for individuals to study their faith community. This requires an understanding of the communal and denominational history, skills for negotiation and conflict management, and awareness of the local culture (language, rituals, symbols, values, norms, relationship patterns, demographics, etc.) To *form and transform self-identity,* individuals need to explore their own life narratives. This involves revaluing past events, awareness of the various contexts and roles through which they have moved and continue to move, social constructs such as gender and race, and the processes and forms they use to connect these aspects. To achieve a faithful *stewardship of the texts of the tradition* requires an understanding of the history and trajectory of the texts. This involves basic literary skills, awareness of how texts have been read in the past, the role of particular passages in the formation of the community's identity, historical issues of the text's production, and the importance of the texts for the next generation. To *sponsor ethical responsibility* requires an understanding of the network of human and nonhuman relationships impacted by the community's actions. This involves description of relationships, actions taken in relationship to others, and the process of study itself. The study process needs to be included in the content of study because of the politics of interpretation. It is important to keep in mind when thinking about issues of educational content that three curricula are always at work simultaneously: the explicit, the implicit, and the null. The explicit curriculum is the material being engaged directly. The implicit curriculum is the content being taught indirectly through the processes. The explicit and implicit may or may not be in harmony. For example, I can explicitly teach that women and men are equal in the church while at the same time teaching the opposite by my conduct toward women in a study group. The null curriculum is what is taught through its absence. For example, many people are taught that women are not to be leaders in the church by lack of reference to women leaders in the past or by their invisibility in the present. Making the process of study part of the content of study moves it from the null to the explicit curriculum. If the process is left in the null curriculum, we may in effect teach that our readings are neutral and universal, when they are anything but that.

2.3 *"What* processes *are desirable in studying the Bible?"*

Attending to processes is important so that explicit content may be treated effectively and may be congruent with and supported by the implicit content of the processes. Educational processes are never value-neutral. They convey powerful messages about central values and assumptions—messages that are often more potent than the explicit content. In general, processes need—both explicitly and implicitly—to foster community, identity formation (including one's spirituality), stewardship of the text, and ethical responsibility. In order to support the purposes of local study, processes need to embody diversity, the liberating impulse of biblical authority, and the meaning-making abilities of individuals and communities. In light of postmodern assumptions about the Bible, methods that broaden hermeneutics from text to context are needed. Ethnographic methods hold a great deal of promise for addressing these process concerns.

Diversity is a pervasive characteristic of the postmodern context and is perhaps the most significant challenge to the formation of communal and personal identity. Educational methods need to reflect the diversity, multiplicity, and differences within and between individuals, communities, media, and sacred texts. Regarding individuals, methods must take into account the realities of developmental stages, learning styles, multiple intelligences, life narratives, and the self as multiple rather than singular. Regarding communities, methods need to take into account differences grounded in gender, class, ethnicity, generational cohorts, education, beliefs, etc. Regarding media, methods need to embrace a range of media forms because of the diversity of individual learning styles and because of the diversity of content produced by each medium. Regarding sacred texts, methods need to reckon with the diversity of readings of a given text, the diversity of perspectives within a canon, and the diversity of canons themselves. Each manifestation of diversity mentioned (and additional ones not mentioned) influences our reading of the text.

The major challenge is for educational methods to embrace this diversity *and* to foster communal and individual identity. For many people these seem antithetical. Indeed, engaging diversity can challenge the strands of commonality and continuity from which identity is woven, to the point where one questions whether people share anything with others and whether sense can be made of the flow of an individual's life events. Embracing diversity can lead to radical individualism. The challenge that diversity presents to the formation of identity is similar to that posed by the diversity encountered in the interpretation of texts. The role of context in interpretation questions whether the meaning of a text extends beyond my group and me. Embracing diversity in relation to interpretation can lead to radical relativism. Radical individualism and relativism both seem to assume an absence of interrelatedness.

People emphasizing commonality and continuity in identity can challenge diversity by forcing uniformity or trivializing diversity. For example, uniformity may be coerced when a gendered interpretation is discounted as distracting from the core "witness" of the text. Diversity may be trivialized when one is asked to leave behind their African-American uniqueness for the sake of unity in Christ. In extremes this can become a denial of diversity, and such denial eventually subverts identity, whether communal or individual. One way or another, that which is denied will eventually surface and unravel the assumed commonality and continuity. Amidst feelings of threat, fear, and even betrayal, people facing up to a diversity previously denied will sense that community has been undermined.

Productive processes that embrace diversity and that construct communal and individual identity inclusive of diversity will assume that identity forms at the boundaries and intersections of social locations as much as at their centers. (This anticipates the discussion of a "decentered" self in the following section.) Individuals uniquely embody the intersections of many social locations. Thus, difference among individuals is a given. Yet people *do* share particular social locations with others, which suggests commonalities. People are unique and interrelated, if in no other sense than having a shared fate of living on this planet. So processes of study might begin by addressing difference, rather than commonality, and then proceed to discover and negotiate commonalities in order to create communal and individual identity. Beginning with assumptions of commonality can put Bible study on a rocky path. Eventually a challenge will arise, let's say a reading informed by gender or race. The different reading may take others aback. They may begin to feel like their relationship with the challenger has been a false one and begin asking whether they can be in fellowship with the challenger. However, if study begins in a hospitable space, with primary attention to differences, commonalities and connections will gradually surface, and, since they are hard won through struggling with difference, they will be more durable and robust. In this approach, interrelatedness across differences is assumed but not taken for granted. The shape of the interrelatedness is negotiated and formed locally during the course of study. Such an approach leads to a sense of individuals-in-community, rather than radical individualism, and pluralism, rather than radical relativism in interpretation. By assuming that readings influence relationships between diverse peoples, pluralistic interpretations do not eliminate norms, as might be the case in relativistic readings, nor do they presume that norms are universal and given, as might be the case in authoritarian readings. Responding to the challenges of diversity moves the interpretation of sacred texts from the arena of epistemology to the arena of ethics.

Methods addressing the *liberating impulse of the biblical traditions* will avoid mere indoctrination by means of "proper" readings, identities and norms. Robert M. Fowler said in the ABS consultation, "We often have the tendency to slip from authority to tyranny. Authority, when it's working at its best, empowers, liberates, and works in the best interest of the other party. By contrast, tyranny dominates, controls, enslaves, dehumanizes, and alienates" (American Bible Society: 13). His characterization of tyranny sounds like Brazilian educator Paulo Freire's description of "banking" pedagogies. Such pedagogies aim to indoctrinate. According to this model, a teacher deposits information into a student whose virtue is the ability to reproduce later what has been deposited. The process creates passivity and seeks to control the learner, because the implicit curriculum teaches that information is static, the domain of experts only, and that the world of the learner does not change. Freire's alternative proposal for liberating pedagogies involves engaging learners in problem posing, naming factors that form the limitations and freedoms of their life and reading, and acting to re-form their world. By engaging their world, learners participate in dialogue and actions that build community and solidarity with each other. The implicit curriculum teaches that knowledge is constructed by people in dialogue and that the world is subject to change.

In light of the increasing democratization and pluralities of readings, methods will need to *support the meaning-making abilities of individuals and communities*. Responding to the demands of diversity and liberating authority requires processes that enable people to negotiate meaning, not only in terms of the text, but also as the text interplays with other authorities and contexts. Local Bible study is a process where laypersons develop their own theologies. This is not a call to return to the days of "Biblical theology," but rather a call for laypersons to take responsibility for their theology. Too often laypersons rely passively on academics and clergy to provide interpretations and theology. Methods need to enhance capacities and competencies for meaning making laypersons.

Here a theological perspective from the Wesleyan tradition may be helpful. According to the "Wesleyan Quadrilateral," theology emerges from the interplay of four sources or authorities: scripture, reason, tradition, and contemporary experience of one's own and others. Interacting with these resources in the search for meaning is a problem-posing process that constantly exposes learners to contrasts. Contrasts are very important in raising consciousness. We become conscious of our physical world as we perceive and process differences in color, shape, texture, tone, etc. In dealing with contrasts, attention needs to be given to create a hospitable space where people are free to risk an encounter with challenging contrasts. Judgment is also needed to know how much contrast is constructive. Too little contrast is uninteresting; too much contrast is threatening and overwhelming. Again, we encounter the central role difference plays in our lives.

Ethnographic, social and psychological methods will all play a role in future Bible study in the local context. *Ethnographic methods* are new on the scene. These methods make available for reflection various aspects of local cultures by listening to the voices of people. When ethnographic methods are used to study congregations, researchers conduct individual and group interviews; participate in and observe worship, classes, fellowship, and ministries; attend to the significance of the architecture, symbols, neighborhood; identify the demographics of the congregation and its surroundings; and focus on the system of interpersonal dynamics and organizational processes. People conducting ethnographic research are described as participant-observers: "participant," in light of their involvement (and thus influence) with the local culture, and "observer," in light of the distance from the local culture created by the act of study. The information gathered from this process is analyzed, looking for common words, phrases, stories, and themes; patterns of communication and interpersonal relationships; meanings of significant symbols and events in their shared history.

Ethnographic methods are particularly important for at least two reasons. First, ethnographic tools enable people to interpret the dynamics of the context shaping meaning-making. Ethnography works in relation to context as critical hermeneutical methods work in relation to texts. Ethnographic processes will help identify cultural themes defining the boundaries of reading and action. Second, ethnographic tools facilitate the discernment of the ongoing revelatory work of God among the people of God. This is another theme emerging from the ABS consultation: "The revelation of God in the universe . . . is going to continue to unfold and the canon is radically open" (American Bible Society: 4). I also think that this desire for discernment is a natural part of Bible study conducted in communities of faith—it is a practice of faith.

Ethnographic work also offers a way to think about local engagement with diverse readings. Narratives that are generated from ethnographic research present a slice of life in a particular place and time. The religious educators with whom I work do not engage in such research to find timeless truths or universal methods applicable to all settings. Generalizations and common themes may indeed be uncovered, but that happens as the researcher compares and contrasts the narrative with that of her own place. The "other" that I encounter in the ethnographic narrative creates a self-consciousness through the contrast of their stories with mine—the researcher is pushed into an awareness of her own context and identity. A similar dynamic may happen in Bible study when people encounter a range of different readings of the same passage. The reading from another's location creates an awareness in me of the particularity, brokenness and implications of my own reading—and very likely also the associated discovery of commonalities. Issues of the truth of the text are thus located in a particular reading community but are also connected to other communities. This process brings one's reading into the content of study. Again, the negotiation of readings is an integral part of addressing the dissonance created by engaging contrasting narratives in the community. Thus, this ethnographic approach is has great potential for building community.

The eclectic and polyphonic aspects of the approach suggested here clearly have issues with which to be concerned. One is whether the eclecticism actually hinders the formation of Christian identity because the range of voices creates identity confusion rather than formation. This is a concern for children as well as those becoming Christians as adults. Given that denominational loyalty and identity are already on the wane, an eclectic approach may raise other concerns about identity formation.

2.4 *"How shall we understand the* people *involved in local Bible study?"*

How one views the people involved in local Bible study significantly influences the educational approach one takes. Several assumptions about the participants in Bible study have already been mentioned in previous sections: people are diverse and interrelated; they are part of the content of biblical study; they constantly engage in meaning making; and there is a communal nature to identity. Two issues regarding participants need more attention here. The first issue is the postmodern understanding of the *self as socially constructed, fluid*, and *multiple*. The second issue concerns *qualifications for leadership* of local Bible study.

A socially constructed, fluid and multiple self is certainly different from the substantial and static self of modernity. James Fowler, in *Becoming Adult, Becoming Christian*, describes the modern self by using the metaphor of building a tepee. By a certain age people were expected to pull together the various poles of their life (gender, politics, family, etc.), cover it with a unifying skin, and then dwell in this identity. The failure to do so by a given time would indicate immaturity or even a form of illness, reflected in comments such as "she has not found herself yet."

To say that people are *socially constructed* means that their identity is woven together from the various threads constituting their socio-historical location. Their self-identity does not pre-exist their socio-historical location. Postmodern theorists differ considerably about the determinacy of the context and the agency of the individual. My view is that we are conditioned but not determined in the process of social construction—creativity, play, and novelty are manifest.

The *fluidity of identity* is a corollary. Identity is not taken as a substance, but rather a process; indeed, a narrative process. Identity is constructed and reconstructed as people use narratives to interconnect and give meaning to the various events in their lives. Through the narrative process, these past events are constantly re-interpreted. Communities provide structures to individuals for this narrative process and in turn are changed through the novelty of the individual narratives.

That the identity of an *individual is multiple* flows from the assumptions of social construction and fluidity. Postmodern people do not exist in just one community, but in a complex network of social locations. Put another way, the postmodern self is not centered in one location, but decentered across many social settings. In each location we assume a particular identity as we narrate ourselves in relation to that context. As I move from home, to the streets, to the office, to class, to the basketball court, to church, etc., I use the "language" of each of those contexts to narrate my identity. In a sense there are multiple Randys in the multiple contexts. The complex aspects of gender, ethnicity, class, and education compound this. At any point in time, which of these aspects is definitive or descriptive of my identity? Lucinda Huffaker, working with feminist and process theologies, suggests that the self is experienced "as multiple feelings, attitudes, and behaviors, and these are often conflicting and ambiguous. We are many selves that must be orchestrated into coherence, an ongoing process that we recognize as our identity" (7). The idea of a multiple self may sound strange to persons within dominant culture; however, the multiple self has long been a part of the experience of marginalized people, such as women and African Americans. Drawing on the work of Mary Catherine Bateson, Huffaker explains:

> life [is] an improvisatory art in which we strive for balance and diversity, coherence and fit—not through the simplification of single-minded purposes, but through the creative blending of simultaneous commitments to different people and projects. Historically, the circumstances of women's lives have given them a particular proficiency at improvisation because their lives have typically been a collage of tasks, interruptions, shifting commitments, and marginality. As a result, women learn to cope with ambiguity and discontinuity. (95-96)

The postmodern assumptions about people parallel the assumptions about the Bible as the content of study. Both the text and the reader(s) are diverse, dynamic, and constructed in relation to context. Just as the canon is in constant construction, so is the narrative of self-identity. The ritual of dancing with the Torah is more than symbolic. The text and its people embrace in a co-creative dance of identity construction.

There are several implications of these observations about participants for local Bible study. Each study session contributes to the ongoing construction of personal and communal identity. Study sessions involve encounters with competing narratives vying to become the coordinating theme for identity. The multiplicity of the self provides opportunities for creating consciousness, if these differences are acknowledged to form creative contrasts. Much of this leads to adopting "negotiation" as a significant metaphor for the study process.

The postmodern view of the self also has significant implications for materials produced to assist local Bible study. The multiple and decentered self means that curricula and study aids aimed for a particular context will ultimately have to address the diversity embodied within the context and the self. That is to say that the materials will need to have a multiple character as well. The current, and necessary, efforts to produce materials for, say, an African-American or Asian-American context may miss the need to address the mix of gender, class, education embodied by the people. Study aids will need to be eclectic in themselves. (More will be said about this in the section about institutional responses.)

The *qualifications for leadership* of local Bible study are the second major issue to take up in this section about participants. Part of the legacy of modern biblical criticism is a rift between lay and professional readers/critics. One explanation for the rift is that lay and professional readings happen in different contexts with different purposes. Another explanation is that the laity, and to some extent clergy as well, have lacked the tools to engage modern criticism. Because the modern framework of biblical study requires the use of technical tools in order to get at the truth of the text, lay readings are almost always considered inferior by default. At the beginning of the twentieth century, a response to this situation came in the form of efforts to professionalize educational leadership in congregations. In order to teach Christians the insights of the modern, critical study of the Bible, professional educators were taught to master these academic skills in order to equip parishioners. A second impetus towards professionalization was the desire for educators to understand and utilize developmental psychology in their educational work. Religious education developed as a quasi-discipline and was taught at seminaries, supported by the Religious Education Association (1903), and practiced by professionals on congregational staffs. In a way, professional educators were to equip laypersons to approximate the interpretive skills of scholars. William Rainey Harper and George Albert Coe of the University of Chicago were champions of this movement.

Responding to the needs of Bible study in a postmodern setting could easily take the form of a new wave of professional leadership development. In addition to mastering developmental, multiple intelligence, and learning theories, the new professional could also become an ethnographer, as suggested by Margaret Ann Crain and Jack Seymour. The new professional could become fluent in multiple reading schemes in addition to "traditional" biblical criticism. Ideally professionals should be equipped to understand texts and contexts so as to produce contextually appropriate, local study materials. Such efforts on the part of seminaries could make a significant contribution to Bible study in the twenty-first century.

However, hopes founded on professional responses should be tempered by several considerations. One consideration is the modest level of effectiveness professional models achieved, in the modern framework, to foster critical, liberating biblical reading, and literacy. Religious educators continue to struggle with being critical, reflective, and age-appropriate when leading Bible study. A second consideration is the constraints placed on religious educators in local settings by conflicting demands on time, education levels/types, and the availability of basic resources. A third consideration is whether professional models can constructively challenge the automatic privileging of "academic" readings over "naïve" or lay readings. This is not likely if leaders see their task as delivering, in a "banking" manner, academic truths. It seems that postmodern biblical study in local settings will need leadership informed by contributions of biblical scholars but also trusting of the interpretive authenticity of the laity.

Overall, this means that postmodern leadership will likely be shaped by the metaphor of negotiation. Regarding the distinction between academic and lay readings of the Bible, Bible study leaders will need to recognize the integrity of both sides and facilitate a local study group's negotiation of the differences. The assessment of each reading's authenticity and integrity will rest more on the contested ground of ethical implications than on the protocols of a school of criticism. This negotiating model of leadership will also be important to apply to the differences in gender, race, and class that a local study group is likely to engage.

A factor in embracing the implications of a postmodern view of self is the developmental readiness of individuals to negotiate constructively diverse and particular readings. For instance, James Fowler's developmental stages of faith would suggest that fairly mature adults, those in *Conjunctive* faith, would be the ones ready for such study. The *Mythic-Literal* faith of children, the *Synthetic-Conventional* faith of adolescents, and the *Individuative-Reflective* faith of young adulthood are either too concrete or dualistic to live with the tensions of negotiation. A counter-argument may be that today's children are growing up and dealing with this diversity everyday and in many ways negotiate difference effectively.

2.5 Summary

Thinking through the questions about the purposes, content, processes, and people involved in local Bible study in the postmodern era has raised several key themes. I have suggested that the *purposes of local Bible study* include formation and transformation of community, formation and transformation of self-identity, stewardship of the texts of tradi-tions, and sponsoring ethical responsibility. Addressing these aspects makes otherwise implicit dynamics explicit and thus more likely to be intentional, constructive, and ethical.

The *content of local Bible study* is concerned with the internal diver-sity of the Bible and the interplay of text and context as the location of meaning. Content also includes elements relevant to the purposes of study: the nature of the local faith community, individual life narratives, the history and trajectory of texts, ethical dimensions of relationships, and the method of study itself. Because of ethical concerns and the assump-tion that no education is value-neutral, attention needs to be given to the three curricular forms in local Bible study: the explicit, implicit, and null.

The *processes of local Bible study* embrace diversity, the liberating impulse of biblical authority, and the meaning-making abilities of individ-uals and communities, and broaden the scope of hermeneutics from text to context. Embracing diversity involves processes that begin by addressing difference, rather than commonality, and then proceed to negotiate and dis-cover commonalities in order to create communal and individual identity. The hope is that this will lead to a sense of individuals-in-community, rather than individualism, and pluralistic, rather than relativistic, interpre-tations. Embracing liberating impulses involves engaging learners in prob-lem posing, naming factors that form the limitations and freedoms of their life and reading, and acting to re-form their world. Embracing meaning-making processes involves intentional negotiation of contrasting authori-ties and contexts. Ethnographic methods are promising because they enable people to interpret their context, discern God's movement in that context, and model a way of engaging diverse readings.

The postmodern world tends to understand the *persons in local Bible study* as socially constructed, fluid, and multiple. If we embrace the multiple and decentered postmodern self, then curricula and study aids will need to be eclectic in order to address the diversity within the con-text and the self. The role of professionals in the leadership of local Bible study will need to be rethought in order to address differences between academic and lay readings of the text. The leader as negotiator may be an apt metaphor.

The next two sections continue the preceding reflections by consid-ering what might be called thought experiments. One deals with institu-tions beyond the local context wishing to support Bible study. The second deals with a possible approach to a study session.

3. Some Options for Institutional Support of Local Bible Study in the Twenty-first Century

The uniqueness of each context for local Bible study presents a major challenge to institutions wishing to be supportive of such study. I am thinking specifically of institutions such as denominational agencies and curriculum publishers, and ecumenical groups such as the American Bible Society. The tendency of such institutions is to address diverse contexts in one of two ways. One way is to develop materials for broad use that are sensitive to diversity. They seek to be inclusive so as to have broad appeal and use. Sometimes this may only involve changing graphics and photos; rarely does it involve intentional treatment of differences. The second way is to develop materials for more focused constituencies, most often in relation to ethnicity. So there are materials designed for African-American, Latina/o, Asian-American, or Native American settings. Even in this approach it is not uncommon for the materials to be adaptations of the curriculum that was developed for the dominant culture. Both approaches are helpful and at the same time challenge the institutions producing the materials. Developing and producing multiple editions of study materials consumes significant resources, often more than is available to address all the contexts. Even if the resources, and the will, are available, the question remains, Does the institution creating the material sufficiently understand the specific constituency? Eventually these approaches encounter the question: When does the diversity within the constituency begin to undermine the effectiveness of the materials? More specifically, does an "African-American curriculum" lose effectiveness if it fails to address African-Caribbean, gender, and urban/suburban differences?

Two alternative approaches are worth considering for the future. Each is an attempt to address the particularities of context, while avoiding the impossible expectation for institutions to produce materials for every conceivable context. These alternatives build on the strength of the connectional function and structures of ecumenical institutions and denominational agencies, which can be further enhanced through electronic means.

One alternative is to work on projects where the larger institution facilitates the creation of curricula in local settings. This approach addresses the problem by shifting the location where the materials are created. This approach is similar to that of developing materials for many specific constituencies. The difference is that the location of production is shifted from the level of the institution to that of the local context.

Congregations would develop their own study resources, or, if they lack the resources, use materials created by a similar congregation. By virtue of being locally produced, the materials would hopefully reflect the unique culture and needs of the context. The larger institution would have three primary roles. One, it would equip local settings with the resources, processes, and building blocks with which to construct materials. Two, it would serve as a clearinghouse and networking structure that makes locally created resources available to other contexts. This function would facilitate discovery of commonalities across contexts and thereby support unity amidst particularity. Three, the institution would provide a means for persons working at the local level to discover blind spots and to avoid being myopic. This function would provide a broader background against which to enrich local meaning.

The second approach addresses the problem by embracing the pervasiveness of difference within local contexts and enriching those contexts with forms of diversity that may be under-represented. In this approach, the materials developed would offer an eclectic and broad range of perspectives and thus could be produced at an institutional level. An example of this type of resource would be an eclectic commentary. This could be organized around a particular book of the Bible or around general themes related to biblical texts. Each section of the resource would have a number of parallel commentaries for a particular passage grounded in various social locations or types of criticism. Materials could have a supplemental section with articles describing the general tendencies of reading from the locations included. For any one biblical text, the institutional task would be to select commentaries that offer fruitful tensions and contrasts. The types of commentaries could change from passage to passage. Interpretations of the text could include provocative perspectives related to gender, ethnicity, historical periods, age, class, nation, theology, inter-religious dialogue, etc. They could be presented in a variety of media and for several learning styles. An eclectic commentary resource may be more realistic in the short term than developing full commentaries from singular reading locations.

The eclectic resource differs from general and inclusive study aids because it is not "a something for everybody" approach. The focus is on using the contrasting perspectives to spark local dialogue and local meaning-making. These materials would facilitate consciousness raising and reflection on local reading through engaging difference. The intentional and structured engagement of the contrasts should make it difficult for the materials to be used merely as a smorgasbord of readings from which to pick. The eclectic resource differs from materials produced for a specific market since it does not assume homogeneous contexts. Materials reflecting the breadth of Christian traditions that facilitate local construction of orthodoxy might be more reflective of the early Church's lively struggles of negotiating a faithful path and assembling a biblical canon in the midst of uncharted waters. The ability to assemble a range of eclectic views should be one of the natural strengths of institutions and agencies.

4. An Option for Approaching Local Bible Study

What might an approach to a local Bible study informed by the previous discussion look like? The following is one possibility for consideration. The educational models developed by Paulo Freire, Thomas Groome, Mary Elizabeth Moore, and Daniel Schipani inform my thinking here. Each model engages issues of liberation, active engagement with contexts, living meaningfully in intersections, identity formation and transformation, and dynamic traditions. The following also has affinities with the study approach developed by Frederick Tiffany and Sharon Ringe in *Biblical Interpretation: A Roadmap*.

4.1 Context Assumptions

It is somewhat difficult to offer this approach in such a decontextualized manner, given all that has been said about the importance of context. I am thinking of these movements as taking place in a congregational small group study setting with a session length of about one and a half hours. The participants are adults who have been in the congregation for about a year but who were also previously nominal members of various different denominations—not a bad assumption given patterns of mobility and low denominational loyalty. Both men and women are present. The group is predominantly European-American but a third is African-American. Economically they are middle class. The session is part of a 12-week series.

It would be wise for study series to begin with session(s) developing group and biblical skills needed for the study approach. This might include dialogue about tolerance, elements other than beliefs that hold a community together, conflict and negotiation skills, and how they recognize "acceptable" readings. Likewise a concluding session that pulls together learnings, reinforces action plans, and brings closure to the study community might be included.

4.2 Movements in the Study

The following is a description of possible steps for one study session.

Create hospitable space. In the opening movement, it is important to create a space in which participants feel safe to take risks and accept the tensions created by engaging differences and consciousness-raising contrasts. Attention needs to be focused on the present social space of this study community. This focusing should not ask participants to leave behind awareness of their circumstances before coming to the study. In fact, each person should be encouraged to share the many contexts that they bring with him or her into the study community. Perhaps in the opening session, individuals may create a poster-size collage of their life settings and who they are in each of those settings. On a weekly basis they may share which parts of the collage are at the front of their consciousness. Such naming honors life issues and allows forward movement after identifying them. This also can be used to create awareness of how individuals narrate their identity from elements of experience and develop forms of interrelatedness, but not necessarily commonality, in the group. Something that orients participants to the text at hand is also needed. Hospitable space may be created through elements such as prayer, a liturgical element, a meal, lighting a candle or incense, attending to physical space, circle dances, personal testimonies, etc.

Encounter biblical text. In this movement the text is encountered at least once and possibly multiple times in various media or different translations. I think it is important to hear the text as well as read it and to have means to mark the text. It may be feasible to read the text in a meditative style, such as *lectio divina*.

Develop initial local interpretation. In this movement individuals and then the group formulate and offer their own initial interpretation of the text. Several things are accomplished by this. First, they have established a reference point for their later engagement of other readings—an initial bargaining position, if you will, in the spirit of the negotiating metaphor. Work in multicultural education suggests that having a position provides a level of personal confidence that lowers defensiveness in encountering voices from different social locations. Second, the initial interpretation establishes the uniqueness of the individuals and the local interpretive community by honoring and making explicit the local reading habits. Third, it avoids making participants passive, which tends to happen when professional interpretations are introduced first. This movement also involves the participants in explaining how they came up with the interpretations they did.

The forms that the initial interpretation take can be diverse and can flow from the various learning styles and multiple intelligences represented in the group. Despite various forms, the interpretations can still be reflective and challenging. For example, forms of interpretations may be simple written paraphrases, symbolic sketches, raps, skits, etc.

Engage and negotiate readings from different settings. Participants are now ready to engage and negotiate with readings from different settings. Again, the presentation of these readings is a very natural place to use a range of media and introduce reflection on the media's role in their understanding the other readings. The number of other readings depends a great deal on the time available and the text at hand.

One reading probably should be informed by scholarship, reflecting historical, cultural and linguistic background for the text. Such a reading supports stewardship of the text and a contrast between the origins of the text and the current community. One or more readings should reflect contrasts based in gender, ethnicity, class, denomination or religion, depending on the text. For example, if the text were the household codes in the Pauline letters, then gender and African-American readings would be helpful. If the text were an account of the conquest of Canaan, then Native American and African-American readings might be offered. Hagar narratives lend themselves to Womanist readings. Texts leading to denominational divisions may call for contrasting denominational readings. Texts reflecting early church attitudes towards Jews may call for post-Holocaust Jewish readings. These contrasting readings will provide opportunities to become aware of the group's identities and ethical responsibilities. They are not intended to offer a smorgasbord of readings from which participants select the reading that suits them. This is where the group should utilize their eclectic commentaries!

Negotiation would mean identifying and describing the contrasts between the different readings and those constructed earlier by the group. This movement fully engages participants in diversity, liberating impulses, meaning-making, and widening interpretations. The contrast presents a problem of meaning and responsibility for the participants. Dealing with the contrasts will likely raise emotions and the energy level of the group, providing motivation for resolution. We often learn best when the adrenaline is flowing. It is also very likely that in the process the group will find commonalities and continuities with the readings. Negotiating the interpretations and responsibilities does not necessarily mean adopting the other's reading. If this were more of a classroom situation, the multiple readings could be presented and negotiated through learning centers incorporating multiple intelligences.

A range of educational methods could be used to help participants deal with the following questions of negotiation. What visceral reactions do you have to the other readings? How do the other readings anger, puzzle, shock, or excite you? How do the group's and the other readings differ? Why do you think the other readers interpret the text the way they do? How do these other readings voice feelings you have longed to say?

Foster awareness of identity in local community. This movement seeks to use the sensitivities and feelings produced from the contrasting readings as pointers to the assumptions and factors shaping the group's original reading of the text, to know better who they are. Here interpretation broadens from text to context. Two questions are central. The first is: What values, commitments, perspectives and assumptions of mine were challenged in the encounter with the other readings? The second is: How did I come to have these values, commitments, perspectives, and assumptions? Assistance can be offered through ethnographic exercises. For example, if the contrast deals with issues of gender or ethnicity, participants could be asked to describe and reflect on the structures of their households. Attention could also be given to who is represented in congregational leadership, the norms and consequences of relating to people of the opposite sex or different ethnic group, or visual symbols in congregational life that implicitly shape gender and ethnic relationships. Awareness should also be raised in relation to how the denominational tradition engages the text, which may evolve into a dialogue with the orthodoxy of the tradition.

Sponsor ethical reading and responsibility. With a fuller understanding of their text and context, this movement encourages participants to take responsibility for the ethics of their study. This would involve addressing several questions. What relationships with others and with creation are brought to attention through this study? Describe what those relationships are like: How just, ethical, or life affirming are the relationships? What claims do the other readings place on you? How have interpretations of the text been used to enhance or limit free, just, and full relationships? What have been oppressive and liberating uses of the text? How does the local congregational culture include and respond to the voices heard in the study of the text? How does taking the voices seriously change community life within the congregation or life in the various other sectors in which individuals move? What concrete actions are called for?

Revise local interpretation. This last movement brings closure to the particular study and also ushers participants into new action and dialogues. Here the initial interpretation is reviewed and revised in light of the study. Important questions include: How has the study changed your view of the text, the way you treat it, value it, share it with others? In what ways has your understanding of yourself and your communities changed? In the collage of your life, where does the text have the most significance?

When a revised interpretation is done, it could be made available publicly through electronic avenues facilitated by connectional institutions, such as denominational agencies or the American Bible Society. This service is well-suited to the mission, function, and location of these institutions. Making local interpretations widely available contributes to a larger fellowship of faith, supports opportunities for negotiating unity, reinforces awareness that laypersons participate in constructing knowledge and interpretation, and invites critique and accountability for the study group. As postings accumulate over time, they may come to form a grass roots "people's commentary." This might serve as a complementary resource with eclectic commentary materials published by institutions. Using the web as a populist publishing outlet would make this material available as an academic resource for understanding congregational life and addressing the issues of privileging academic readings over lay readings. In the interest of integrity, I believe the posting of revised local readings should be limited to subscribers committed to an intentional communal study process. However, once posted, the interpretations should be made available to all for the purposes of their own study, critique, and response.

5. Conclusion

The challenges and opportunities of the postmodern context give good reason for religious educators to rethink local Bible study. Just as responses to modernity spawned "classic" models of religious education, postmodern religious education models will emerge. Intentionally addressing difference, constructing meaning and identities at boundaries, and engaging the ethics, power and forms of relationship across difference will be characteristic of these models. Perhaps negotiation will serve as a key metaphor for a postmodern model.

Works Consulted

American Bible Society
     N.D.   *Futuring the Scriptures: The Bible for Tomorrow's Publics.* New
              York: American Bible Society. [report on conference by same title
              held on February 6, 1999, at Bible House, New York City]
Cobb, John B., Jr.
     1993   *Becoming A Thinking Christian.* Nashville: Abingdon.
     1994   *Lay Theology.* St. Louis, MO: Chalice.
     1995   *Grace and Responsibility.* Nashville: Abingdon.

Crain, Margaret Ann and Jack Seymour
    1996   "The Ethnographer as Minister." *Religious Education* 91
           (Summer): 299-315.
Dykstra, Craig and Dorothy C. Bass
    1997   "Times of Yearning, Practices of Faith." Pp. 1-12 in *Practicing Our
           Faith*. Ed. Dorothy C. Bass. San Francisco: Jossey-Bass.
Fowler, James W.
    1984   *Becoming Adult, Becoming Christian*. San Francisco: Harper and
           Row.
Freire, Paulo.
    1996   *Pedagogy of the Oppressed*. Trans. Myra Bergman Ramos. New
           York: Continuum.
Groome, Thomas
    1980   *Christian Religious Education*. San Francisco: Harper and Row.
Gottwald, Norman K.
    1995   "Framing Biblical Interpretation at New York Theological
           Seminary." Pp. 251-261 in *Reading from this Place*. Vol. 1. Eds.
           Fernando F. Segovia and Mary Ann Tolbert. Minneapolis: Fortress.
Huffaker, Lucinda A. Stark
    1998   *Creative Dwelling*. Atlanta: Scholars Press.
Lynn, Robert W. and Elliot Wright
    1980   *The Big Little School*. Birmingham, AL: Religious Education Press.
Moore, Mary Elizabeth
    1983   *Education for Continuity and Change*. Nashville: Abingdon.
    1998   *Ministering with the Earth*. St. Louis, MO: Chalice.
Patte, Daniel
    1995   *Ethics of Biblical Interpretation*. Louisville: Westminster John
           Knox.
Schipani, Daniel
    1997   "Educating for Social Transformation." Pp. 23-40 in *Mapping
           Christian Education*. Ed. Jack L. Seymour. Nashville: Abingdon.
Schmidt, Stephen A.
    1983   *A History of the Religious Education Association*. Birmingham,
           AL: Religious Education Press.
Segovia, Fernando F.
    1998   "Introduction: Pedagogical Discourse and Practices in
           Contemporary Biblical Criticism." Pp. 1-28 in *Teaching the Bible*.
           Eds. Fernando F. Segovia and Mary Ann Tolbert. Maryknoll, NY:
           Orbis Books.
Segovia, Fernando F. and Mary Ann Tolbert, eds.
    1995   *Reading from this Place*. Vol. 1. Minneapolis: Fortress.
Tiffany, Frederick C. and Sharon H. Ringe
    1996   *Biblical Interpretation: A Roadmap*. Nashville: Abingdon Press.

Afterword

Between the Past and What Has Nearly Arrived

Martin E. Marty

Two themes remembered from my own starting-out years came to mind as I read these essays on new paradigms of approach to the Bible. After the next paragraph I'll take a moment to say why these two quotations came to mind and seemed appropriate in the present context.

First, however: the editors sent me the chapters that you have read as they came in to them. This means that I did not know—and did not *want* to know—in what order they were to appear. This more or less random—no, this *totally* random sequencing in my reading pattern in some ways matches the plot of the book itself. That is, no one can come from reading its chapters with a sense that much of anything is settled. Those who desire metaphorically firm ground on which to stand for their intellectual pursuits are likely to feel that they are at sea, perhaps on a raft. To suggest that would not be an insult to the editors. They would say that in biblical studies, in the use of the Bible as a document relating to faith, and in assessments of the Bible as literature, we are currently "between paradigms." We are no longer secure in what many presumed had been settled. We have not arrived at any new synthesis, system, or, again, agreed-upon paradigm. If that situation turns out to be unsettling to some, so be it, say the editors and authors: "that's how things are." I picture the essayists saying, in effect, "While we can no longer stand where we did, and while we do not inhabit the future, individually and collectively we will help things unfold and develop—we will help to shape 'how things will be.'" I imagine the editors saying, "If the jumbling of these essays is a stimulus to the imagination, well and good."

With that as background, it is time for the first of two framing bits of literature. This one is from poet Rainer Maria Rilke, in the form of lines that helped me locate the apparently dislocating circumstances from which the eleven authors here wrote:

> Each torpid turn of the world has such disinherited ones,
> To whom neither the past belongs, nor yet what has nearly arrived.[1]

(Note that throughout this Afterword I will be putting the simple word "past" and the phrase "what has nearly arrived" in quotes, treating them as technical terms, references to premodern and modern circumstances in the first case and the postmodern in the second.)

The second literary snippet that will frame another part of my Afterword is designed to minister to the intellectual and perhaps the existential interests of many readers. I picture some of them, devoted to classic canons of literature and thus at home with the Bible as a book secure in the canon, approached through traditional means of interpretation, skeptical of any claims that a new paradigm is not only emerging but that it shows promise for literary students and critics. Are most of these authors voguish postmodernists, deconstructionists, trashers of what has come down to us from the past? My second quotation will shortly be adduced as a kind of plea for patience, for developing curiosity, for promise.

I also picture other readers who might describe themselves as Bible-believers, people whose faith is grounded in a scriptural revelation, who cherish the Book, and who feel pushed around or cast adrift. To take but two examples: two of the essays in this volume examine the phenomenon of the marketing of the Bible, as if it were an ordinary commodity. Two other essays, not necessarily prescriptive but generally positive in tone, suggest that the Internet, virtual reality, cyberspace, and the digital revolution represent a qualitatively different challenge than have the critical approaches to the Bible of the past two centuries.

It is with these two sets of readers in mind that I tell a little story about patience in the face of change and enthusiasm in the face of experiment. When I mentioned above that these bits came from my starting-up years, it is certainly the case in the present quotation. A half-century ago as a theological student I was editing a magazine called *The Seminarian*. At the end of an academic year, during summing up, I ended a column called "The Theologbook" with a quotation. ("May we print a parable we're afraid we'll lose if it isn't printed?" "We" were the editor, so, of

---

[1] The translation is by Stephen Mitchell, in *The Selected Poetry of Rainer Maria Rilke* (New York: Random House Vintage International, 1982), p. 188. The original reads:
> Jede dumpfe Umkehr der Welt hat solche Enterbte,
> denen das Frühere nicht und noch nicht das Nächste gehört

course "we may." I must not have lost it, because after five decades it has remained fresh in my mind.)

It was from the *Protevangelium Le Corbusiana,* which must have reached me through some unconventional route. The text came from the Abbey of St. Denis in Paris, "where Gothic architecture began." Here it is:

> On a May morning the Abbot Suger walked in his garden amid those good thoughts that were his familiar poursuivants when there came to him Brother Tomas, well versed in antique theology who, having received permission to break the silence, spoke to him, saying, "Father, I would bring to your mind the young architect who is vaulting our aisled choir. He builds the arches, not in the good round Roman manner made venerable by ancient use, but broken, having a pointed form like arches of the barbarous Persians. Let him be reproved, I pray, lest he profane further the crescent temple of our Holy Martyr." To whom the good abbot, having remained a moment in meditation replied, saying, "These forms are indeed strange to me, my son, and yet I think they are not without purpose. Let us be patient. Some good thing may yet grow out of them."

I

To take up first the theme that treats the "torpid turn of the world" between paradigms theme: Some of the essayists evoke a world somewhat less given to "torpid turning," because they deal with some confidence concerning "the past" in approaches to the Bible. One thinks of John G. Stackhouse chronicling the world of evangelicals, that one-fourth of the United States population—and presumably of the Canadian, with which Stackhouse is so familiar—that describes itself as being most persistently the religion of the book. Or Randy G. Litchfield, who deals with the scene in which people gather, as they have long gathered, for "local Bible study." While Stackhouse speaks of "challenges" and Litchfield deals with change, both of them relate to a horizon where one senses, or glimpses, elements of continuity, of stability.

It is difficult to read their essays, however, after reading the other nine, without seeing threats to inheritance from the past. One might even say that many who cling to "the old time religion" as anchored in the book as it has been studied in the local circles are living with blinders or illusions. Why? Because those who do such clinging also inhabit the same world of electronic and now digital disruption, discontinuity, and instability, as do the enthusiasts of postmodernity and experimentation. Many of them are ahead of liberals and modernists in adapting their ways to those of the computer-universe.

Meanwhile, essayists here who observe what the digital revolution is doing to consciousness and to objects such as printed scriptures, evidently intend to jostle complacent readers. They seem to be most aware of and have become impatient with the heritage of the past in approaches to the Bible. Some of them even construct a vision of the past in which there seemed to have been more rootedness, more rock-solidity in relation to the Bible, than most historians who study social history actually find. However accurate their assessments of the legacy of the past, in any case, they depict and often seem to welcome "what has nearly arrived" as a shaper of biblical faith and determiner of biblical scholarship in the new millennium.

Aspects of that envisioned future have, of course, made their way into the consciousness and habits of millions who would not use words like "digital revolution" or "postmodernity." Just what are the revolutionaries talking about, one might ask, in a world where hundreds of millions who deal with the Christian scriptures—in ways analogous to the ways millions of others, in Judaism and Islam, two other "religions of the book"—shape approaches that on first appearance are untouched by or resistant to the erosions and storms of postmodernity?

In that questioning sentence I am referring to all those movements that go by code-names such as "Fundamentalism." In the United States and Canada, as in much of the Christian world, the prospering religious movements tend to be those that urge reading the Bible as if nothing has changed. Or in such a way that change does not reach a particular body of defensive and defending believers. Such fundamentalists, some of them in the "evangelical" and "local" camps described in two essays here, are confident that God spoke to and through prophets and apostles who infallibly inscribed onto scrolls inerrant words that *are* the Word of God. Being saved, being brought into the orbit of obedience and grace connected with God's action, to them means to rely on what one gets from printed words which for some centuries have been gathered into books, into The Book. Are these Bible-believers not "saved" from what Stackhouse calls challenges to their approach, which means, are they not secure? Are they not effectively insulated from the storms of postmodernity, safe within the walls of libraries of the mind, within communities in which words on the page still matter supremely?

Not likely, if one pays attention to essays such as those of Mark Fackler, who speaks of "niche markets" for new custom-tailored biblical productions, or of R. S. Sugirtharajah, who speaks of "packaging" and "peddling" Holy Writ. Why bring up entrepreneurship? Because it is precisely in the communities among whom the Bible is a holy object, a secure collection of words, a book of continuities and stability, that most marketing, packaging, and peddling goes on. One asks just how much the Bible-believers who make up such communities can make use of the marketplace without having their consciousness and habits to large degrees shaped by it.

To shift to the world of proper nouns: one would not expect to prosper by merchandising biblical material that focuses on the Unitarian-Universalist world, where the Bible is at best one of the many influences available to seekers and celebrators. Even the Roman Catholic one-fourth of America, or much of the mainstream Protestant or the Orthodox communities, are not so fatefully engaged with printed pages of the Bible as are fundamentalists, evangelicals, pentecostals, conservative Baptists, and the like. The latter cluster is the one most at home with the Bible market. Among them are those who operate the thousands of "Bible bookstores" in which Bibles contend with thousands of titles written by fallible humans who are prone to produce errant texts. And, alongside the Bible in such stores, one finds non-books, non-Bibles, objects (T-shirts, mugs, banners, balloons, CD-ROMs, games, video-creations, dolls) all vying for attention among those who often like(d) to describe themselves as people of the Book, of *one* book. When do the spin-offs overwhelm that from which they originally spun: printed words on pages in bound books, especially the Bible? When they do, what happens to the stable Bible market and the Bible itself?

Reinforcing such questionings is the essay by Mary E. Hess, herself not a member of the evangelical community and someone evidently not as close to local Bible study groups as others are. Hers is an essay that focuses on popular culture. Paradoxically, here again the religious communities that had once been described as liberal or modernist have often turned out to be more conservative in their cultural expressions than are the advocates of Bible-based old-time religion. It is among Episcopalians, Presbyterians, Lutherans of the ELCA sort, and United Methodists where one is likely to find classical forms of worship, Revised Standard Versions of the Bible (with accent on "Standard") instead of the translation of the week, "traditional" as opposed to "contemporary" worship, and sermonic references to classical authors. (I would not overdo this accent; many in the Catholic and Protestant mainline have copied the ways of the evangelicals, but they have not thrown themselves so wholeheartedly into the embrace of popular culture.)

Of course, the conservative Bible-believers do not always engage in that embrace of the market culture uncritically. But in their understandable zeal for what Fackler and Sugirtharajah would call "the market share" and growth in the community of believers, they have often been more alert to what popular culture provides than those liberals and others whom they regard as less devoted than they are to printed scriptures. Often their strategy has been one that pays the compliment of imitation. Thus ambitious and creative evangelicals, having heard the challenge of rock music to the loyalty of their Christian offspring, and having grown tired of resisting the musical beat they or their parents had once attributed to Satan himself, have picked up the beat. Hence, Christian Rock, a billion-dollar-a-year industry at this turn of the millennium, reflects the consciousness and reinforces the habits usually associated with secular rock fans. The performers dress like their pagan counterparts. The music sounds the same as that issuing from the festivals of the rock-bound heathen. But some biblical words replace those of the profane world, so the Bible stands, theoretically the same as always, yet manifestly it has turned into an expression of a new paradigm.

When one comes to the essays locating the reception of the Bible in particular communities, it is clear that what belonged to the past no longer belongs to the disinherited. Kwok Pui-lan locates, which means "finds a house" for, the biblical figure Ruth. This house shows up in contexts of gender and sexuality that were always latent but not readily developed back when people of the male persuasion monopolized biblical scholarship. After Kwok is finished, the reader no longer will find good old Ruth at her traditional home, serving as a model for loyal women in what were once presumed to have been conventional, even normative family situations. No, say some of Kwok's scholars, we might now watch for lesbian undertones, even overtones, in the relation of Ruth to Naomi. We have to pay attention to the complex politics of male-female and generational relations between Ruth and Boaz. The cast of characters in the book of Ruth remains the same as before, but "no longer what's been" holds the stage as they are seen acting in it.

Similarly, as Lamin Sanneh discusses how the Bible is used for "ethnic mobilization" in Africa or Abraham Smith discusses "postcolonial interrogation" among African-Americans, the reader who cherishes and would perpetuate "what's been" receives another jolt. In the old paradigm familiar to most North Americans of any race or gender, men of European descent determined for others how the Bible was to be received, interpreted, and put to work. They have certainly not disappeared, as anyone who consults current bibliographies or attends meetings of the Society of Biblical Literature can discern with a quick eye-scan. But they do not have the field to themselves, and even in their corners of the fields, they do things differently now after having been made aware of how the Bible sounds in other settings and among diverse communities.

How far these paradigms have moved became clear to me as I noticed how few of the proper names on these pages survive from the scholarly and ecclesiastical communities with which senior generations grew up. There are few references to "historical criticism," "form criticism," "redaction criticism," and the like, though it is true that the results of schools of thought symbolized by such terms are taken for granted here. Now a whole new vocabulary appears, employing language no doubt not recognized as new by the younger generation whose consciousness and habits are no longer "what's been." Thus in the search for long-familiar proper names in these chapters one blink of an eye can lead a reader to overlook the rare citations of biblical scholars as notable as Rudolf Bultmann and those in his generation who represented old new paradigms. Of course, there is always some displacement of major figures in each generational "torpid turn of the world." But much of what is in the present book signals the asking of a very different set of questions than the earlier scholars, ecclesiastics, and popularizers asked.

Readers who have felt pushed by proclamations of the already mentioned new paradigms have good reason to be jostled, even jolted, as I was, when reading the remaining essays. What can happen to the worded-book called the Bible if A. K. M. Adam is right in projecting a "dispelling [of] the mystique of words" themselves? For both those devoted to faith and devotees of literature, what happens if words lose their mystique? Critic George Steiner years ago anticipated Adam's kind of essay in his own reckoning that in the modern world numbers, mathematics, the language of science, had challenged the mystique and function of words when it came to giving an accounting of the real world. Adam is on a parallel track to Steiner's, a track on which if anything he goes further in his comment on "dispellings" of what words, once upon a time unchallenged, spelled out.

Most difficult to grasp in the "what has nearly arrived" zone are the digital figurings of Robert S. Fortner, who sees the digital or post-electronic phenomena as a "cultural metaphor" that is based on realities that our generations are coming to take for granted, though not always thoughtfully. Reaching even further away from the domain of pages and books, from words that take the form of molecules of ink on molecules of paper, is Richard Thieme, whose paradigm has us "entering sacred digital space" in the cybersphere.

What has happened to all the biblicists, the fundamentalists, the firm-footed evangelicals with whom Stackhouse would reacquaint us? What indeed will happen to them, since they are as reflexively connected to the world of the web, as at home in the abodes of virtual reality, as disembodied as are the signals in cyberspace, as anyone, including those to whom the book had mattered less? Is everything that "belonged in the past" disappearing, to be displaced only by "what has nearly arrived?"

At this turn someone with psychological or pastoral concerns may be tempted to speak reassuringly of the enduring "past." That is, one can point to continuities in the face of displacements, to survivals of reassuring aspects of old paradigms in the face of the new.

One available and attractive strategy at such a moment would call one to deal critically with the extravagant and sometimes obscurantist character of much postmodern talk. It has been and is clotted with jargon, given to neologisms that turn antique within a decade.

A second way of fending off the challenge of unsettling new paradigms is to point to the low yield that has come from most envisionings and predictings in the past. The history of bad guesses in respect to technological futures and cultural adaptations can provoke pathos or hilarity. It may well be that some of the projections in this book will turn out to be such wide-of-the-mark guesses, fancies that turn out to have been fantasies and fads.

A third approach would move one to resort to the language of The Preacher in the Bible and simply contend that there is nothing new under the sun. Only apparently new.

II

Having noted such strategies of evasion and given them their due as qualifiers of any impulses one might have to settle for breathless announcements that new paradigms are safely here, one can add a fourth strategy. That is, to accept, with fingers crossed and with guard up, most of the depictions of new paradigms in this book and then to ask what they mean. Or, back to Abbot Suger's plea for patience, to suggest "some good thing may yet grow out of them."

Thus in the case of John Stackhouse's essay, one that seemed most congenially rooted in "old paradigms," though admittedly "challenged" by them: something may come of the evangelical community's insistence on biblical narrative in the midst of the changes described throughout this book. Stackhouse offers a helpful, succinct historical definition of the bewilderingly complex evangelical house, an ever-enlarging house that is still being inhabited by millions long after it was supposed to have been condemned as metaphysically uninhabitable. Instead of being razed, it has been remodeled. Might not such evangelicals, or members of analogous communities, learn from other essays in this book about the ways they may have over-adapted to markets and the digital revolution? If so, and if they henceforth relate more critically, or are able to spell out better than they have to date how they can make all the adjustments into market "niches" and digital culture without losing their soul or their narrative, they can serve the larger community of believers and readers.

If some readers find the realities, virtual and otherwise, of our cyberspatial, digital world to be too encroaching, too imperial, too irresistible, too global and cosmopolitan, Randy Litchfield's accent on local communities of readers may show promise. Philosopher Stephen Toulmin has dealt with the paradoxes of living in an age of cosmopolitanism and noting how it has stimulated responses attentive to the local. Here is a case of readers thinking cosmopolitanly, maybe even with universalizing intent, but acting locally with new awareness and purpose.

To illustrate: in 1993, in an off-year election, Republican candidates often prevailed. The still rather new, post-honeymoon President Bill Clinton consoled himself and reached out to the public by saying that in no way were those voting totals referenda on the state of the nation. They were local, as is all politics—Congressman Tip O'Neill having contended thus. The next day columnist William Safire came back: yes, Mr. President; yes, Mr. O'Neill; all politics is local. What they had not noticed was that today the local *is* the national.

In a way those in local Bible reading communities reflect that same awareness. They may be increasingly able to live with the revelations and technological developments described by Fortner, Adam, and Thieme, yet they are also able to view such changes through the prism of experience tested close to home. In the days of the emergent new paradigms, they seek aspects of community, self-identity, stewardship, and ethical response in liberating ways. They know and embody the "fluid identity" mentioned by Litchfield and others; they know old landmarks have gone. Yet they find ways to "negotiate" with the surrounding reality and achieve equivalents, in their time and experience, to some features of formation that came with old paradigms when what belonged to "the past" still ruled. They are, in effect, saying that some good thing may yet grow out of the experiments and changes—but that in their experience not everything is threatened.

Similarly, the essays by Sugirtharajah and Fackler on the topics of "peddling" and "marketing" for new niches do not represent wholly new zones of response to the Bible. Several essayists here display an historical sense that leads them to remember that the communities of faith and reading not only survived but also expanded in the face of some previous, pre-electronic, pre-digital revolutions. We refer especially to the invention of movable type and the expansion of the worlds of printing and book-making in the fifteenth and sixteenth centuries. Far from finding that earlier revolution nothing but a challenge to the church, because it eroded old-style clerical authority—the clerics having previously been the custodians of the Book—that revolution led not only to a passion for reading but also to an enlargement of the community—or, one must say, communities—of faith. Yes, some of that enlargement meant vulgarization, misrepresentation, and lay enterprise that may have strayed from orthodoxies, as the clerics saw them. But "some good thing," most now would say, "came of it," namely book-printing, new literacy, fresh communities of faith and renewal of old ones. Must digital communication be seen as nothing but a subversion of verities and communities that cling to what was valid in the old?

As for the popular culture described by Mary Hess, something that has certainly "arrived," though adaptations to it by the communities shaped by the Bible may still be relegated mostly to the "what has nearly arrived" sphere: one is tempted to ask, "So what else is new?" A major strand of social history in recent decades, as it has been spun out of reflection on what used to be called "Reformation History" (late fifteenth to early seventeenth century Western Europe), has been the discovery of popular culture in the Catholic and then the Protestant worlds of the time. Some historians, Jean Delumeau among them, suggest that popular culture in the form of devotion to relics and pilgrimages meant that Europe had still been largely pagan when Martin Luther came along. Luther introduced the Bible and literacy and orthodoxy, at the expense of devotion to the "superstitions" of the day.

However, these social historians continue, in the wake of Luther and his contemporaries in movements called evangelical or Protestant, popular culture still continued to hold its sway. All one has to do is read the sermons of prophets and whiners on Protestant soil in the sixteenth century to find a depiction of what the laity and the unlearned clergy of the time, for all their access to the book, *really* believed. Yet the book prospered and provided some sort of coherence for multitudes. The book as we have known it may some day exist only as electronic impulses in cyberspace, signals that can appear on a screen and then disappear. But such signals are likely to be received by future generations who will take elements of the biblical narrative and fuse them with other stories, other cultural productions—as believers and scholars always have done. Out of the mix of high-cultural biblical interpretation and popular cultural expression can come chaos and mayhem, it is true. But one can also observe signs that suggest "some good thing may yet grow" out of this mixture.

Similarly, the three essays that relocate the dislocated contexts of the old (male, Western European-dominated) paradigms in settings where women, Africans, African-Americans—and, if this book had space for more, an indefinite number of Asian, Native American, and many more interpreting communities—take command, do not represent only an assault on the book and the Bible. The overall experience, as authors Kwok Pui-lan, Sanneh, and Smith make clear, has not been one of abandonment of the Bible or all that old paradigms offered. Instead, these particular communities, while challenging what has belonged to "the past," also enlarge the understandings of those who have been partially blinded by their own cultural, gendered, and racial settings.

It may be discomforting for ordinary believers and scholars who have instinctively fashioned and imagined a white Gentile Christ, one who has historically been appropriated among people influenced by Greek and German philosophy, now to face grasps of Biblical faith and learning among people who had seemed quite distant from such images and influences. Yet we are far enough into the revolution occasioned by "the women's movement" and "ethnic and racial communal readings" to see how these have cast light on shadowed biblical narratives and themes. When the black community or the company of the poor or the abused gained a voice and spoke up or wrote about the Bible in their experience, they were more likely to relate to some of the scriptures' main themes—freedom from oppression being among them—than were those who were closer to the established powers.

Today heirs of both kinds of traditions can and do meet, sometimes learning enough from each other to give confidence to Suger-ish counsel: "some good thing may yet grow out of it." Those jostled from complacency might come to the point of urging others to keep on representing "the Other." Those representing "the Other" might hope that not all would be merged too quickly into something resembling again that which had been too familiar, already too well known, in the traditional male Western reading communities. Too much is lost if everything and everyone are prematurely or crudely blended into a harmonious new whole. Mary Hess, by accenting the particularity of texts and contexts, shows good reason for interactions of "Self" and "Other," interactions that imply movement from and receptivity among both "sides." So her work belongs with that of Kwok, Sanneh, and Smith: devotees of popular culture need not become universalists. They are another community of particularists of their own sort, offering challenge and promise to shapers of new paradigms: "some good thing may yet grow out of it," is their counsel to the impatient. The trio who here treat gender and racial and regional particularities know that those of whom they write had long been regarded as marginalized. In the new paradigm no one is marginalized because everyone is; everyone is established because no one is. Or may be.

That trio of essays which many might find, as I did, the most dislocating and upsetting, those by Adam on the mystique of words and Fortner and Thieme on the digital revolution, seem and no doubt are furthest from what belongs to "the past" and are the clearest attempts to discern "what's coming." If the three authors are correct, it is not likely that a stable definition of a new paradigm is in the offing at all. Yet, ill-defined as the new paradigm may be, it also has its promising along with its challenging side—as the three authors demonstrate by their own ready welcome of the changes. (Throughout the book, there is little whining about change, about "what has nearly arrived," even where there is caution and criticism).

Adam describes a surrealistic scene that speaks of deception and exposing of deceptions. He criticizes those who would rely too unreflectively on a printed book. Yet he does not envision a future of desolation but of possible enlargements and enhancements. Some of the changes can bring tomorrow's communities to share much with those who pursued faith and learning before the invention of printing. Back then they relied on oral stories, relics, objects, music, stained glass windows, arts high or popular, and other embodiments of the Word. The book as such does not have to disappear tomorrow. But what its readers found the book to offer, they may even find amplified after the mystique of only-the-word has been dispelled. Might there then be a recovery of religious art? Something good may still grow of these alternatives to the reliance on the printed book of words alone.

Until I read Fortner and Thieme, I was not aware of how drastic the breach is between the artifacts and achievements of the "electronic" and the "digital" revolutions. It is well known that some faith communities adapted more enthusiastically to the electronic revolution than did others. In North America, at least, Roman Catholics, the Orthodox, Jews, and mainline Protestants were less capable of embracing and utilizing the inventions of modernity, radio and television, than were the anti-modern "old-time religionists" who practically came to own the religion channels on television.

Now comes the digital revolution, which is much more capable of fragmenting, isolating, and dislocating individuals in community than is the still thriving electronic version. What happens when books, chapters, paragraphs, words, and letters become pixels? What can there be of continuity in a world of the kinetic, of that which is always being revised, the scene that virtual reality dominates? What is virtual? What is real? The communities derived from and dependent on faith and learning inspired by the printed page are faced with the blurring of the line between what they presumed happened and was recorded in books, on one hand, and, on the other, self-creations that may seem more real in their "virtualness" than the presumed reality "behind the text" of old ever was.

I once visited a gift shop at a battlefield commemorating a battle of the American Civil War. The store was called "The Blarney Stone." What did that Irish artifact have to do with the War Between the States? Upon examination I further found that the shop was owned by a couple from Germany. And their chief product for sale was Southwest Native American jewelry. When I first told that story years ago, it would be greeted with chuckles of recognition by others who had also been thrown off balance by such cultural juxtapositions and jumbles.

No more. Today, after millions have experienced the manufactured realities of Disney World, have captured images with their digital cameras or controlled the plots on television with the by now apparently neolithic tool called the zapper, few are even moved to hear the account as strange. The early postmodern assemblage of phenomena is part of the taken-for-granted world.

Fortner and Thieme ponder what fleeting digital phenomena do to communities that had been at home with the book and approved interpretations of it. Still, there are manifest precedents for the less stable, less permanent approaches signaled in the spheres where the book once dominated and inspired community. More centuries of Israel's and the Christian community's lives have been mediated by the spoken word than have been inspired by the written word; by images in glass and stone and wood than by what was in bound books. One thinks of Martin Luther, no mean devotee of the scriptures, insisting that the word must be *geschrieen*, "cried out," and not only *geschrieben*, "written"; that the church in which worship occurred was not a *Federhaus*, a "writing-pen house," but a *Mundhaus*, a "mouth-house," for the creation of a new reality among congregants.

Yes, Fortner and Thieme do envision a future far removed from what belongs to "the past" and their depiction of the digital world and its effects cannot be shrugged off as old stuff, with a "been there, done that." Yet believing and reading communities have done enough blending of spoken-word and written-word, have seen enough of the momentary mingled with aspiration to the permanent, to suggest that among those entirely resistant to new paradigms, Suger's word about the invention of the Gothic is valid counsel: here, too, "something good may still grow out of it."

Index

A

Abbey of St. Denis, 252
Abbott, Edwin, 19
Abbot Suger, 252, 260
Abeokuta, 173
Aboriginal, 152
Abraham, viii, ix, 90, 111, 132, 165, 255
Abrahamson, Vickie, 41, 45
Academic, 3-5, 14, 16, 24, 105, 110, 115, 125, 128, 130-132, 137, 153, 154, 178, 184, 192, 200, 226, 238-240, 247, 251
Academy, 114, 135, 138, 188
Ackroyd, Peter, 91, 94, 97, 107
Acts of the Apostles, 109
Adam, viii, 3, 25, 35, 167, 256, 258, 261
Adam, A. K. M., 3
Adi Granth, 202
Adrados, Francisco 129
Adult, 56, 91, 196, 201, 207, 214, 236, 248
Adventures in Odyssey Bible, 76
Africa, 155, 157-162, 164, 165, 167, 168, 171-181, 255
African, ix, 52, 74, 90, 111-113, 115-119, 121, 124, 130-134, 157-159, 161, 164-167, 170-176, 178-180, 182, 232, 237, 238, 241, 243, 245, 255, 260
African-American, ix, 74, 118, 131, 133, 232, 238, 241, 243, 245
biblical hermeneutics, see African-American, biblical scholarship
African-Caribbean, 241
African Methodist Episcopal Church, 90
Afro-America, 116
Ajayi, J. F. Ade, 170, 173, 174, 176, 180, 182
Albanian, 65
Alien, 52, 144, 155, 210, 211
Alienness, 210

see also other/others; otherness
allegory, 5, 14, 96
Allen, Charlotte, 180
Alpert, Rebecca, 143, 152
Alpha program, 197
Alsace, 172
Althaus-Reid, Marcella María, 141, 152
America, 35, 41, 76, 116, 124, 130, 131,133,152, 155-157, 161, 192, 197, 199, 201, 202, 205, 225, 254, 261
American, 5, 6, 33, 38, 40, 56, 58, 72-75, 77, 82, 110-112, 115, 116, 118, 124, 130-133, 135, 136, 145, 151, 155, 159, 181, 183, 192, 195, 197, 198, 201, 204, 205, 207, 218, 226, 232, 238, 241, 243, 245, 247, 260, 262
American Bible Society, vii, viii, x, xi, 183, 207, 218, 226, 241, 247
American Indian, 151
Analog culture, 33. 35
Ananias and Sapphira,92
Anderson, Christopher, 99, 108
Anderson, Herbert, 209, 216, 223
Angel Bible, The, 75
Anglican, 197
Anglo-American
Anglo-European biblical scholarship, 114
annihilation, zone of, 58, 59, 66, 113, 146
animation, 14, 24, 44, 218
anthropology, 52, 139, 158, 168, 174, 178, 179, 213, 217, 219
anthropologist, 209
anti-Semitism, 151
antislavery movement, 161, 173, 174, 179
apartheid, 160
Apocalypse of John, 120 see Revelation
Apocalyptic, 41, 66, 119
Apologetics, 191, 196, 202
Aquinas, Thomas, 198
Aramaic, 5, 184

263

I

N

About the Authors

A. K. M. Adam teaches New Testament at Seabury-Western Theological Seminary, Evanston, Illinois. His books include *Making Sense of New Testament Theology, What Is Postmodern Biblical Criticism?, Handbook for Postmodern Biblical Interpretation,* and *Postmodern Interpretations of the Bible.* He began working in the field of computer graphics in 1980 and left full-time professional work in that field in 1983, when he estimated that there was no future in it.

Edith Blumhofer is Professor of History and Director of the Institute for the Study of American Evangelicals at Wheaton College, Wheaton, Illinois. Her research interests include American evangelicalism and pentecostalism. She is currently writing a biography of the hymn writer, Fanny J. Crosby.

Mark Fackler is Professor of Communication Arts and Sciences at Calvin College, Grand Rapids, Michigan. He is co-author of *Media Ethics: Cases and Moral Reasoning* and is the author other books and articles investigating professional ethics and public life. He also lectures and conducts research in East Africa.

Robert S. Fortner is Professor of Communication Arts and Sciences at Calvin College, Grand Rapids, Michigan. His current research projects include a comparative history of the moral imperatives affecting the development of radio in Canada, Great Britain, and the United States; developing a Christian theory of mass communication; and continuing work on the implications of the developing information revolution around the globe.

Robert M. Fowler is Chairperson and Professor of Religion at Baldwin-Wallace College, Berea, Ohio. He is the author of *Let the Reader Understand: Reader-Response Criticism and the Gospel of Mark,* and he collaborated in the writing of *The Postmodern Bible.* His current research

interest is the media history of the Bible, particularly the electronic muta-
tions of the Bible in cyberspace.

Mary E. Hess is Assistant Professor of Educational Leadership at Luther
Seminary, St. Paul, Minnesota. She is a Roman Catholic layperson whose
research focuses on the challenges posed to religious education within
media culture contexts. She is also a member of the International Study
Commission on Media, Religion and Culture. Her work is regularly published in the journal *Religious Education*, and she maintains a web site at
www.luthersem.edu/mhess.

Kwok Pui-lan is William F. Cole Professor of Christian Theology and
Spirituality at the Episcopal Divinity School, Cambridge, Massachusetts.
Born in Hong Kong, she has published extensively in Asian feminist the-
ology, biblical hermeneutics, and postcolonial criticism. Her recent books
include *Discovering the Bible in the Non-Biblical World* and *Introducing
Asian Feminist Theology*. She has also co-edited *Beyond Colonial
Anglicanism: The Anglican Communion in the Twenty-First Century* and
Postcolonialism, Feminism, and Religious Discourse.

Randy G. Litchfield is Associate Professor of Christian Education at the
Methodist Theological School in Ohio, Delaware, Ohio. He is also
Executive Secretary of the Association of Professors and Researchers in
Religious Education. His research interests include the impact of post-
modernity on religious education, particularly regarding Christian identi-
ty, vocation, and holiness.

Martin E. Marty is the Fairfax M. Cone Distinguished Service Professor
Emeritus at The University of Chicago, Chicago, Illinois, and the George
B. Caldwell Senior Scholar in Residence at the Park Ridge Center for the
Study of Health, Faith, and Ethics, Chicago, Illinois. He is the author of
over fifty books.

Lamin Sanneh is Professor of History at Yale University and the D.
Willis James Professor of Missions and World Christianity in the Yale
University Divinity School, New Haven, Connecticut. He is the author of
*Abolitionists Abroad: American Blacks and the Making of Modern West
Africa, Translating the Message: The Missionary Impact on Culture*, and
*Encountering the West: Christianity and the Global Cultural Process:
The African Dimension*.

Fernando F. Segovia is Professor of New Testament and Early Christianity in The Divinity School of Vanderbilt University, Nashville, Tennessee. His research interests include method and theory in biblical studies; non-Western and minority interpretation of the Bible; non-Western and minority theological studies; and gospel studies.

Abraham Smith is an ordained National Baptist USA Inc. minister and an Associate Professor of New Testament at Perkins School of Theology. He has published numerous articles on cultural studies and has written articles for several important study Bibles. His most recent work is a commentary on 1 and 2 Thessalonians in the New Interpreter's Bible Series.

John G. Stackhouse, Jr., is the Sangwoo Youtong Chee Professor of Theology and Culture at Regent College, Vancouver, Canada. He is author and editor of several books and hundreds of articles on the history and theology of North American evangelicalism.

R. S. Sugirtharajah is Professor of Biblical Hermeneutics, School of Historical Studies, University of Birmingham, Birmingham, England. His books include *The Bible and the Third World: Precolonial, Colonial and Postcolonial Encounters* and *Asian Biblical Hermeneutics and Postcolonialism: Contesting the Interpretations*. He has also edited and contributed to *The Postcolonial Bible, Vernacular Hermeneutics*, and *Dictionary of Third World Theologies*.

Richard Thieme, "a father figure for online culture," according to the *London Sunday Telegraph*, is a former Episcopal priest who speaks, writes, and consults on the human dimensions of technology and work. He has explored technology and spirituality and the emergence of cyber-religion for two decades. His work is published in many languages and taught in universities in Europe, Canada, and the U.S. He is the CEO of ThiemeWorks, based in Milwaukee, Wisconsin.

.